THE MEMORY LANE cookbook

ÉTIENNE POIRIER, JR.

KEY PORTER·BOOKS

For Adelle Davis,
who started it all.

Royalties from the sale of this book will help finance a 24-hour-a-day free hotline for senior abuse victims. It will be operated by the Annie & Étienne Poirier Foundation, the international, community-based non-profit organization working to prevent and curtail financial, psychological and physical abuse of senior citizens, a growing problem in all countries.

Memory Lane ® is a registered trademark of the Foundation.

Canadian Cataloguing in Publication Data
Poirier, Étienne
    The memory lane cookbook

Includes index
ISBN 1-55013-567-8

1. Cookery.   2. Sugar-free diet – Recipes.
23. Low-calorie diet – Recipes.   I. Title

TX714.P75 1994   641.5'63   C94-931241-X

Key Porter Books Limited
70 The Esplanade
Toronto, Ontario
Canada M5E 1R2

Distributed in the United States of America by National Book Network, Inc.

Book design and production: Counterpunch/Linda Gustafson
Printed and bound in Canada

CONTENTS

Preface   iv

Acknowledgements   viii

Introduction   1

1. SOUPS   24

2. BEEF   53

3. PORK   75

4. POULTRY   97

5. FISH AND OTHER SEAFOOD   112

6. PASTA AND RICE   124

7. BEANS AND VEGETABLES   146

8. SALADS AND SALADA DRESSINGS   173

9. SAUCES   194

10. BREADS   207

11. RELISHES, PICKLES AND CHILI SAUCES   233

12. CONSERVES AND MARMALADES   244

13. DESSERTS   248

More Food for Thought   286

Index   289

PREFACE

Annie Poirier arrived in Canada in 1919 as a war bride. A cosmopolitan Londoner, she had married Étienne Poirier, a decorated war hero. Not only did she suffer culture shock on her arrival in New Brunswick (she spoke little French), her marriage in the Church of England was deemed invalid by the Catholic Church. A second wedding was therefore hastily celebrated in the Église Saint-Benoît, Balmoral, New Brunswick, where the couple were settling. Their first child, Patricia, was rechristened.

The three-storey, pine log family house in front of the church was comfortable and efficiently organized. Huge farm meals were served on time every day by in-laws anxious to please the glamorous "dame anglaise" from "way over there." Nevertheless, Annie was nostalgic for good old-fashioned English cooking and was annoyed to find no cookbooks in any of the stores in nearby towns. She wrote home for favorite recipes and began planning a cookbook. She submitted recipes to newspapers and magazines and several were published, but by then, Annie had become an activist for various causes and had increased her family by three sons.

In her search for recipes, she wrote to chiefs of state and religious leaders, appealing for help on behalf of impoverished natives and French-Canadian families. The Canadian prime minister, W.L. Mackenzie King, always replied to her letters within hours. (One surviving letter is dated New Year's Eve, 1939.) So did others, including Eleanor Roosevelt and Mary Baker Eddy. In seven decades, Annie wrote more than 10,000 letters soliciting recipes. She also met many political leaders and members of the Royal Family.

In March 1957, her husband, Étienne, succumbed to health problems brought about by an inoperable war injury. Declining several offers of marriage from local widowers, Annie decided to devote her time to favorite causes. She now wrote more letters than ever while bemoaning the rising cost of stamps and deteriorating postal services. She greeted Princess Diana and Prince Charles on their first visit to Canada. The Knights of Columbus declared Annie "Citizen of the Year," and New Brunswick premier Richard Hatfield showed up to present her with a plaque.

Suffering from diabetes and osteoporosis, Annie refused to budge from a new ranch bungalow her husband had built for her in the early 1950s. She continued to receive daily visitors and reluctantly agreed to have a nurse come by twice a week "to make sure you're taking your medication and sticking to that low-calorie diet." In late April 1987, Annie, trying to reset a grandfather clock, fell and suffered a shattered vertebra and cranial concussion. Five hours later, the visiting nurse found her lying on the floor. She spent a month in hospital and was visited daily by her daughter, Patricia, and son Étienne. Assured that she would remain in hospital for at least another month, they left, just as Victor Barry Poirier, her eldest son, flew in from Alberta on his first visit in fifteen years. He and his brother Francis Vaughan Poirier removed Annie from the hospital – ostensibly to have "a look" at her Balmoral house – but took her to Francis's place, where she was forced to sign a deed of cession and power of attorney, leaving her legally homeless for the last seventeen months of her life. She was not allowed to re-enter her own home to recover memorabilia. When she died at the age of 90, she was living with a former Red Cross worker.

Before her death, her situation was given coverage by newspaper and radio and TV reporters. As a result, more than a million Canadians signed the Annie Poirier Petition, which asked for legislation to curtail and prevent financial, physical and psychological abuse of senior citizens, the plague that now hits more than 4% of citizens aged 65 and over. More than a hundred watchdog committees sprang up in various communities, and the work spread to other countries.

The grass-roots movement culminated in the Annie & Étienne Poirier Foundation, chartered by the federal government. Seeking to raise funds, the Foundation decided to produce a cookbook based on Annie's recipe collection. Profits from the sale of the cookbook would finance a free hotline for victims of senior abuse. However, it had to be more than a cookbook. It had to be a call to healthy, joyful living, and appeal to all ages.

The Foundation also established non-profit cooking schools and the Annie Poirier Home Cooking Institute. The Institute recruits and trains volunteer chefs to demonstrate healthy meal preparation in various centers. Seniors no longer have to lunch on tea and toast. Children can go to school well fortified for the tasks of learning and loving. Adults can quickly prepare healthy, nutritious office lunches. All can once again gather around the table for an evening of sustenance, great taste and sound nutrition. (We believe that the family that eats together stays together and will seldom abuse their elders.)

How Recipes Were Selected

After Annie had left her home, it was vandalized, resulting in the loss of many letters and recipes. The estate and Foundation launched a public appeal to recover her lost papers, so her recipes could be reproduced in the cookbook. The appeal was partially successful and the response from neighbors and friends was gratifying. However, there were not enough recipes to warrant a cookbook. The Foundation launched an international contest; the public was invited to submit heritage recipes – the kind grandchildren recall with nostalgia, the kind that stir memories of family gatherings around the hearth, the kind that produce those unmistakable aromas of food prepared with savoir-faire and love. We wanted the recipes to be affordable for those on even the tightest budgets. We looked for recipes that could be frozen, as well.

All contestants were advised that recipes would be triple-tested by volunteer chefs and adapted to drastically reduce or eliminate such ingredients as butter, egg yolks, salt and sugar. Only when the chefs and tasters were satisfied that the adapted recipes were identical in appearance, taste and texture with the originals could they be included in *The Memory Lane Cookbook*.

Once recipes were okayed, the problem was what to call them. Why not name them after famous personalities our parents and grandparents loved and admired? We contacted as many descendants as we could locate and all enthusiastically approved. (When they learned of the cause, some even mailed donations to the Foundation!) Research did the rest. We had to make sure that each recipe "fit" the personality honored by *The Memory Lane Cookbook*.

When the Canadian team won the 1992 World Culinary Olympics in Germany against formidable competition from many countries – including France and the United States – we were all terribly proud of our cooks,

especially the native chefs, whose dishes caused a sensation with sophisti-
cated European gourmets. Canadian cuisine had not only come of age,
but in the opinion of the startled judges, our cooking methods were on a
par with, and in many ways superior to, all others.

The volunteer teams behind the Memory Lane project were delighted
but not surprised. After all, Canada's cuisine was not born yesterday but
some 40,000 years ago when the first Asians crossed what is now known as
the Bering Strait and spread throughout the New World. This explains
why native dishes figure in the book you just bought.

Since a dinner is more than a gourmet feast, we also hope the com-
ments that precede many of the recipes will stimulate conviviality and
friendly conversation. According to a major 1994 study by scientists, nega-
tive emotions can lead to cardiac problems. Duke University in the United
States and the Montréal Heart Institute in Canada were involved in the
research.

The most important contribution this book can make is to encourage
people to select healthy foods and prepare them properly, as the great
Adelle Davis would put it. Even diabetics and those on rigorous diets will
find recipes that delight the senses and satisfy healthy appetites. Both
Annie and Adelle would be proud of the recipes in this book and the cause
that has led to their collection.

Acknowledgements

Dietitians, gourmet chefs and home economists worked in teams to make sure that every recipe in this book is a winner for appearance, ease of preparation, taste and nutritional value. Each contains little or no fat, cholesterol, sugar or sodium. Nevertheless, people on medically prescribed diets should consult a dietitian to see how the Memory Lane recipes fit specific meal plans.

Kitchen tests were carried out in Montréal, New York, Paris and Toronto by volunteers from the Annie Poirier Home Cooking Institute and the Annie & Étienne Poirier Foundation under the direction and supervision of maître chefs Émile Lemieux, Antoine Lagacé, Miriam Davis, Brent Thrall, Rosalyn Turner, François Bernard and Jean-Marie Cloutier. Nutrient values of foods specified in the recipes were analyzed and tallied by Marjorie Clarke, M.Ed., R.D.; M.J. Carswell, M.S., R.D.; Peter Di Santo; Maria Pires; Jocelyne Vézina; and Thérèse Leblanc. Invaluable editorial advice was provided by Wendy Thomas and Jonathan Webb.

A small army of volunteers collected information about and researched food hazards, and tried, with the editor, to separate fact from fiction. We are also indebted to the Center for Science in the Public Interest, whose book *Safe Food* should be required reading in all medical schools. Their award-winning newsletter is available by writing CSPI, 1875 Connecticut Ave., N.W., Suite 308, Washington, DC 20009.

INTRODUCTION

A Word About Budgets

You don't have to be rich to serve delicious, nourishing meals. You do have to be cautious, wise and creative. Here are some general tips on penny pinching for gourmets.

• Shop during off-peak hours when stores are less crowded and you can spot the bargains. Don't forget to take store coupons – it's easy to remember them if you keep them in one of the many junk mail envelopes that come into our homes.

• Plan your meals around the supermarket specials of the week. Check the newspaper ads, make a list and stick to it. If an item is out of stock, obtain a raincheck.

• Make sure you know what's in the fridge, freezer and cupboards. If necessary, keep a separate list on a special kitchen notepad. Don't wait until the stuff rots. Use it!

• When buying favorite items, check the unit price. Don't purchase a huge bag of flour or rice if it's going to sit there for two years. Buy the size that suits you at the lowest unit price.

• Unless you absolutely need help, shop alone. You cannot concentrate on what you're doing if you have to cater to a grumpy spouse, free-wheeling children and chatty friends. Budget shopping is both an art and a science.

• Buy only as many fresh items as you can consume within three to seven days. Items such as fish are no longer "fresh" once they reach the showcase. If you're not planning a fish dinner within ten hours, buy frozen fish. If you buy more meat than you need, wrap it in moisture-proof bags, label it, date it and freeze it.

• Buy your herbs and spices in bulk at the local health-food store. They're cheaper and fresher. Take along some prepared labels to identify your purchases – sometimes it's hard to tell marjoram from thyme, for example.

• Cut down on meat and eat more beans, pasta, rice and potatoes. Try being a vegetarian once or twice a week. Prepare a gourmet meal of soup, vegetarian casserole, salad and favorite dessert (minus the fat, sugar and salt). Check out some tofu recipes.

• Use less expensive, low-fat dairy products. Powdered skim milk is the cheapest and makes the best kitchen yogurt. In a favorite recipe, replace imported cheese with domestic.

• Canned soups are expensive and contain questionable ingredients (salt *and* sugar, if you please!). Make your own chicken, meat and vegetable stocks. Defat and freeze them in ice-cube trays and other containers.

• If a sandwich filling is well-seasoned, why add butter or margarine? Try a home-made mild mustard, light mayonnaise or relish as a spread, as well.

IRRADIATED FOOD

Many people are concerned that food irradiation can lead to cancer. All the facts about irradiation are not yet known, so why take a risk? Countries such as Canada have advanced food distribution systems in place, and in our homes we have good preservation and storage facilities. Is further preservation by irradiation really necessary?

In the irradiation process, radiation energy passes through the food, which absorbs a small amount. The amount absorbed kills organisms, extends shelf life and prevents fast ripening. It also destroys some of the vitamins A, C, B_{12}, B_6, carotene and thiamine; causes chemical changes in the food; and results in new food components (radiolytic products) being formed.

To date no irradiated foods, with the exception of spices, are being sold in Canada; but it is likely that pressure from the food industry will force politicians to open the border.

THE NEW MILK: CAN IT ENDANGER YOUR HEALTH?

The U.S. Food and Drug Administration (FDA) allows farmers to inject cows with recombinant bovine somatotropin (rBST), a genetically engineered growth hormone that increases the amount of milk produced by up to 25%. Fewer cows are required to produce the same quantity of milk, and farmers using the synthetic hormone gain a competitive advantage over those who don't. For Monsanto, the corporate giant which holds the license under the trade name Prosilac, and farmers who use the hormone, it's a win-win situation.

Although the hormone has not been approved for use in Canada, this dramatic development has the Annie Poirier Home Cooking Institute deeply concerned. Some scientists believe rBST will increase the risk of breast cancer among premenopausal women. One scientist is the respected Samuel Epstein, professor of occupational and environmental medicine at the University of Illinois school of public health. Drinking or using treated milk, he warned the FDA, could lead to premature breast enlargement in young children. Furthermore, cows treated with rBST tend to develop severe cases of udder infections, or mastitis. More antibiotics are required and their residues appear in milk despite careful screening.

Labels on the product sold to farmers in the United States must bear a warning that Prosilac is associated with health problems in cows that lead to their receiving further medication. No such warning would appear on Canadian labels. Furthermore, in a move obviously aimed at organic farmers and health-food stores, dairies are not allowed to label their milk rBST-free.

The hormone was approved for use in the United States in February 1994 after a six-month moratorium imposed by the government to allay public fears. Similar action in Canada is opposed by the National Dairy Council of Canada and a House of Commons agriculture committee. Meanwhile, in the United States, the American Medical Association has called for further studies to determine if "the bovine insulin-like growth factor is safe for children, adolescents and adults." In that country, a backlash against milk and dairy products has developed and sales are down as consumers let their views be known by holding back their grocery dollars.

A TASTE OF THINGS TO COME: NO TASTE

The latest bad news comes from those scientific tinkerers working, for the most part, in well-funded university labs. At a conference in Los Angeles billed as Science Innovation '92, one enthusiastic biology professor forecast that genetic engineers can not only get vine-ripened tomatoes to distant store shelves but will soon be able to feed the overpopulated Third World – he neglected to add that these engineered products will be tasteless.

He and his colleagues involved in biomedical research are working on genetically breeding out the male portion of corn plants to clear the way for cheaper and more productive hybrids. The flavor and texture of the end result are less important than high-yield crops.

The U.S. Food and Drug Administration, after nine years of study, approved the McGregor tomato in May 1994. The California inventor is now seeking permission to sell it in Canada. The softening gene has been installed backwards to allow longer vine ripening before shipping. The *Washington Post* said it tastes better than tomatoes shipped from afar but not as good as ones ripened in the backyard.

There is also a clear danger that biotechnology will spark allergies in some people. "Anything that you transfer raises a question," warns Dr. Hugh Sampson, pediatrician and food allergy specialist at Johns Hopkins University School of Medicine. Millions are already allergic to nuts and other foods. Eating these can cause hives or a life-threatening asthma attack. Since it is now possible to genetically manipulate corn, tomatoes, squash and countless other foods, the risks are enormous and more difficult to avoid. What if material from a Brazil nut is put into soybeans which then end up in everything from baby formula to bologna? (Scientists can now move genetic material from plant to plant, animal to plant, bacteria to plant and virus to plant.)

The end result, of course, will be an even greater assault on biodiversity, which contributed so much to the aroma and taste we all used to enjoy in the Memory Lane kitchens of our grandparents. (For more information on this vital subject, please see What You Should Know About Apples, page 11.)

NUTRITION IS COMMON SENSE

For decades, medical students were taught very little, if anything, about nutrition. Small wonder that many doctors continue to downplay the important role of nutrients, vitamins and minerals. But things are changing.

Why are fractured hips, stooped shoulders and crippled joints more common among older women than men? These are symptoms of osteoporosis – the debilitating condition caused by calcium loss. Calcium is important in everyone's diet, but women's needs make it vital for them. During pregnancy and breastfeeding, the need for calcium increases. If the diet doesn't supply enough, the body takes the calcium from the bones. After 35, women begin losing bone mass at a rate of 1% a year; in men, the process starts after 55. Common sense would therefore dictate that everyone – especially women – consume adequate calcium throughout their lives. Calcium protects older bones and guards against colon cancer and high blood pressure.

Avoid consuming fat in the dairy products you ingest for their calcium by purchasing low-fat, non-fat and skim-milk products. Most stores offer a wide choice of these products, such as reduced-fat cheeses, which are as tasty and nutritious as the regular kind.

The U.S. Department of Agriculture, pressured by nutritionists for the past three decades, has now designed a new Eating Right Pyramid. Certain commercial interests tried to block its publication, but the recommendations make sound nutritional sense. Everyone should eat, on a daily basis, six to eleven servings from the vegetables group; two to four from fruits; and two to three from both dairy foods and meats. Keep portions small and varied.

We would go even further and agree with Dr. Art Mollen of the Southwest Health Institute in Phoenix whose "anti-aging diet" downplays animal protein. He says we should eat only about a quarter of our current levels.

The average person who ingests 130 grams of protein a day should lower this intake to 50 or 60 grams. "Half of that can be from animal protein and the rest from vegetable sources," says Dr. Mollen. The result will be fewer calories, more money, less disease and longer lives.

Mortality rates for certain types of cancer and coronary artery disease are much higher in North America than in China. The Chinese consume one-third less protein than we do and only 7% of that comes from meat, dairy products and fish. The rest comes from rice, soy and other beans. No drastic changes are called for if we adopt similar eating habits – the dinner plate will look just as full of food. Protein and fat simply take up less room. So from now on, let protein be the extra. Dr. Mollen advises that meat, poultry and fish become side dishes, and pasta or vegetable recipes be served as the main course.

Legumes, nuts, seeds and soy products such as tofu are plant-based proteins and should form a part of everyday eating.

CAN YOU PREVENT CANCER AND HEART DISEASE?

If further evidence is needed to convince you, here are recent findings about the relationship between nutrition and cancer:

- Most people can reduce the risk of cancer by adding a green salad and a glass of juice to their daily diet, says the U.S. Cancer Institute.
- People should eat at least five servings of fruits or vegetables daily. The current average is only 3 1/2. "Five a day is the minimum," says U.S. Health and Human Services Secretary Louis Sullivan. "Nine servings a day are better for you." He recommends a glass of orange juice in the morning, a lettuce and tomato salad at noon, apple or carrots for a snack and broccoli or another vegetable at dinner.
- Nutrients in fruits and vegetables protect against cell damage that leads to cancer, according to Dr. Peter Greenwald, director of cancer prevention at the National Cancer Institute. Worldwide studies prove that the more fruits and vegetables consumed, the lower the cancer rate.
- Men consume more food than women but eat fewer servings of fruits and vegetables. Their cancer rate is also higher.
- Don't imitate former president George Bush's aversion to broccoli. Its cancer-fighting ability is now verified by scientists. In a 1994 study published in the *Proceedings of the National Academy of Sciences*, Johns Hopkins University researchers report that sulforaphane – a chemical found in broccoli – helps protect animals against cancer. Physician Paul Talalay, a co-author of the study, told the Annie Poirier Home Cooking Institute, "The results are really quite dramatic."

RECYCLE THOSE EXTRAS!

Creative cooks never throw good food out. Leftovers can be transformed into new culinary delights. Here are some tips:

Bananas: Freeze whole with skin on, wrapped in plastic. Thaw, peel and mash for use in breads or layer sliced bananas with graham cracker crumbs and a low-calorie instant pudding in a baking pan. When set, cut into squares.

Bread: Freeze bread and pastries before mold appears. Use stale bread for bread pudding, bread salads, croutons or bread crumbs.

Casseroles: Leftover casseroles make great fillings for tortillas. Add grated cheese then roll each tortilla in a paper towel. Microwave on high (100% power) for 30 seconds. Eat whole or slice for hors d'oeuvres.

Cereal: Perfect for crumb toppings on desserts and baked sweets. Corn flakes can be ground in a blender or food processor and used to thicken soups and stews.

Cheese: Mix with bread crumbs or chips to top hot broccoli, cauliflower or cabbage.

Dips: Use leftover dip instead of mayonnaise for sandwich spreads.

Jelly: Whip leftover jelly in blender or food processor with low-fat sour cream or yogurt and serve as Bavarian cream. Use 1/2 cup (125 mL) jelly and the same amount of sour cream or yogurt. This makes a terrific low-cal topping for strawberries, fruit cocktails and pies. If desired, add Splenda granular sweetener to taste.

Meat: Make a pâté with leftover meat. Purée it with raw or cooked vegetables. Leftover meat, fish and poultry make terrific sandwiches, fajitas, tacos, quesadillas, pasta dishes or casseroles. Or cover cooked veal or chicken with tomato sauce and heat in the oven.

Potatoes: Mash, add white of an egg, press into a pie plate and freeze. Use as a crust for meat pie. Or combine mashed potatoes with leftover meat, poultry or vegetables, spray a skillet and convert into hash browns by tossing them over medium heat in the skillet.

Vegetables: Combine equal proportions of cooked vegetables with chicken stock, purée in a blender and serve as a hot or cold soup.

SOME FOODS KILL ... HANDLE WITH CARE!

On a car trip with two friends, we pulled into an ultra-modern service center on a highway to gas up and grab a coffee. The other two ordered hamburgers with "the works" but I didn't like the look of the patties thawing on the counter. I opted for a muffin. Four hours later, after we'd settled for the night in our motel rooms, I was awakened by groans and calls for help. The man and his wife were crawling around on the floor and had to be rushed to hospital. They had been poisoned.

Health and Welfare Canada says that 30 to 60% of all ground beef sold in Canada contains the *E. coli* bacterium, which causes hemolytic uremic syndrome, a kidney failure that can be fatal to children. Patients may require blood transfusions, kidney dialysis and even kidney transplants. An outbreak in January 1993 – traced to undercooked burgers in fast-food restaurants in Washington state – caused four deaths and hundreds of illnesses. The lesson is clear: Don't eat your ground beef pink!

In some countries, there's also a risk of being infected with trichinosis if pork is undercooked. (Canada is applying to the World Health Organization to have the country declared trichinosis-free.) And you can contract salmonella from raw eggs or poultry of any type. Never sample uncooked pork sausages or feed raw chicken or pork to pets. The muscle deterioration and inflammation caused by trichinae (live microscopic organisms) can lead to a very painful death.

In meat recipes throughout this book, we stress the importance of kitchen hygiene. In an overpopulated world, there are simply not enough government inspectors to check everything sold in butcher shops and stores. Those are the facts of life in the modern age. As soon as you've prepared such foods for cooking, wash your hands in hot, soapy water. Do the same right away with utensils, dishes and the cutting board. And sterilize your meat grinder each time you use it.

There's no need to become paranoid and overcook everything. Pork is safe if you cook it to an internal temperature of 167°F (75°C); use a meat thermometer to ascertain the internal temperature.

Finally, you won't find any recipes in this book for steak tartare, sushi, sashimi, ceviche or gravlax. Too many people contract hepatitis every year from eating uncooked fish and meat. In an overpopulated world, even the oceans are now polluted, as oceanographer Jacques Cousteau sadly noted.

SOME BASIC EQUIPMENT FOR THE KITCHEN

Although we have included microwave versions of many traditional recipes, we remain unconvinced of the safety aspects of this kitchen appliance. Some believe microwave ovens pose a radiation hazard; others pooh-pooh such concerns. We have not found any great time-saving advantages and have noted that constant attention is required in order to make sure that food is evenly and thoroughly cooked. In some recipes, taste and texture leave a lot to be desired. And never cook stuffed poultry in the microwave; uneven heat and warm, moist conditions are perfect breeding grounds for harmful bacteria.

Microwave cooking does offer two benefits: (1) it retains a greater amount of essential minerals and vitamins and (2) it is terrific for defrosting and cooking frozen food or reheating leftovers. Just make sure that defrosted food is cooked right away!

In the opinion of our chefs and health experts, a far better investment, whether you're a young person starting out or an older couple scaling down, would be a small convection oven and a pressure cooker, long a staple in Grandma's kitchen.

Before we get to their benefits, though, we must warn you that both are rather heavy to handle and difficult to clean. Fat tends to accumulate in the top filter of the convection oven; you'll need a screwdriver to remove it for a thorough washing. Cleaning the pressure cooker is no easier due to its weight. For both the bottom bowl of the convection oven and the pressure cooker, you'll need to rinse well (a double sink is handy). No one enjoys the taste of detergent in an otherwise excellent meal. The rubber ring in the pressure cooker must be replaced at least every two years.

That said, consider the benefits. A convection oven makes a breeze of cooking bacon to crisp perfection (the most popular models use hot air forced down from the top heating element); most of the fat accumulates in the bottom of the bowl and there is no splattered grease on kitchen tops. Sausages can be cooked with little mess. Cover them for five minutes then remove the cover and prick the sausages with a fork. Contrary to TV commercials, you cannot cook vegetables on a rack *beneath* the meat since they will be smothered in fat. Space in most convection ovens is very limited indeed; the largest item it will handle is a small chicken or a sirloin roast for two. (Larger models are available.) However, it produces no harmful radiation rays and saves energy, thanks to an adjustable thermostat. And unlike microwave ovens, it cooks food evenly.

A pressure cooker is ideal for turning tough meat into a succulent treat worthy of the most expensive restaurant. It retains almost all the minerals and vitamins. Soups and stews are, if anything, even more delicious than those cooked in the conventional way. If you want to can or preserve fresh produce, a large pressure cooker is a must. It also consumes only a little more electricity than a microwave oven and is not at all dangerous.

For absolute beginners, we recommend stainless steel pots and pans and a cast-iron frying pan or two. Some words of advice are in order:
• Never, ever, scour stainless steel with metallic pads in order to remove coagulated fat. The scouring can scratch the protective stainless steel coating and the underlying alloys produce dangerous oxides which then enter the food. Use plastic scouring pads, bleach and – if absolutely necessary – good old oven cleaner. Follow the directions on the labels of these cleaners and avoid inhaling their fumes. (Every kitchen and bathroom should be equipped with powerful fans to draw out noxious fumes; clean the filters every two months, the conduits themselves at least once a year.)
• Before cooking anything in a new cast-iron pan, coat it all over, inside

and out, with canola or safflower oil. Place in a plastic bag and let it "age" at room temperature for three days and two nights. Then wash with soapy detergent (Palmolive is among the best and least expensive, according to Consumers Union, the non-profit watchdog organization which evaluates goods based on actual tests), rinse thoroughly in warm water and place on a heating element. Turn heat to high until all the water drops evaporate. Remove from heat and your new pan is ready to use. If you leave the pan to dry next to the sink, it will rust.

Do not use any aluminum equipment in your cooking or food preparation. Some medical scientists believe that it is the main cause of Alzheimer's disease, an epidemic now almost as severe as that of senior abuse. We would even extend this warning to the rolls of foil used – and overused – in outdoor barbecuing.

Another item to be avoided is any utensil coated with a substance that prevents food sticking. After only a few months of regular use, the coating is inevitably scratched. If the metal underneath is aluminum, it will infect any food cooked in the pan. Another metal to avoid is copper; any excess causes nausea, vomiting and diarrhea.

A far better choice – and much cheaper – is cast iron. Apply a touch of cookware spray and you have a stick-proof surface. If you prefer, dab on a little canola or safflower oil and smooth it around with a paper towel. This technique can also be used in any recipe calling for cookware spray. With proper care, cast iron will outlast you and become a family heirloom.

Corning Ware and Pyrex dishes are safe, but some imitations made in low-wage countries are fragile and substandard. The FDA warns against using ceramic cookware from China, India, Hong Kong and Mexico; these countries use lead in the glazes, which leaches into food. Avoid lead crystal plates and glasses for obvious reasons. Even at low levels, lead is very dangerous – especially for children and fetuses. When buying coffee mugs, insist on brand-name porcelain. Nothing is a bargain if it's going to ruin your health.

If in doubt about lead leaching from the glazing of ceramics and pottery, use a home-test kit. Two we recommend are Leadcheck Swabs (HybriVet Systems, Box 1210, Framingham, MA 01701) and Frandon Lead Alert (Frandon Enterprises, 511 N. 48th St., Seattle, WA 98103). Both sell for about $25 U.S.

In the final analysis, it's your life. Treat it as a sacred trust.

WHAT YOU SHOULD KNOW ABOUT APPLES

Believe it or not, when North America was young and supermarkets did not exist, our ancestors enjoyed more than 600 varieties of apple. On my family's farm in Balmoral, New Brunswick, we had six different kinds, each with its own taste and aroma. In today's stores, we are limited to McIntosh, Spy, Cortland, Spartan and Delicious, types that withstand fork-lifts and trucking. The markets don't give a hoot what consumers want; it's a question of durability over taste.

Appalled, some enthusiasts formed the North American Fruit Explorers, a group of growers dedicated to the finest fruits and nuts. Walda and Fred Janson are two of these. At their Pomona Orchard in Rockton, Ontario, they grow Gilliflower of Gloucester, Greensleeves, Honeygold, Coe's Golden Drop, King Cox, King of the Pippins, Riston Pippin, Rusty Coat and Royal Russet alongside such European delights as Chenango, De l'Estre, Drap d'Or, Karin Schneider, Signe Tillisch and Zuccalmaglio's Reinette. The orchard is named after the Roman goddess of fruit.

Many other concerned orchardists in Canada and the United States have taken similar initiatives; their delicious, heritage apples are sold in farmers' markets and at roadside stands from summer until late fall. Don't miss an occasion to buy and taste them. If you have space in the yard, plant a few varieties. Like good wines, all classic apples are gastronomic delights.

A good cooking apple is one used principally for pies, tarts, cobblers, strudels, fritters, applesauce and stuffings. It should have a tarter flavor and firmer texture than an eating apple. All are rich in vitamins C and A, potassium and other minerals. (It was King Solomon who declared the apple to be a cure-all.) Each contains only about 80 calories.

A member of the rose family (as are pears, plums and peaches), an apple tree may live for 100 years. It can be duplicated only by grafting, not by seed, and is one of the few gifts the Europeans brought with them. Johnny Appleseed (his real name was John Chapman) did his bit in the 1800s, roaming barefoot through Pennsylvania, Ohio and Indiana.

The all-purpose McIntosh, which originated in Ontario, is an excellent cooking apple. Others are Rome Beauty, Winesap, Granny Smith, Stayman and York Imperial.

It's best to store all apples in a plastic bag in the fridge. Since they give off ethylene gas, do not place near other fruit unless you want to hasten ripening. Wash only before using and do so with a stiff brush and warm, running water to remove possible wax coating and pesticide residue. Use a stainless-steel knife for cubing, and avoid coring devices. To benefit from all the minerals and vitamins, do not peel. An apple a day keeps the doctor away only if it's unpeeled.

Eggs

Regardless of advertised claims, there's no such thing as a cholesterol-free egg. A large egg will give you at least 210 mg of cholesterol and 5 g of fat. All the cholesterol is in the yolk. Solution: don't use the yolk – make do with the egg white.

Brown eggs are not nutritionally superior to white ones. The color is determined by the breed of hen laying the eggs and has nothing to do with nutritional content or taste.

Farm-Fresh Egg Substitute

Developed by the Annie Poirier Home Cooking Institute, this home-made substitute is much cheaper than commercial frozen brands. To cut cholesterol and convert your favorite recipes, use 1/4 cup (50 mL) for each whole egg called for. (Note also that powdered non-fat milk, sold in health stores, is not the same as ordinary brands of instant skim milk powder. The latter does not work in this recipe.) Commercial frozen egg substitute delivers a whopping 204 calories per 1/4 cup (50 mL)!

You can use the substitute to make scrambled eggs. In a non-stick skillet, just fry as you would whole eggs, then season with freshly ground pepper.

PREPARATION TIME: *4 minutes*
SUITABILITY FOR FREEZING: *excellent*
MAXIMUM REFRIGERATOR LIFE: *1 week*
PER 1/4 CUP (50 mL): *85 calories. Excellent source of potassium. Good source of protein.*

6	farm-fresh egg whites	6
¼ cup	powdered non-fat milk	50 mL
1 tbsp	canola oil	15 mL
	Drop of yellow food coloring (optional)	

1. In a bowl, using a fork, mix together all ingredients until smooth.

2. Use immediately or seal, label and refrigerate or freeze.

HERBS AND SPICES

For maximum flavor – and a tangible link to the past – grow some herbs in your backyard. Herbs prefer a pH of 6 to 7.5 (neutral to slightly alkaline). If the soil is too acidic, add some lime.

Some favorite and easy-to-grow herbs are basil, cilantro (coriander), chives (regular or garlic chives), dill and parsley. Simply follow the seed packet directions. Remember that many herbs deter insect pests, which is why knowledgeable people plant them as edging for vegetable beds or flower gardens.

Hardy perennials such as sage (*Salvia officinilis*) and thyme (*Thymus vulgaris*) will last for years. Even in colder regions of North America, you can grow French bay, rosemary and tarragon in pots sunk in the ground. Lift the pots in the fall and set them on a sunny windowsill for the winter.

Valued for centuries, garlic is a must for anyone interested in healthy eating. The latest confirmation of its health benefits comes from the *Annals of Internal Medicine*, which reports that one-half to one clove per day helps decrease total serum (blood) cholesterol levels by about 9%. This fall, simply break off a few garlic bulbs into cloves and plant base-down, one to two inches (2.5 to 5 cm) deep, six inches (15 cm) apart.

When fresh herbs such as basil, dill, marjoram, mint, parsley, rosemary, sage, savory and tarragon are at their peak, rinse them in water, dry and freeze them on an open tray. Pack them into freezer bags, remove air, seal and label. They'll retain garden-fresh flavor for up to a year. Chopped parsley can be put in ice-cube trays with a little water. When frozen, remove and pack the cubes into bags; use for soups and stews.

REMOVING FAT CAN SAVE YOUR LIFE

You might wonder why fat must be removed from beef and chicken before you eat the results. The reason: fat is bad for your heart and general well-being. To know how much fat you are buying, it's important to know what's on a label and what isn't.

Ground beef labeled "75% lean" does not contain only 25% fat. The label is misleading. The store with this type of label is referring to fat *by weight*, not the number of *calories*. Thus percentage of fat by weight is useless in-formation because most customers don't bother translating this into calories per portion. What the stores should really tell us is the percentage of calories supplied by fat instead of the percentage of fat (or lean) by weight.

After frying or broiling, a 4-ounce (113 g) burger made with "75% lean" weighs 3 ounces (85 g). It gives you 260 calories, 171 of which come from 0.68 oz (19 g) of fat. The average burger in a fast-food restaurant is made from "75% lean." Even at 85% lean (so-called extra-lean), half the calories in the cooked product come from the fat.

This leaves health-conscious cooks with two choices: either get rid of the fat in ways recommended in our recipes or have a butcher trim and grind your own lean cuts. Remember that each gram of fat gives you nine calories.

The U.S. Department of Health and Human Services calculates that about 40% of the calories in the typical North American diet come from fat. For a healthy lifestyle, cut this in half. Use this formula to determine the percentage of fat in your daily caloric intake:

- Determine the grams of fat in a food (by reading the label or a government guidebook).
- Multiply the grams of fat by 9 (1 g of fat = 9 calories).
- Divide by the total number of calories.
- Multiply by 100 to get the percentage of calories from fat.

The Memory Lane Cookbook specifies polyunsaturated margarines in some recipes. Oils and margarines should be low in trans and saturated fats. Trans fat raises the harmful LDL cholesterol level and lowers beneficial HDL cholesterol. It is linked to heart disease, certain cancers, diabetes and obesity.

Although labels don't list trans fat separately, you can quickly work out how much your favorite margarine contains. Simply add up the polyunsaturates, monounsaturates, saturates and cholesterol (if any). Deduct this figure from the total fat content on the label. The result gives you the trans fat content. The healthiest choice is a margarine with no trans fat whatsoever.

GROUND BEEF

You must have absolute confidence in the honesty of the butcher where you buy your meats. Government inspectors cannot check every shop every week and it's easy to incorporate everything from chicken giblets to pork with beef and pass it off as ground beef. Three pounds of fresh red meat can be mixed with a pound of green decaying meat to yield four pounds of red ground meat. And many retail outlets use commercial grades and imported frozen beef rather than Canadian Grade A.

Government standards for maximum fat content are: regular, 30%; medium, 23%; and lean, 17%. These standards are seldom enforced so, generally speaking, you're better off buying so-called regular, and cooking it in ways to get rid of the fat. In testing our recipes, we often collect as much fat from "lean" as we do from "regular."

Ground beef deteriorates rapidly, so wrap and freeze any you will not be using within 24 hours. Make sure the freezer-wrapped portions are the right size for later use. Label and date each one.

Avoid buying soy burgers. Make your own. Soy is a source of bacteria and can be used to mask subquality meats by an unscrupulous outlet. Even a trained inspector cannot tell how much soya-water paste has been mixed with the beef.

DAIRY PRODUCTS

Milk: Milk labeled 2% (98% fat-free) means 2% *fat by weight*. The fat in this milk supplies 38% of the calories (whole milk is 3.5% fat by weight but derives 50% or more of its calories from fat). The only solution is *skim milk*, which is fat-free.

Is 2% milk as nutritious as whole milk? More so. Lower-fat milks have almost twice as much vitamin A as whole milk. The vitamin level fluctuates through the year with the highest concentrations in the peak summer months. Lower-fat milks also have slightly more calcium, phosphorous, potassium, sodium and B vitamins than whole milks.

Dairy fat is dangerous because it's saturated. High consumption leads to heart disease, some cancers and obesity. If you drink two glasses of milk per day, switch to skim milk and save yourself 18 g of fat!

All recipes in this book specify and have been kitchen-tested with skim milk and give delicious and nutritious results.

Whipped Cream: At about 400 calories per cup (250 mL), whipped heavy cream is the ultimate no-no. However, there's nothing wrong with enjoying the real thing for special occasions – for example, when the first crop of field strawberries is ready for picking. After all, life must have some rewards. Just don't overdo it.

You can make an acceptable substitute with chilled evaporated skim milk. Be sure to also chill the bowl and beaters. One cup (250 mL) yields five cups (1.3 L) of topping. Add a teaspoon (5 mL) of sugar or Splenda granular sweetener and a half-teaspoon (2 mL) of pure vanilla extract. For a firmer texture, combine 1/4 cup (50 mL) of the unwhipped mixture with 1 1/2 teaspoons (7 mL) of unflavored gelatin. Heat gently until the gelatin melts. Chill and add to the mixture. Chill after whipping.

Substitutes for whipped cream are sold in stores but some contain hydrogenated, and therefore largely saturated, oils. Some have less than half the fat and calories of real whipped cream. The following chart gives the calorie and fat content of some of these products based on a 1/4-cup (50 mL) serving.

Product	Calories	Fat (g)
Cool Whip (non-dairy)	48	4
Cool Whip Lite	32	3
Reddi Whip	40	4
Reddi Whip Lite	24	2
Pet Whip	56	4
La Crème	65	4
Rich Whip	48	4
Light whipping cream, whipped	88	8
Heavy cream, whipped	104	11
Evaporated skim milk, whipped	13	0

Manitou Water

Since water is a fundamental ingredient in many of the low-cal recipes in this book, we had to find the best in North America. Our requirements were few but very strict. The selected brand must contain enough dissolved mineral salts to be conducive to good health while retaining the clear, fresh taste of natural spring water characteristic of the age before the world population explosion – and the march of so-called industrial progress – began to infect the water of life with dangerous pollutants.

We tasted more than three dozen national and international brands. We then tested them in four distinct recipe categories: beverages, breads, soups and stews. The taste and recipe testing was conducted blind; i.e., participants (more than four groups of 16 each) were not told which brands were being used. The taste tests were conducted with both chilled and room-temperature water samples. Participants voted as people do in a regular election – with ballots and pencils under controlled conditions.

The clear winner was a new, relatively unknown brand bottled and distributed by a native Ojibwe corporation, Manitou Water Inc. (Eau Manitou, inc.). Although the water is bottled at three different geographical locations (presumably to cut down on transportation costs), we were impressed with the hygienic and sanitary conditions strictly adhered to at the bottling plants and the firm's fanatical insistence on quality standards. In fact, even shelf life in health-food stores – where we purchased our samples – is routinely controlled. Unlike imported brands, bottles of Manitou Water are replaced with fresh ones after a short time.

The name, of course, is from the Ojibwe for the Great Spirit. The corporation's head office is on Manitoulin Island, the largest fresh-water island in the world. Further laboratory testing showed that Manitou Water has 306 parts per million of dissolved mineral salts, including vital quantities of fluoride ions, bicarbonates, calcium, iron and potassium. And nothing is added or taken away. The company does very little advertising and relies on word of mouth. If your favorite grocery store still doesn't stock this remarkable spring water, speak to the management and insist. You, too, will be able to actually taste the difference.

If Manitou Water is not yet available in your area, try to find another one whose properties, according to the label, come closest to this exceptional brand. Read the label carefully and make sure the water is non-carbonated and naturally iron free and salt free.

PORK

Everyone wants to eat leaner meat, and you may be surprised to know that one of the leanest is Canadian pork, unavailable in our great-grandparents' time. (Farmers in those days raised only the fatty kind.) Pork also contains certain elements essential to health that cannot be found in other meats such as beef or poultry.

For skeptics, here is how chicken breast compares with pork tenderloin (per 90 g cooked):

	CHOLESTEROL	FAT
Chicken breast (skin removed)	76.4 mg	3 g
Pork (lean only)	61.7 mg	4 g

For the raw articles, Health & Welfare Canada comes up with the following (per 120 g):

	Cholesterol	Fat
Skinless chicken breast	77 mg	11 g
Polyunsaturates		2.4 g
Monounsaturates		4.6 g
Saturates		3.2 g
Pork tenderloin	68 mg	3 g
Polyunsaturates		0.3 g
Monounsaturates		1.3 g
Saturates		1 g

All the pork recipes in this book have been kitchen-tested with a view to removing even more of the fat content while still maintaining tender cuts. If you're watching calories and cholesterol, count the new pork in!

SALT AND SUGAR

Many people still do not understand the dangers posed by such items as canned soups and other so-called convenience foods. Read the labels. Unbelievably, the soups contain not only salt but sugar, both of which are addictive. Both tend to reduce life expectancy – in some cases, more so than cigarette smoke.

Some recipes call for canned soups, but note that no additional salt or sugar is required – and for good reason. These prepared goods are already loaded! *None should be served as soups.* The best soups in the world are always home-made. Build up a stock to keep in the freezer. That way, you need never be caught short-handed and your loved ones will enjoy more productive and longer lives.

Whatever you do, don't use cuisines like those of most North Americans or Japanese without adapting them. Americans and Canadians eat far too much fat and the Japanese eat too much salt.

When people from Japan move to California, their death rate from heart disease jumps from 1.3 to 3.7 per thousand. A typical American or Canadian gets 40% of his or her calories from fat, compared to 10 to 15% for the Japanese.

"If you prepare a Japanese recipe, cut the salt and the pickling," says Dr.

John H. Weisburger, director of the American Health Foundation's Naylor Dana Institute. "The Japanese love salt and have problems with strokes," agrees Dr. George Sopko, head of a cardiovascular risk-reduction center at St. Louis University. There's a correlation between cancers of the stomach and esophagus and exposure to high levels of nitrite and nitrate.

The Poirier Foundation's medical panel recommends avoiding such high-sodium items as miso and soya sauce and the nitrites in smoked fish. Any soya sauce specified in recipes is the reduced-sodium kind.

We give the last word on this subject to Bonnie Liebman, nutritionist with the Center for Science in the Public Interest, Washington: "Stay away from sodium and pickled and smoked foods. The Japanese consume great amounts of sodium and have a higher incidence of high blood pressure."

HONEY VERSUS SUGAR

North Americans consume their weight in sugar and corn sweeteners every year. Just thinking about it is enough to make your blood curdle.

Sugar is not too bad if you just look at the calories – each teaspoon (5 mL) contains only 16 calories – but it's a prime cause of tooth decay and other ills. Many of the sugars we consume are hidden in processed foods and beverages. Cream-style corn, for instance, derives 23% of its total calories from sugar.

Some people think honey is better for you than sugar. There's no evidence for this at all. In fact, honey scores 87 on the glycemic index, whereas sucrose registers only 59. The index measures how different forms of sugar affect circulating blood glucose levels. Pure glucose gets a score of 100. Sugar is therefore the lesser of the two evils.

If you have children under one year of age, do not under any circumstances feed them honey. Honey sometimes contains dormant *Clostridium botulinum* spores, causing infants to develop botulism. Honey is safe for older children.

The fact of the matter is that sugar is sugar and the body has to break it down into glucose. It doesn't matter if it's corn syrup, brown sugar, processed white sugar, honey or maple syrup.

Just as this book was being written, a new low-calorie sweetener, Splenda, appeared on the market. All our desserts had been kitchen-tested with aspartame despite lingering doubts in some quarters about its safety. Since

Splenda contains maltodextrin, a corn-derived starch, and sucralose, a sugar substitute actually created from sugar, we decided to retest all recipes with the new natural product. One advantage became immediately clear. Unlike aspartame, Splenda does not lose its sweetening power in recipes calling for long cooking periods. *It also tastes like sugar and contains only two calories per teaspoon (5 mL).* Most important, in cooking and baking, 1/2 cup (125 mL) of sugar adds 406 calories but the same amount of Splenda granular will provide only 50 calories. It measures spoon-for-spoon like sugar and is priced competitively with such brands of aspartame as Equal. We are certain you'll agree we did the right thing.

For those who do not have to worry about weight, diabetes or tooth decay, we have retained the sugar option. (Instead of Splenda granular sweetener, use an equal amount of sugar. All calorie counts are for Splenda only.) Be aware, however, that sugar and fats contribute to heart disease.

At the 14th Congress of the European Society of Cardiology, Dr. Larry Scherwitz presented the results of the San Francisco Heart Trial. A group of heart patients experienced dramatically improved health on a regimen of low-fat vegetarian foods, little alcohol, regular moderate exercise and relaxation techniques. Which of these factors was the most important? The low-fat diet, according to Dr. Scherwitz. The study proved this was the most significant factor in improving the health of the patients. It is therefore possible to reduce the risk of serious heart problems without the use of drugs while living a normal life.

Take it from there. Take it to heart. And if you do decide to go vegetarian now and then, you'll find terrific recipes in this book and you'll be in great company: Da Vinci, Gandhi, Jesus, Plato, Pythagoras, Shaw and Tolstoy – to name but a few – were all vegetarians.

THE FRENCH PARADOX

If you insist on eating fat, smoking and avoiding physical exercise, at least take a tip from the French and enjoy your meals with a little alcohol, preferably dry red wine.

The American TV investigative journalism show *60 Minutes* recently focused on *Le Paradoxe français*. The paradox? The French, who consume 30% more fat than North Americans, smoke more and exercise less, also suffer fewer heart attacks.

So what's going on? Our first reaction was to note that the French are fine cooks, that they take two-hour lunches (or used to until so-called market globalization), that they smoke pungent cigarettes, that they know how to relax and interact while enjoying their esteemed cuisine. Hard questions remain: Why aren't the French keeling over like all the rest who love fatty foods? Why do they have fewer heart attacks?

Believe it or not, the answer is alcohol, according to Dr. Serge Renaud, director of the National Institute of Health and Medical Research in France. He gives the specific credit to dry red wine, which cleanses the platelets from artery walls. Red wine in moderation at mealtime combats the buildup of fatty deposits. When this was announced in such papers as the *New York Times*, sales of red wine shot up by 40%.

Dr. Renaud also gave passing credit to the age-old gastronomy of the French, their spiritual respect for good food and the care and attention given to preparing and eating it.

A more recent study indicates that drinking two glasses of wine a day cuts the risk of heart disease by at least 40%. Wine (not the de-alcoholized kind) has an anti-clotting effect on particular blood cells.

Researchers compared farmers from Var, in southern France, who drink more than two glasses of wine a day, to farmers from southwest Scotland, who drink one glass or less. The activity of blood platelets was much lower in the French group.

"Alcohol taken in moderation may be one of the most efficient drugs for protection from coronary heart disease," they declared, and all groups, including smokers, can benefit.

The new study shed light on the "French paradox." In Toulouse, the annual heart-disease death rate per 100,000 is 78 for men and 11 for women; in Glasgow, the figures are 380 and 132 respectively. Both diets are rich in fat.

If further proof is needed, scientists at the Organization for Applied Scientific Research in Leiden, The Netherlands, did their own study and concluded that moderate alcohol consumption with meals reduces the risk of heart disease. The protective effects of alcohol are strongest in the evening, when fats from the dinner meal circulate throughout the bloodstream, the researchers concluded.

Apart from preventing the formation of blood clots, a few glasses of beer, wine or spirits may dissolve blood clots that already have formed, the study found. The benefits of two to three glasses of wine with the evening meal were also stressed in a 1994 report of the *British Medical Journal*.

If you'll pardon the pun, we have in this cookbook taken the matter to heart. After all, the Good Book enjoins us to "eat thy bread with joy, and drink thy wine with a merry heart" (Ecclesiastes 9:7). Like the early Christians, we urge all good cooks and their guests to drink a little wine for the sake of their stomachs and general well-being. Prepare your meals with enlightened gusto. Light the candles, converse and fraternize. We also urge all governments to reduce taxes on the finer alcoholic beverages, especially dry red wines. It's a matter of life and death.

KNOW YOUR VITAMINS

When a newsmagazine with the impact of *Time* runs a cover story on vitamins ("The New Scoop on Vitamins"), as they did in their April 6, 1992, issue, people who dismiss the faithful as crackpots sit up and take notice.

The few doctors who take courses in nutrition are well aware of the problem: food is not what it used to be and people still don't eat enough broccoli, Brussels sprouts, cabbage and carrots. How fruits and vegetables are grown, where they are grown, how they're harvested and shipped to market all determine whether you're getting your daily ration of minerals and vitamins.

According to a Canadian study, people who take high daily doses of vitamins C and E cut the risk of cataracts by at least 50%. Since cataracts afflict 20% of people over 65, it would appear prudent to take supplements. Think of the cost savings in health care!

At Toronto General Hospital, rabbits injected with vitamin E showed 78% less damage to heart tissue than anticipated. Vitamin E helps preserve heart muscle and prevents free radicals from injuring the organ. In seniors, it boosts the immune system and wards off the effects of tobacco smoke, car exhaust and other pollutants.

Vitamin E is a powerful antioxidant, a nutrient that protects other substances from oxidation caused by inhaling pollutants. So is beta carotene, abundant in carrots and cantaloupes. The body turns it into vitamin A as needed. In Japan and Norway, where diets are rich in beta carotene, there are far fewer cases of lung, colon, prostate, cervical and breast cancers than in Canada or the United States.

And feeding children twice the recommended amount of calcium helps them grow denser bones and may ward off fractures later in life, according to a new study of identical twins in Indiana.

The twins were given calcium tablets. "Adding calcium beyond the RDA seemed beneficial in terms of skeletal mineral development," reported Dr. Charles W. Slemenda (*New England Journal of Medicine*, July 8, 1992). Those who benefited significantly were children who had not yet reached puberty.

And though it might not be your favorite vegetable, broccoli is known to fight cancer. A 1994 study published in the *Proceedings of the National Academy of Sciences* pinpoints sulforaphane – a chemical found in broccoli – as the cancer-battling agent.

Unfortunately for seniors, eating alone is the fastest way to become undernourished, according to a survey by Katherine Tucker of the Human Nutrition Center on Aging at Tufts University in Boston. She studied 700 people from age sixty through their nineties and was shocked to find that a table set for one is the biggest risk factor for poor nutrition. The Annie Poirier Home Cooking Institute, whose volunteer chefs demonstrate recipes in a growing number of cities, is only too conscious of the fact that, for too many seniors, lunch consists of tea and toast. An obvious solution, though not the complete answer, is for physicians to prescribe more vitamin supplements to their elderly patients.

The news that vitamins and minerals help ward off major diseases is not news at all to those of us who read and follow these things, ignoring critics in the heavily financed scientific community. Three decades ago, Adelle Davis researched and wrote three books: *Let's Eat Right to Keep Fit*, *Let's Get Well* and *Let's Have Healthy Children*. She advocated a balanced diet, high in fiber-rich foods free of pesticides.

As Stephen T. Sinatra, M.D., chief of cardiology at Manchester Memorial Hospital in Connecticut, put it recently: "Nutritional awareness is on the leading edge in preventing many degenerative diseases, including cancer and coronary heart disease."

Soups

Basic Chicken Stock

Preparation:

10 minutes

Cooking: 3

hours

Freezing:

excellent

Per cup (*250*

mL): *31 calories.*

Excellent source

of calcium and

potassium.

Tips

- To save time and electricity, use a pressure cooker.
- When stock is made, cooled and defatted, freeze small portions in ice-cube trays to make gravies. After freezing, remove and store in freezer bags.
- Use leftover chicken bones, cooked or uncooked, frozen or fresh.
- Vinegar, which evaporates, helps draw out the protein from the bones.
- Canned stocks or broths are loaded with salt so use them only in an emergency. (The Institute's medical panel links excessive salt consumption to high blood pressure, kidney disease and loss of sexual prowess.)

4 lb	chicken bones or carcasses	2 kg
1	onion	1
3	cloves	3
1	leek, scrubbed thoroughly and trimmed	1
1	carrot, scrubbed and cut into 3 or 4 pieces	1
2	garlic cloves, peeled	2
1	bay leaf	1
2	sprigs fresh parsley	2
2	celery stalks, chopped in sections	2
1 tsp	dried thyme	5 mL
6	black peppercorns	6
3 quarts	spring water	3 L
1 tbsp	sea salt	15 mL
¼ cup	white vinegar	50 mL

1. Place all ingredients in an 8-quart (8 L) stockpot and bring to a boil.
2. Reduce heat and simmer for 3 hours.
3. Strain through a colander lined with cheesecloth. When warm to the touch, cover and place stock in refrigerator.
4. Use a slotted spoon and a lifter to remove congealed fat from surface.
5. Stock must be fat-free and absolutely clear. If uncertain, bring to a boil, remove from heat, refrigerate overnight and repeat Step 4.
6. You may, if you wish, reduce the stock by simmering, uncovered.
7. To clarify completely, add 1 beaten egg white and 1 crushed eggshell (thoroughly scrubbed first under running lukewarm water with a stiff brush). Bring stock to a boil and stir with a whisk. Remove from heat. Strain through a colander lined with several thicknesses of cheesecloth or a clean linen towel wrung out in cold water. Don't hurry the process; just let it drip and drain slowly.
8. Pour into plastic containers, cool and refrigerate or freeze.
   Yield: 12 cups (3 L).

Basic Beef Stock

Instead of chicken bones, use 4 lb (2 kg) beef bones, 3 lb (1.5 kg) marrow-bones and 2 veal knuckles. Proceed as above and simmer 4 hours. Cool and refrigerate or freeze.
Yield: 12 cups (3 L).

Turkey Stock

Use the entire carcass from a roast turkey and any other frozen chicken bones you may have on hand. Proceed as in Basic Chicken Stock. Cool and refrigerate or freeze.
Yield: 12 cups (3 L).

Basic Fish Stock

PREPARATION:
8 minutes

COOKING:
35 minutes

FREEZING:
excellent

MAXIMUM
REFRIGERATOR
LIFE: *8 days*

This stock is excellent for poaching fish or using in recipes from this book. Label and freeze small quantities for use as required.

3 lb	fresh fish bones (plus heads and tails)	1.5 kg
4 quarts	spring water	4 L
1 tsp	thyme	5 mL
3	bay leaves	3
3	cloves garlic, unpeeled	3
2	onions, quartered	2
12	peppercorns	12
3	carrots, coarsely chopped	3
2	stalks celery with leaves	2
3	sprigs fresh parsley	3
¼ tsp	salt	1 mL

1. Wash bones in two changes of water.
2. Put bones and water in a large kettle and boil 5 minutes.
3. Add other ingredients. Simmer uncovered 30 minutes.
4. Strain and cool.
   Yield: 3 quarts (3 L).

Basic Chinese-Style Stock

PREPARATION:
3 minutes

FREEZING:
excellent

This is the traditional base of wonton soup. The idea is not to overpower the savory fillings.

6 cups	chicken stock (page 24)	1.5 L
4	green onions, chopped	4

1. Bring ingredients to a boil in a saucepan.

2. Simmer for 3 minutes.
   Yield: 6 cups (1.5 L).

ANNIE POIRIER'S CLAM CHOWDER

PREPARATION:
6 minutes
COOKING:
20 minutes
FREEZING: *not recommended*
PER CUP (250 mL): 94 calories. Excellent source of calcium, potassium and vitamin A.

After being diagnosed as diabetic and advised to adopt a low-fat diet, Annie – a Londoner who never lost her love of seafood – devised a method of enjoying the full taste of Atlantic clams with the velvety smoothness of the traditional New Brunswick chowder. Today's guests will appreciate this low-calorie dish.

1	can clams (5 oz/142 mL)	1
1 tsp	cornstarch	5 mL
2 tbsp	spring water	25 mL
½ cup	dry white wine	125 mL
1	onion, coarsely chopped	1
2	carrots, sliced	2
2	potatoes, cubed (preferably unpeeled)	2
¼ tsp	dill weed	1 mL
	Pepper to taste and/or cayenne	
1 cup	green beans, diced (frozen or fresh)	250 mL
1 cup	skim milk (or 2% evaporated)	250 mL

GARNISH:

1 tsp	fresh parsley, chopped	5 mL

1. Drain clam juice into saucepan and set clams aside. In a cup, mix cornstarch with the water. Add to saucepan with wine, vegetables (except beans), herbs and pepper. If liquid seems insufficient, add water.

2. Simmer for 15 minutes, stirring occasionally. Add beans and cook another 5 minutes. Add clams and milk and heat but do not boil. Garnish before serving.
   Yield: 2 to 3 servings.

TIPS

- If using fresh beans, they will be crisp. If you prefer a softer consistency, simmer them an extra 5 minutes before adding clams and milk.
- Do not boil after adding clams and milk. If you do, the clams will harden and milk may curdle.
- Omit beans or use frozen peas instead.
- Use thyme instead of dill weed.

CARLETON-SUR-MER FISH CHOWDER

PREPARATION:
4 minutes
COOKING:
approximately 25
minutes
FREEZING: not
recommended
PER CUP (250
mL): 153 calories.
Excellent source
of folate, niacin,
potassium and
vitamin A.

Carleton-sur-mer is a Québec haven on the north shore of the Baie des Chaleurs. We refuse to provide any further directions in case this sanctuary becomes infested with even more tourists than it already is. The chowder was developed by French settlers when fish was plentiful, and this version is a nostalgic and nutritious tribute to the past.

1	large onion, chopped	1
1 tbsp	oil	15 mL
1	clove garlic, minced	1
3	potatoes, diced (1 lb/500 g)	3
1	carrot, diced	1
½ cup	sweet red pepper, diced	125 mL
⅓ cup	celery, diced	75 mL
2 cups	spring water	500 mL
1 lb	fish (fresh or frozen)	500 g
	Touch of dried dill or cumin	
¼ cup	fresh parsley or 2 tbsp (25 mL) frozen	50 mL
2 cups	skim milk	500 mL
1 cup	corn kernels (frozen or canned)	250 mL
	Black pepper, freshly ground	

GARNISH:

Soy bacon bits and/or sweet paprika

1. In a saucepan, cook the onion in the oil for 5 minutes over low heat until transparent but not brown.
2. Add garlic, potatoes, carrot, red pepper, celery and water. Simmer, covered, until potatoes are almost tender (about 15 minutes).
3. Cut fish into chunks and add to saucepan. Cook, covered, for 3 minutes for fresh fish, 10 minutes for frozen.
4. Add cumin or dill, parsley, milk and corn. Season with pepper to taste. Heat but do not boil.
5. Serve immediately with toasted wholewheat bread or unsalted cream crackers.
6. Offer guests paprika for light dusting.

Yield: 4 to 6 servings.

TIPS

- Instead of parsley, use fresh dill.
- If a creamier texture is desired, thicken with 1 tablespoon (15 mL) corn-starch, made into a paste with water, before Step 3.

SOUPE AUX POISSONS DE PERCÉ (PERCÉ FISH SOUP)

The Gaspé is noted for its awesome scenery and fresh seafood. The latter is threatened by overfishing. If you can't find fresh mackerel, substitute any other fish.

PREPARATION:
20 minutes
COOKING:
35 minutes
FREEZING:
excellent
PER CUP (250
mL): 215 calories.
Excellent source of
calcium, folate,
potassium, protein
and vitamin A.

2 oz	lean salt pork	50 g
2 tbsp	unbleached white flour	25 mL
3 cups	spring water	750 mL
1 ½ cups	unpeeled, diced potatoes	375 mL
½ cup	diced leeks (white and light green parts)	125 mL
½ cup	chopped onion	125 mL
3	cloves garlic, minced	3
¼ tsp	white pepper, freshly ground	1 mL
½ lb	boneless cod	250 g

½ lb	boneless mackerel	250 g
¼ lb	unshelled small shrimp	125 g
1 cup	skim milk, fresh or reconstituted	250 mL

GARNISH:

| 2 tbsp | fresh parsley, chopped | 25 mL |

1. Boil salt pork 5 minutes. Discard water and rinse. Remove rind and cut into small cubes. Fry over low to medium heat until crisp and golden, about 10 minutes. Discard fat and rinse pork in boiling water.

2. Make a paste of the flour and 1/4 cup (50 mL) water. Put the paste in a large saucepan and add potatoes, leeks, onion, garlic, remaining water and pepper. Stir well. Cover and simmer for 15 minutes.

3. Cut cod and mackerel into 1-inch (2.5 cm) pieces. Shell and devein shrimps. Add all three to soup. Cover and simmer for 5 minutes. (Note: Cool and freeze, if desired. Thaw overnight in refrigerator, heat, and proceed with Step 4.)

4. Stir in milk. Simmer gently for 3 to 5 minutes. Adjust seasoning. Do not cook more than 6 minutes. Serve with garnish. *Yield: 5 servings.*

LAZARE POIRIER'S OYSTER CHOWDER

Lazare was a great woodsman and fisherman like his brother, Étienne (my father). Like all the Poiriers of his generation, he was also a fantastic cook. He lived to be 94.

1 tbsp	canola oil	15 mL
1	onion, chopped	1
1	stalk celery, chopped	1
1	carrot, diced	1
2 tbsp	unbleached white flour	25 mL
¼ cup	spring water	50 mL

PREPARATION:
6 minutes
COOKING:
15 minutes
FREEZING: *not*
recommended
PER CUP (*250*
mL): 76 *calories.*
Excellent source
of calcium,
niacin, potassium
and vitamin A.

½ cup	dry white wine	125 mL
1	can oysters (5 oz/142 g)	1
1	clove garlic, minced	1
1 cup	diced, unpeeled potatoes	250 mL
1 tsp	dried or fresh thyme	5 mL
	Black pepper, freshly ground	
2 ¼ cups	skim milk, fresh or reconstituted	550 mL
2 tbsp	chopped fresh parsley	25 mL

1. In a saucepan, sauté in oil the onion, celery and carrot. Cover and simmer for 5 minutes on very low heat.
2. In a cup, make a paste of the flour, adding water gradually until all lumps are gone. Add wine and blend with mixture in saucepan. Stir.
3. Partially open can of oysters. Drain liquid into saucepan.
   Stir. Set can of oysters in refrigerator.
4. Add garlic, potatoes and thyme. Simmer, uncovered, until potatoes are tender (10 minutes should do). Season with pepper to taste.
5. Add oysters, milk and parsley. Heat but do not boil.
   Yield: 4 servings.

VARIATIONS

- Use 2% evaporated milk, diluted, instead of skim milk. (Calorie count will increase by 16%.)
- Use fresh oysters instead of canned.
- Instead of wine, use 1/2 cup (125 mL) Basic Fish Stock (page 26) or prepare some, using powdered fish stock sold in farmers' markets and health food stores.
- Instead of flour, use 1 tsp (5 mL) cornstarch. If thicker consistency is desired, add more cornstarch paste.

Ragoût de Louisbourg
(Louisbourg Seafood Chowder)

PREPARATION:
10 minutes
COOKING: 53
minutes
SUITABILITY
FOR FREEZING:
excellent
PER CUP (250
mL): 146 calories.
Excellent source
of folate, niacin,
potassium and
vitamin A.

In the last part of the 20th century, young men and women depict life as it was in the summer of 1744 when the Fortress of Louisbourg was the bastion of Nouvelle-France and the most expensive for Louis XIV. From May to October, thousands of people visit this historic walled town which includes l'Hôtel de la Marine tavern and an excellent restaurant, l'Épée Royale, where this award-winning chowder is served.

1	onion, chopped	1
2	cloves garlic, minced	2
2 tbsp	canola or safflower oil	25 mL
1	green or red pepper, chopped	1
½ lb	mushrooms, sliced (2 ½ cups/625 mL sliced)	250 g
1 lb	new potatoes, unpeeled, washed and cubed	500 g
1 cup	fish stock (page 26) or clam juice	250 mL
½ cup	dry white wine	125 mL
1	can plum tomatoes (28 oz/796 mL), mashed	1
1 tsp	lemon rind, grated	5 mL
2 tsp	fresh sage, chopped, or ½ tsp (2 mL) dried	10 mL
	Dash of cumin	
1 lb	frozen cod, haddock, bluefish or scallops	500 g
	Black pepper, freshly ground	

1. In a heavy soup pot, sauté onion and garlic in oil over medium heat for 2 minutes. Add green or red pepper, stir, and continue cooking another 3 minutes.
2. Add all other ingredients except seafood and black pepper. Cover and simmer 40 minutes.
3. Stir in seafood, cover and simmer until scallops are opaque or fish flakes easily (about 8 minutes).
4. Season with pepper.
   Yield: 4 servings.

VARIATIONS

- If fresh garden basil is available, chop 1/4 cup (50 mL) and use in place of the sage.
- Instead of potatoes, use 2 cups (500 mL) chopped fresh garden vegetables (asparagus, beans, snowpeas, zucchini and so forth). Reduce simmering time by about 20 minutes or cook until vegetables are crispy-tender.

LAS VEGAS CUCUMBER SOUP

The immortal Marlene Dietrich's first 1953 live performance in Las Vegas, then the entertainment capital of the world, was a triumph. Other show-biz celebrities started flying in from all over the world to catch her act at the Sahara. She gave the audiences what they had come for, including such memorable songs as "When the World Was Young," "Lili Marlene" and "The Boys in the Back Room." This classic soup was on the menu for opening night. Try it at home and, when serving, play a Dietrich CD for your awed and fascinated guests.

PREPARATION:
6 minutes
FREEZING: *not recommended*
REFRIGERATOR STORAGE LIFE:
4 days
PER CUP (250 mL): *70 calories. Excellent source of calcium, folate and potassium.*

3	fresh cucumbers (about 1 ½ lb/750 g)	3
¼ tsp	cumin	1 mL
1	clove garlic, minced	1
1 ½ cups	no-fat plain yogurt	375 mL
	Pepper, freshly ground	

GARNISH:
Parsley, fresh mint or sliced cucumbers

1. Scrub cucumbers under luke-warm water. Rinse in cold water. Do not peel. Cut into chunks.
2. In blender or food processor, blend cumin, garlic and cucumbers.
3. Transfer to a bowl. Add yogurt. Stir well. Chill for 4 hours.
4. Add pepper to taste. Garnish with parsley, mint or sliced cucumbers.

Yield: 4 servings.

Soeur Saint-Victor's Heavenly Carrot Soup

PREPARATION:

12 minutes

COOKING: *45 to*

60 minutes

FREEZING:

excellent

PER CUP (*250*

mL): 175 calories.

Excellent source

of beta carotene,

calcium,

potassium and

vitamin C.

Soeur Saint-Victor was one of Étienne Poirier's five sisters. A conscientious nun, she could not bear to see even the simplest of God's bounties wasted. This recipe produces a smooth soup so divinely flavored, it will convert even the most ardent carrot-hater.

2	unpeeled potatoes, scrubbed and quartered	2
4	unpeeled carrots, scrubbed	4
1	onion, chopped	1
2	cloves garlic, chopped	2
¼ cup	canola or safflower oil	50 mL
6 cups	defatted chicken stock (page 24)	1.5 L
	Pinch of celery salt	
½ tsp	nutmeg	2 mL
½ tsp	coriander	2 mL
	Pinch of ground ginger	
2 tbsp	unbleached white flour	25 mL
1 cup	aged white Cheddar cheese, grated	250 mL
	Black pepper, freshly ground, to taste	

1. Steam potatoes until cooked and mash. Chop carrots in the food processor.
2. In a saucepan, sauté onions and garlic in half the oil over low heat for 5 minutes or until translucent. Do not brown.

Add carrots and cook a further 5 minutes.

3. Add the chicken stock and heat to a simmer. Add potatoes, celery salt, nutmeg, coriander and ginger. Stir and simmer for 10 minutes.

4. In a cup, mix remaining oil and flour to make a paste and add to the soup, stirring constantly. Cover, reduce heat and simmer 5 minutes. (Note: Cool and freeze, if desired. Thaw overnight in refrigerator, heat, and follow steps 5 and 6.)

5. Stir in half the grated cheese and pepper. At this point, remove from heat and do not simmer or cheese will separate.

6. Serve immediately. Garnish each bowl with remaining cheese.
   Yield: 8 servings.

Potage Saint-Quentin (Cabbage Soup)

This traditional recipe from the hills of Saint-Quentin, New Brunswick, is chock-full of vitamins and minerals. It's guaranteed to recharge the batteries after a hard day at work. Cool the wine while you prepare the soup. Cabbage is loaded with vitamin C and helps prevent cancer of the colon.

PREPARATION:
20 minutes

COOKING: 75 minutes

FREEZING: excellent

FREEZER LIFE: 3 months

PER CUP (250 mL): 34 calories. Excellent source of calcium, potassium and vitamins A and C.

½ cup	pinto or other beans, washed, soaked overnight and drained	125 mL
3 cups	chicken stock (page 24)	750 mL
3 cups	spring water	750 mL
2	carrots, cut in cubes	2
1	stalk celery, chopped	1
1	potato, unpeeled, washed and diced	1
1	large onion, chopped	1
3	cloves garlic, chopped	3
1	can tomatoes (28 oz/796 mL), chopped	1
1	bay leaf	1
5	peppercorns	5
½ cup	any leftover, defatted, cooked chicken or meat (optional)	125 mL
3 cups	shredded cabbage	750 mL
¼ cup	fresh lemon juice	50 mL

3 tbsp	corn syrup	40 mL

Dash of cumin (optional)

GARNISH:

Chopped parsley and grated cheese

1. In a heavy soup pot, combine beans, stock, water, carrots, celery, potato, onion, garlic, tomatoes, bay leaf and peppercorns. Simmer covered for 45 minutes then add leftovers, if using. Simmer for another 15 minutes.
2. Add cabbage and continue simmering for 15 minutes.
3. Stir in lemon juice and corn syrup. Adjust seasonings and add a touch of cumin if you wish.
4. Light candles and serve the chilled white wine.
5. Ladle the elixir into bowls, top with parsley and cheese, and serve with crusty wholewheat rolls.

Yield: 6 servings.

VERDI'S GARLIC AND PEPPER SOUP

PREPARATION:
10 minutes
COOKING: 30
minutes
FREEZING:
excellent
PER CUP (250
mL): 62 calories.
Excellent source
of folate,
potassium and
vitamin C.

For a break from composing, the great Giuseppe Verdi insisted that the garlic in this amazing soup nourished the soul of his immortal music. One bowl served with crusty bread and he was ready for another three or four hours' inspired work. (He completed the opera *Falstaff* in his 80th year and used part of his fortune to establish a retirement home for musicians.) Of course, the chicken stock also provides nourishment, and the bell peppers, vitamin C. If mascarpone is not available in your locale, use low-fat creamed cheese or sour cream.

3	medium red bell peppers	3
2	large cloves elephant garlic or 1 clove ordinary garlic	2
1 ½ cups	chicken stock (page 24)	375 mL
½ cup	Alfie Duncan's El Cheapo Tomato Sauce (page 195)	125 mL

½ tsp	black pepper, freshly ground	2 mL
1 ½ tsp	clover honey	7 mL
1 ½ tsp	fresh basil, chopped,	7 mL
	or	
¼ tsp	dried basil	1 mL

GARNISH:

| 4 tsp | mascarpone creamed cheese, low-fat cottage cheese | 20 mL |
| | (mashed with a fork), or low-fat sour cream | |

1. Scrub and wash red peppers in warm water, rinsing with cold. Slice in quarters and remove seeds and pith.
2. Peel garlic and chop coarsely.
3. In a blender or food processor, purée peppers and garlic to a smooth paste.
4. In a saucepan, combine purée and other ingredients except garnish. Bring to a gentle simmer and continue simmering 30 minutes. (Note: Cool and freeze, if desired. Thaw, warm and follow Step 5.)
5. Garnish each bowl with 1 tsp (5 mL) of chosen garnish. *Yield: 4 servings.*

SAUGEEN CREAM OF MUSHROOM SOUP

This low-fat creamy mushroom soup beats the canned variety by a mile and contains no salt or sugar. The talented Ojibwe chefs of Chief's Point and Saugeen reserves on Lake Huron use wild morels in season. Different versions of our low-calorie recipe have been enjoyed for centuries.

3 cups	fresh morels or mushrooms	750 mL
2 tbsp	canola oil	25 mL
2	small onions, finely chopped	2
2	cloves garlic, minced	2
5 cups	chicken stock or beef broth	1.25 L

PREPARATION:
15 minutes
COOKING: *25 to*
30 minutes
FREEZING:
excellent
PER CUP (*250*
mL): *132 calories.*
Excellent source
of calcium,
niacin and
potassium.

2 tbsp	dry white wine	25 mL
2 tbsp	unbleached white flour	25 mL
3 tbsp	spring water	40 mL
1 cup	evaporated skim milk	250 mL
	Black pepper, freshly ground, to taste	
½ tsp	ground nutmeg	2 mL

GARNISH:

| ½ tsp | paprika | 2 mL |

1. Wash mushrooms (saving a few for garnish), chop and sauté in oil. Add onions and garlic, frying lightly for 4 minutes.
2. Transfer to a pot. Add stock and wine. Simmer for 15 minutes.
3. In a cup, form a thin paste with the flour and water. Stir well. Add to soup and stir.
4. Cool slightly. (If freezing, cool completely, transfer to tightly sealed containers, date and label. Thaw overnight in the refrigerator, warm and proceed with Step 5.)
5. Add milk and seasonings except paprika.
6. Serve at once. Garnish with reserved mushrooms and paprika.
   Yield: 6 to 8 servings.

SOUPE AUX POIS DE LA BOLDUC (LA BOLDUC'S PEA SOUP)

Of Irish ancestry, Madame Bolduc (née Mary Travers) became French-Canada's first great folklore singer. Her concerts were invariably sold out. La Bolduc's 78 RPM recordings are family heirlooms now in thousands of homes. Her nutritious recipes are also treasured.

1 lb	whole dried yellow peas and water for soaking	500 g
3 quarts	spring water	3 L
½ lb	lean salt pork	250 g
½ cup	diced carrots and turnips	125 mL

PREPARATION:

10 minutes

COOKING: *4*

hours

FREEZING:

excellent

REFRIGERATOR

STORAGE LIFE:

1 week

FREEZER LIFE:

3 months

PER CUP *(250*

mL): 168 calories.

Excellent source

of calcium,

niacin,

potassium,

protein and

vitamin A.

1	large onion, chopped	1
2	cloves garlic, chopped	2
	Freshly ground black pepper	

GARNISH:

Fresh parsley, chopped

1. Pick over and wash peas in a colander. Soak 12 hours in water or use quick method (see page 147).
2. Rinse peas and put in a pot with spring water and salt pork.
3. Bring to a boil, add vegetables and simmer 4 hours. Add pepper to taste.
4. Serve unstrained, garnished with parsley.
   Yield: 6 servings.

TIPS

- If preferred, use lean ham, cubed, rather than salt pork. Add during last hour of simmering.
- If soup becomes too thick, add water.

TOMATO CHOWDER BEAUSÉJOUR

An Acadian favorite, this chunky dish is a superb warmer-upper on a crisp autumn day when you're wondering how to use the last of the season's tomatoes. It freezes well in small plastic tubs.

¼ cup	canola or safflower oil	50 mL
1 tbsp	crushed garlic	15 mL
1 cup	diced onions	250 mL
1 cup	diced carrots	250 mL
2 ½ cups	fresh tomatoes, crushed	625 mL
4 cups	canned tomatoes, crushed	1 L
½ cup	tomato purée	125 mL
1 tbsp	basil	15 mL

PREPARATION:

12 minutes

COOKING: *72*

minutes

FREEZING:

excellent

PER CUP *(250*

mL): 88 calories.

Excellent source

of beta carotene,

calcium and

vitamin C.

| 1 cup | spring water | 250 mL |
| 1 cup | evaporated skim milk | 250 mL |

GARNISH:

Fresh parsley

1. Put the oil in a large saucepan. Add garlic, onions and carrots. Sauté over low heat for 30 minutes, stirring now and then. Do not brown the onions.

2. Blanch whole tomatoes in boiling water for 2 minutes. Pour off hot water and replace with cold. Peel tomatoes and crush with a potato masher. Crush the canned tomatoes in the same way and add all the tomatoes, with the purée, to the saucepan. Simmer for 40 minutes.

3. Add basil, water and evaporated milk. Heat but do not boil or it will curdle.

Yield: 12 servings.

PREPARING THE SOUP FOR FREEZING:

• Add water but omit the milk. Fill plastic tubs to within 1/2 inch (1 cm) of top. When cool, cover, label, date and freeze.

USING THE FROZEN SOUP:

• To thaw, place tub in hot water for a few minutes to loosen the frozen soup.
• Transfer to the top of a double boiler.
• When the soup is hot, add the evaporated milk and serve immediately. The flavor is even more superb after freezing.

ANDY WARHOL'S
CREAM OF TOMATO SOUP

PREPARATION:
6 minutes
COOKING: *3
minutes*
FREEZING: *not
recommended*
PER CUP *(250
mL): 87 calories.
Excellent source
of calcium,
potassium and
vitamin C.*

The Prince of Pop and Pied Piper of New York's underground shocked the art world with his Campbell's soup cans in the 1960s and died prematurely in 1987 following surgery to remove gallstones. Sotheby's auction of his memorabilia yielded $25.3 million. Canned soups contain huge amounts of salt and sugar. This version, created with the help of one of his kitchen-whiz friends, does not. They used a homemade sauce similar to Alfie Duncan's. The taste is sublime.

1 cup	Alfie Duncan's El Cheapo Tomato Sauce (page 195)	250 mL
3 cups	chicken stock (page 24)	750 mL
1 cup	evaporated skim milk	250 mL
¼ tsp	black pepper, freshly ground	1 mL

GARNISH:

Chopped chives, basil or dash of nutmeg

1. In a blender, purée sauce until smooth.
2. In top of double boiler, combine sauce and remaining ingredients and heat.
3. Garnish before serving.

Yield: 4 servings.

Mata Hari Chicken Soup

PREPARATION:
20 minutes
COOKING: 40
minutes
FREEZING:
excellent
PER CUP (250
mL): 82 calories.
Excellent source
of calcium and
potassium.

Why this version should be named after the exotic spy is one of those great mysteries. We do know that it is nourishing and comforting. The fenugreek plant is almost as mysterious, multifaceted and versatile as Mata Hari herself; the seeds make a laxative tea, and the leaves contain *coumarin*, an artificial maple flavoring, and *diosgenin*, a steroid used in birth-control pills!

1 cup	spring water	250 mL
½ cup	basmati rice	125 mL
5 cups	cold tap water	1.25 L
¾ lb	chicken breast or leg with back attached	375 g
1	onion, chopped	1
3	cloves garlic	3
½ tsp	fresh ginger, chopped	2 mL
1 cup	spring water	250 mL
1 tsp	tomato paste	5 mL
¼ cup	turmeric	50 mL
½ tsp	Hungarian sweet paprika	2 mL
½	stick cinnamon	½
¼ tsp	black peppercorns	1 mL
1	large cardamom pod	1
¼ tsp	cumin	1 mL
½ tsp	ground coriander	2 mL
6	cloves	6
2 tbsp	lemon juice	25 mL
5 cups	spring water	1.25 L
1 tsp	dried fenugreek leaves	5 mL
1 cup	evaporated skim milk	250 mL

GARNISH:

Chopped fresh coriander or parsley

1. In a saucepan, boil 1 cup (250 mL) water. Add rice, cover and simmer over very low heat for 20 minutes. Turn off heat.

2. In another saucepan, bring 5 cups (1.25 L) tap water to a boil. Add chicken and simmer over medium heat for 10 minutes. Drain. Run cold tap water over chicken and remove fat and skin. Cut chicken into small strips and discard bones. Put chicken in a large pot. Wash and dry hands.

3. Purée onion, garlic, ginger and 1 cup (250 mL) water in a blender or food processor.

4. Put the mixture in the pot with the chicken, then add tomato paste, turmeric, paprika, cinnamon, peppercorns, cardamom pod, cumin, ground coriander, cloves, lemon juice and spring water. Bring to a boil, stirring frequently, reduce heat and simmer 25 minutes over medium or low heat. Remove cinnamon stick.

5. Add cooked rice and simmer another 5 minutes. Add fenugreek leaves and milk. (Note: If freezing, omit milk. To use, thaw, heat gently, then add milk but do not boil.) Serve with garnish.

Yield: 4 to 6 servings.

MA PARKER
QUICK-GETAWAY BEEF SOUP

Robbing banks can take a lot of energy out of even the most devoted practitioners of the art. This soup from the Bonnie and Clyde era of the Great Depression provides all the protein you'll need to keep your wits about you, energy for quick reactions and no fat to clog arteries and slow you down. Please be kind to the tellers; they only work there.

	Cookware spray	
1 lb	lean ground beef	500 g
1 tbsp	dry white wine	15 mL
8 oz	potato or rice flour, sold in health food stores	250 g
2 quarts	spring water	2 L

PREPARATION:
15 minutes
COOKING: 60
minutes
FREEZING:
excellent
FREEZER LIFE:
3 months
PER CUP (250
mL): 46 calories.
Excellent source
of potassium,
protein and
vitamin A.

1 cup each	diced onions, carrots and celery	250 mL each
3	cloves garlic, minced	3
1	can plum tomatoes (28 oz/796 mL)	1
1 tbsp	B-V or Bovril beef base	15 mL
	Black pepper, freshly ground	
	Dash of cumin	
	Dash of cayenne or Tabasco	
1 cup	frozen corn niblets	250 mL
1 cup	frozen peas	250 mL

1. Apply spray to a skillet and sauté beef with the wine for 20 minutes over low heat, stirring frequently. To remove all fat, drain in a colander and pour boiling water over beef. Alternatively, simply remove with a slotted spoon. (You can always refrigerate soup after cooking and lift any congealed fat off the top.)

2. Put all ingredients except frozen vegetables in a soup pot, bring to a boil and simmer for 45 minutes.

3. Add frozen corn and peas and simmer for 5 minutes.
   Yield: 8 servings.

NOTE:

Refrigerating overnight improves flavor. If frozen thaw in refrigerator overnight before using.

FIRST NATIONS' MANOMIN POTAGE (WILD RICE SOUP)

PREPARATION:
25 minutes
COOKING: 90
minutes
FREEZING:
excellent
PER CUP (250
mL): 129 calories.
Excellent source
of calcium,
potassium and
vitamin A.

Wild rice has grown in northwestern Ontario since the first Ojibwe arrived there 36,000 years ago. *Manomin*, as the natives call it, could become an important annual crop if the northern lakes aren't overwhelmed by southern Ontario's self-destructive population explosion. The rice on these lakes is a far better quality than the kind grown on commercial paddies in California and Minnesota. Alas, since humanoids appear determined to breed themselves into extinction (according to the United Nations), enjoy this ancient delicacy while you can. The soup is not only delicious but nourishing.

¼ cup	wild rice with sufficient water to cover	50 mL
¼ cup	spring water	50 mL
	Cookware spray	
1	onion, chopped	1
2	cloves garlic, minced	2
2 tbsp	unbleached white flour	25 mL
2 tbsp	spring water	25 mL
2 ½ cups	chicken stock (page 24)	625 mL
1	bay leaf	1
1 cup	evaporated skim milk	250 mL
	White pepper, freshly ground	

GARNISH:

Soy bacon bits

1. Cover rice with cold water and let stand for 30 minutes. Strain in a fine sieve and rinse under running cold water. Cover and simmer 30 minutes in 1/4 cup (50 mL) spring water. Set aside.

2. Spray a saucepan and in it sauté onion for 10 minutes over low heat. Add garlic. Cover and simmer 5 minutes.

3. In a bowl, make a paste of the flour and 2 tbsp (25 mL) water. Add chicken stock to the paste. Stir well.

4. Combine all ingredients except rice and simmer, covered, another 30 minutes. Remove bay leaf. Add wild rice. Simmer for 15 minutes or until rice is tender.

5. Freeze some of the soup at this point if you wish. To use, thaw, heat gently and proceed with Step 6, adjusting milk quantity.

6. Stir in evaporated skim milk and season to taste with pepper. Reheat but do not boil. Serve immediately, sprinkling each bowl with "bacon" bits.

Yield: 3 to 4 servings.

POTAGE BAS-BALMORAL (LENTIL SOUP)

PREPARATION:
20 minutes
COOKING:
1 1/2 hours
FREEZING:
excellent
PER CUP (250
mL): 92 calories.
Excellent source
of calcium, folate,
niacin, potassium
and vitamin A.

In the old days, soup did not come out of a tinfoil envelope or a can. It came from experience – centuries of it. The folks living in the main part of Balmoral (Bas-Balmoral or "Lower Balmoral") were determined to make a better lentil soup than their cousins living higher up in the hills (Haut-Balmoral or "Upper Balmoral") in New Brunswick. I recall as a ten-year-old pedalling my bike from one part of the village to the other in order, naturally, to sample both versions in the aromatic kitchens of obliging gourmet cooks. I could not make up my mind then and still cannot recall which was better since both recipes produced superb results. Both are great sources of vitamins and minerals.

1 cup	red lentils	250 mL
½ cup	canned tomatoes and juice, or equivalent fresh	125 mL
1 cup	chopped onions	250 mL
5	green onions, chopped	5
4	garlic cloves, minced	4
1	bay leaf	1
5 tbsp	chopped fresh parsley (or 2 frozen parsley ice cubes)	65 mL

5 tbsp	fresh coriander leaves, chopped	65 mL
	or	
¼ tsp	dried coriander	1 mL
2 tsp	ground ginger	10 mL
2 tsp	turmeric	10 mL
2 tsp	sweet paprika	10 mL
2 tbsp	vegetable oil	25 mL
2 tbsp	peanut oil	25 mL
1 tsp	black pepper, freshly ground	5 mL
2 cups	spring water	500 mL
3 cups	vegetable stock	750 mL
1 tbsp	powdered cumin	15 mL

1. Pick over lentils. Rinse.
2. In a soup pot, combine all ingredients except cumin, bring to a boil, reduce heat and simmer for 1 1/2 hours.
3. Cool and refrigerate to improve flavor.
4. Label and freeze if you wish.
5. When serving, sprinkle a touch of cumin atop each bowl.
Yield: 8 servings.

POTAGE HAUT-BALMORAL (HERB, LENTIL AND TOMATO SOUP)

Here's the potage from Upper Balmoral. See if you can pick your favorite – I can promise you it won't be easy. The first settlers named the village after Balmoral in Scotland where the Royal Family has its country home. They claimed the soup was a favorite with Queen Victoria. The French added the Gallic touch with the seasonings. We adapted the recipe to eliminate fat.

2 cups	red lentils and water for soaking	500 mL
2 cups	spring water	500 mL
2	bay leaves	2

PREPARATION:
12 minutes
COOKING: 42
minutes
FREEZING:
excellent
PER CUP (250
mL): 79 calories.
Excellent source
of calcium, folate,
potassium and
vitamin A.

3 tbsp	canola or safflower oil	40 mL
2 tbsp	minced garlic	25 mL
2	celery stalks, chopped	2
	Cumin (pinch)	
1 tbsp	marjoram	15 mL
1 tbsp	savory	15 mL
½ tsp	thyme	2 mL
2 tsp	black pepper, freshly ground	10 mL
1	can plum tomatoes (28 oz/796 mL), chopped in the can with a knife	1
2 cups	defatted chicken stock (or vegetarian stock)	500 mL
¼ cup	evaporated skim milk	50 mL
	Drop of Tabasco sauce (optional)	

GARNISH:

Chopped fresh parsley, dandelion leaves and/or grated carrot
or hard cheese

1. Soak lentils in cold water for 10 minutes. Drain and wash again carefully, using a fine sieve. Put in saucepan with spring water and bay leaves.
2. Simmer over medium heat about 25 minutes or until lentils are tender. Most of the water will be gone. Set aside.
3. In another saucepan, sauté in oil the onions and garlic. Do not brown.
4. Add celery, herbs and pepper. Simmer for 2 minutes.
5. Add chopped tomatoes and juice. Simmer for 15 minutes.
6. Stir in lentils. Add stock and heat at moderate setting.
7. Just before serving, stir in evaporated milk.
8. Garnish with chopped fresh parsley, dandelion leaves and/or grated carrot or hard cheese. *Yield: 6 servings.*

Mary Pickford's University Avenue Potage

PREPARATION:

18 minutes

COOKING: 15

minutes

FREEZING:

excellent

PER CUP (250

mL): 89 calories.

Excellent source

of calcium,

potassium and

vitamin A.

America's Sweetheart, Gladys Marie Smith, saw the light of day in 1893 at 175 University Avenue in Toronto. When the house was torn down in 1943, she had 20 bricks shipped to her in Hollywood. *The Film Encyclopedia* describes her as "the most popular star in screen history." This easy-to-prepare Canadian soup was served many times to blasé but appreciative guests at fabulous dinner parties in her gracious home, Pickfair, according to Hedda Hopper.

5 cups	chicken stock (page 24)	1.25 L
2 cups	mixed vegetables, unpeeled, scrubbed and grated	500 mL
3	cloves garlic, minced	3
½ cup	noodles or shell pasta	125 mL
½ cup	chopped fresh parsley	125 mL
2 cups	greens, chopped or torn (see below)	500 mL
	Black pepper, freshly ground	

GARNISH:

Seasoned croutons and/or grated cheese

1. Bring stock to a boil. Add vegetables (carrots, green onions, yellow turnip, celery, green peas or any combination of what you have on hand) and garlic and simmer for 4 minutes.
2. Add noodles or pasta. Simmer for 4 minutes.
3. Add parsley and greens (washed spring dandelion, spinach, Romaine lettuce, celery leaves or any combination of what you have on hand). Simmer for 3 minutes. Add pepper, taste, adjust seasoning and turn off heat. Serve within 10 minutes with seasoned croutons and/or grated cheese.

Yield: 4 servings.

VARIATION

- Today's Hollywood chefs occasionally add a few garden-ripe tomatoes or even chopped zucchini as part of Step 1. Let your imagination dictate ingredients. Just make sure they're fresh.

Dr. Banting's
July Heat Wave Soup

PREPARATION:
6 minutes
FREEZING: *not*
recommended
PER CUP (250
mL): 112 calories.
Excellent source
of calcium,
potassium and
vitamin C.

With the discovery of insulin, Canada's Frederick G. Banting changed the lives of millions of diabetics throughout the world.

This refreshing summer soup, one of the great scientist's favorites, should be served well chilled.

⅛ tsp	dried dill	0.5 mL
1 ½ cups	low-sodium tomato juice	375 mL
2	cloves garlic	2
1 cup	no-fat yogurt	250 mL
	Dash of hot pepper sauce (such as Tabasco)	

1. Rub dill between fingers and add to juice. Add garlic, crushed in a garlic press. Add yogurt and dash of hot sauce.

2. Whisk thoroughly, cover and chill several hours.
   Yield: 2 servings.

TIPS

- Replace dill with mint, fresh or dried.
- Add 2/3 cup (150 mL) diced, unpeeled cucumber.

Sir Harry Oakes's Bahamian Soup

PREPARATION:
4 minutes
COOKING: *10
minutes*
FREEZING:
excellent
PER CUP (*250
mL): 225 calories.
Excellent source
of calcium, folate,
potassium and
vitamin A.*

Oakes, an old codger of a millionaire mining magnate, met a most untimely end, but while ensconced in his luxurious, tax-free retirement mansion among the palm trees, this Canadian lived life to the hilt. If you believe the advertising, "everything's better in the Bahamas," including its unusual banana soup. Sir Harry found it sexy (probably because of its high potassium content).

5	very ripe bananas, peeled	5
1 quart	skim milk, fresh or reconstituted	1 L
1 tbsp	grated orange rind	15 mL
⅛ tsp	ground nutmeg	25 mL
¼ tsp	cornstarch	1 mL
2 tbsp	spring water	25 mL

GARNISH:
Sliced kiwi fruit, sliced bananas and/or fresh mint leaves.

1. In a blender or food processor, pulse bananas until smooth. Add milk, rind and nutmeg and blend.
2. Make a paste of the cornstarch and the water. Add to mixture in blender or food processor. Blend.
3. Pour into saucepan and simmer over low heat, uncovered, for 10 minutes or until it thickens. Serve chilled. Garnish each bowl with fruit or mint.
Yield: 4 servings.

Salt Lake City Melon Soup

PREPARATION:
4 minutes
FREEZING: *not recommended*
PER CUP (250 mL): 64 calories. *Excellent source of calcium, folate and vitamins A and C.*

Nothing is more refreshing on a hot summer night than a chilled melon soup. Making this one, a favorite with members of the Mormon Tabernacle Choir, is a breeze.

1	ripe cantaloupe	1
1 cup	no-fat plain yogurt	250 mL
3 tbsp	lemon juice	40 mL
¼ tsp	ground ginger	1 mL

GARNISH:

| 2 tbsp | chopped fresh mint | 25 mL |

1. Remove and discard seeds from cantaloupe.
2. Remove pulp and combine it with other ingredients in blender.
3. Blend until smooth. Refrigerate.
4. Garnish with fresh mint.
   Yield: 2 to 4 servings.

BEEF

 ## ALICE B. TOKLAS'S BORJUPAPRIKAS (LOW-CAL HUNGARIAN VEAL GOULASH)

PREPARATION:
25 minutes
COOKING:
1 hour
FREEZING:
excellent
PER SERVING:
299 calories.
Excellent source
of protein and
vitamin C.

A veal is a veal is a veal. Gertrude Stein. Gertrude Stein. Gertrude Stein. Cubist writer. Poet. Cubist collector. Mentor. Hemingway and Fitzgerald. Alice and Gertrude were companions for 40 years. Alice did the gardening, the banking and the cooking. And she pushed Gertrude to write, write, write. Alice's cuisine was international and as creative as Gertrude's literary work.

1 tbsp	sweet paprika, or more to taste	15 mL
2 lb	boneless veal, cubed (1 ½ inches/3.75 cm)	1 kg
	Cookware spray	
2 cups	thinly sliced onion	500 mL
1 tbsp	beef stock (page 25)	15 mL
1	small green pepper, seeded and chopped	1
2	cloves garlic, minced	2
1 cup	tomatoes, peeled and coarsely chopped	250 mL
1 cup	Alfie Duncan's El Cheapo Tomato Sauce (page 195)	250 mL
2 tbsp	low-fat plain yogurt or light sour cream	25 mL
½ tsp	fresh lemon juice	2 mL

1. Sprinkle half the paprika over the veal cubes and let stand 10 minutes.
2. Spray a heavy saucepan and sauté onions with the beef broth over low heat until translucent, about 10 minutes. Add green pepper and stir.
3. Add veal and cook over medium heat until it loses its bright redness. Stir.

4. Add garlic, paprika, tomatoes and tomato sauce. Cover and reduce heat to low. Simmer 1 hour or until veal is tender.
5. Combine yogurt and lemon juice. Swirl in just before serving. Serve immediately over rice or noodles.
Yield: 8 servings.

MICROWAVE METHOD

1. Follow Steps 1 and 2 above.
2. Transfer to a 2-quart (2 L) casserole.
3. Add all ingredients except lemon juice and yogurt.

4. Cover and microwave 25 minutes or until veal is tender.
5. Remove and let stand for 5 minutes before stirring in lemon juice and yogurt.

PRESSURE COOKER METHOD

1. Follow Steps 1, 2 and 3 in main recipe.
2. Add garlic, paprika, tomatoes and tomato sauce.
3. Cook at 15 lb (6.8 kg) pressure

for 15 minutes. Cool under running cold water.
4. Remove cover and reheat. Add lemon juice and yogurt.

TO FREEZE

1. Omit lemon juice and yogurt. Cool and freeze.
2. When ready to use, thaw in refrigerator overnight and reheat.

3. Add lemon juice and yogurt just before serving.

CORNER BROOK BRISKET OF BEEF

PREPARATION:

20 minutes

COOKING:

4 1/2 hours

FREEZING:

excellent

PER SERVING:

412 calories with

defatted sauce.

Excellent source

of niacin,

potassium and

protein.

Now that cod stocks have been decimated, Newfoundlanders are turning to beef for their protein. This recipe rates five stars by any criteria. Don't be afraid of the garlic. It becomes sweet and odorless.

6	large onions, sliced	6
10	garlic cloves, peeled and halved	10
6 lb	brisket of beef	3 kg
1 cup	Alfie Duncan's El Cheapo Tomato Sauce (page 195)	250 mL
1 cup	spring water	250 mL
½ cup	ketchup (preferably Heinz)	125 mL
3 tbsp	red wine vinegar	40 mL
2 tbsp	Dijon mustard (preferably Aristocrate)	25 mL
3 tbsp	Worcestershire sauce	40 mL
1 tsp	hot pepper sauce (such as Tabasco)	5 mL
1 tsp	black pepper, freshly ground	5 mL

1. Place half the onions and garlic in the bottom of a large pot with a tight cover. (The tight cover is important.)
2. Put the brisket in the pot and cover with remaining onions and garlic.
3. Mix all remaining ingredients in a small bowl and pour over the brisket. Cover tightly.
4. Bake for 4 hours at 325°F (160°C). Check 4 times to make sure there is at least 1 cup (250 mL) of liquid in the pot. If not, add boiling spring water.
5. Remove lid. Raise oven temperature to 350°F (175°C) and bake another 30 minutes.
Yield: 12 servings.

All-Day Cooking

We tried this at 225°F (110°C) for those who leave early for work and don't feel like cooking extravagantly when they arrive home from the evening rush hour. After 10 hours, the beef was exquisite and very tender. At this low temperature, no extra spring water was required.

Freezing

Allow brisket to cool, then slice and transfer to freezer containers. Top with mixture from pot and spring water to cover, allowing room for expansion. Cover tightly, label and date. To use, thaw overnight in refrigerator, heat and serve.

Calgary Stampede Beef and Sauce

Preparation:
12 minutes
Cooking: 20 minutes
Freezing: excellent
Per serving: 394 calories.
Excellent source of niacin, potassium, protein and vitamin C.

A delicious way to convert leftover roast beef into another gourmet item. The Stampede is an annual event in ranch country and every restaurant in town seems to have its own version of this traditional Western recipe.

¼ cup	chopped celery	50 mL
¼ cup	chopped onion	50 mL
1 cup	sliced mushrooms	250 mL
1 tbsp	canola oil	15 mL
2	cloves garlic, chopped	2
¼ cup	chopped green pepper	50 mL
½ tsp	minced fresh or preserved ginger	2 mL
	or	
¼ tsp	ground ginger	1 mL
¼ cup	brown sugar	50 mL
1 ¼ tbsp	cornstarch	20 mL
1 tbsp	Worcestershire sauce	15 mL
1	beef bouillon cube	1
2 ¼ cups	tomato juice	550 mL
2 cups	leftover roast beef or meat loaf, slivered	500 mL

1. In a skillet, sauté celery, onion and mushrooms for 3 minutes in hot oil, stirring.
2. Add all other ingredients except beef. Stir and continue simmering over low heat for 15 minutes.
3. When slightly thickened, stir in beef. Simmer for 2 minutes.
4. Serve over hot rice or noodles. *Yield: 4 servings.*

ROBERT MORLEY'S BARBECUED SIRLOIN

A seasoned cosmopolitan in more ways than one, the world-traveled actor returned with this delectable recipe after a trip to Asia. No salt is used in our adaptation because it will toughen the fibers and draw out the juices.

PREPARATION:
4 minutes
COOKING: *14 to 20 minutes*
FREEZING: *excellent (after Step 2)*
PER SERVING: 327 *calories. Excellent source of niacin, potassium and riboflavin.*

3	cloves garlic	3
1/2 tsp	black pepper, freshly ground	2 mL
2 tbsp	sesame oil	25 mL
2 lb	sirloin steak 1 1/2 inches (3.5 cm) thick	1 kg

1. Peel garlic and mash in a garlic press. Add oil and pepper.
2. Rub mixture into both sides of steak. Set aside while you prepare the barbecue (or cover and leave to marinate in refrigerator).
3. Grill 7 minutes on each side for rare, a few minutes longer for medium.
4. Remove and let stand 6 minutes before carving thinly. *Yield: 6 servings.*

NOTES
- Steak sauce and mustard, if desired, should be applied after steak is cooked.
- Sesame oil is sold in specialty stores; if unavailable, use canola or safflower.

Jean Drapeau Bifteck au Poivre Vert (Sirloin Steak with Green Peppercorn Sauce)

PREPARATION:

4 minutes

COOKING: *10, 20*

or 30 minutes

(rare, medium or

well-done)

FREEZING:

excellent

PER STEAK: *286*

calories.

Excellent source

of niacin,

potassium and

protein.

Jean Drapeau is the Montréal mayor who declared that Expo 67 could no more run a deficit than "a man could have a baby." Ah, well, it was a great party and the whole world came. He also opened a fancy restaurant but it sank in a sea of red ink. Ah, well, people can be fickle. His maître chef was absolutely right in featuring this dish, however. It's simple, low-cal and outrageously good. Green peppercorns, which are preserved in brine or vinegar, are less pungent than their black and white brothers.

1	sirloin steak, 1 ½ inches (3.5 cm) thick	1
	Cookware spray	
½ cup	spring water	125 mL
1 tbsp	Ontario brandy	15 mL
1 tbsp	polyunsaturated margarine	15 mL
1 tbsp	crushed green peppercorns	15 mL
¼ cup	evaporated skim milk	50 mL
½ tsp	Dijon-type mustard, preferably Aristocrate	2 mL

GARNISH:

Chopped fresh parsley

1. Trim all fat from the steak.
2. Dip steak in cold spring water and drain. Do not pat dry.
3. Spray a frying pan, preferably cast-iron. Place on high heat.
4. When frying pan is hot, sear steak on both sides quickly. Lower heat to low-medium. Add spring water and continue cooking (10 minutes for rare, 20 for medium and 30 for well-done). Add water as required.
5. Place steak on a warm plate while preparing sauce.

6. Add brandy to frying pan and stir to deglaze.

7. Combine margarine and peppercorns. Roll into a ball and add to pan. When melted, add milk. Stir and simmer until gravy is desired consistency.

8. Add mustard to gravy, stir, and pour over steak. Garnish and serve immediately.

VARIATION

If green peppercorns are unavailable, use freshly ground black or white pepper. Dip steak in water, sear rapidly and sprinkle with pepper to taste while cooking.

CAFÉ BUDAPEST BOEUF STROGANOFF

The waiter cooked the beef strips over a fire at the table when we tried this in Berlin in 1961. Our low-calorie version of this traditional feast will astound and delight the senses.

PREPARATION:
6 minutes + 2 to
3 hours'
refrigeration
COOKING: 10 to
15 minutes
FREEZING:
excellent (after
Step 5)
PER SERVING:
352 calories.
Excellent source
of niacin,
potassium and
protein.

1 ½ lb	boneless sirloin	750 g
	Black pepper, freshly ground, to taste	
½ tsp	canola oil	2 mL
1	medium onion, sliced	1
1	can sliced mushrooms (10 oz/284 mL), drained,* rinsed in cold water to remove salt and drained again (or fresh mushrooms)	1
1 tbsp	unbleached white flour	15 mL
10 oz	condensed beef bouillon or consommé (preferably homemade)	284 mL
1 tsp	Dijon mustard	5 mL
	or	
½ tsp	dry mustard	2 mL
1 tbsp	tomato paste	15 mL
1 tbsp	Worcestershire sauce (optional)	15 mL
3 tbsp	low-fat sour cream or plain yogurt	40 mL
¼ cup	fresh parsley, washed and finely chopped	50 mL

Set mushroom liquid aside.

1. Remove fat and gristle from the meat and cut it into strips 2 inches (5 cm) long and 1/2 inch (1.25 cm) thick. Season with pepper and refrigerate for 2 to 3 hours.

2. In a heavy frying pan, heat oil and brown meat quickly on both sides. Add onion and canned or fresh mushrooms. Sauté for 5 minutes, then remove mixture to a hot platter.

3. Blend flour with beef bouillon and add to frying pan.

4. Stir in mustard, tomato paste and Worcestershire sauce, if using. Add beef and onion.

5. Stir vigorously and simmer until sauce is smooth. If too thick, add mushroom liquid or water.

6. Blend in sour cream or yogurt and heat for 3 minutes. Add parsley. Serve immediately on broad noodles or unpeeled chopped and steamed potatoes. *Yield: 4 to 6 servings.*

LAZY BONES CASSEROLE
CABBAGE ROLLS

This has all the flavor and texture of the traditional rolled kind minus the fuss. Serve with a good dry white wine. Nifty for entertaining; you can prepare it three days in advance, cover and chill in the refrigerator. Reheat at 325°F (160°C) for 25 minutes.

PREPARATION:
8 minutes
COOKING: 100
minutes
FREEZING:
excellent
PER SERVING:
166 calories.
Excellent source
of calcium,
niacin,
potassium,
protein and
vitamin C.

1 lb	lean ground beef	500 g
	(or cooked Bay of Fundy Gourmet Meat Loaf, page 66)	
1 tbsp	oil	15 mL
2	cloves garlic, chopped	2
1	onion, chopped	1
	Black pepper and/or cayenne to taste	
	Dash of powdered cumin	
1 tsp	Worcestershire sauce (optional)	5 mL
3 tbsp	raw long-grain rice	40 mL
1	can condensed cream of tomato soup (10 oz/284 mL)	1

1	soupcan of Manitou spring water or dry red wine	284 mL
3 cups	shredded cabbage (coarse)	750 mL
	Grated sharp cheese (optional)	

1. If using raw ground beef, fry in oil for a few minutes at medium heat. Pour off any fat (or place beef in colander and pour hot water over it). If using leftover meat loaf, chop or shred coarsely. To either meat, add garlic, onion, seasonings and rice. Sauté gently for 3 minutes. Add soup and water.

2. Place raw cabbage in a sprayed casserole. Stir meat mixture well and spoon it over the cabbage. Do not stir. The idea is to have two distinct layers intermingling their flavors.

3. Cover and bake for 1 1/2 hours at 325°F (160°C). If topping with cheese, uncover after 1 hour, sprinkle with cheese, recover and continue baking. *Yield: 8 servings.*

RED DEER TACO MIX

PREPARATION:

3 minutes

There are direct flights from Denver and other midwestern points to Calgary. This must explain how the recipe reached Canada's West. Since it has no salt or sugar, it beats the store-bought kinds.

¼ cup	instant minced onion	50 mL
1 tbsp	garlic powder	15 mL
2 tbsp	cumin	25 mL
1 tsp	cayenne	5 mL
1 tbsp	cornstarch	15 mL
2 tsp	oregano, crushed*	10 mL

1. Mix all ingredients.

2. Spoon into two plastic bags. Seal.

*To achieve fine texture, place herb in the palm and rub with two fingers of the other hand.

RED DEER TACOS

PREPARATION:

2 minutes

COOKING: 30 to

45 minutes

FREEZING:

excellent

(after Step 3)

PER SERVING:

117 calories.

Excellent source

of calcium,

niacin, potassium

and vitamin C.

1 lb	lean ground beef, veal, pork or chicken	500 g
½ cup	spring water	125 mL
1 or 2 tbsp	ketchup, preferably Heinz	15 or 25 mL
1 bag	(¼ cup/50 mL) Red Deer Taco Mix (previous page)	1
6	taco shells	6

Tomatoes, shredded cheese, green peppers and other favorite toppings

1. In a heavy skillet, cook and break up ground meat over low heat for 30 minutes.
2. Transfer meat to a colander. Pour hot water over meat to remove fat.
3. Wipe skillet with paper towel.

Return meat to skillet and add spring water and ketchup. Add Taco Mix. Stir. Simmer to evaporate water, about 15 minutes.

4. Spoon into taco shells. Add toppings.

Yield: 6 servings.

CHARLES BOYER REAL CHILI

When he got to Hollywood, the French screen lover developed a certain love affair with American foods. One of these was chili, which, he insisted, should be "authentic." Translation: no beans. The International Chili Society defines the dish as "any kind of meat, or combinations of meats, cooked with chili peppers, various other spices, and other ingredients with the exception of items such as beans or spaghetti which are strictly forbidden." In cookoffs in Texas, where it's been officially declared the state dish, they sometimes include rattlesnake. There's no rattlesnake in this recipe and no beans, so we've named it in honor of Charles Boyer.

PREPARATION:

15 minutes

COOKING: 3

hours 20 minutes

FREEZING:

excellent

PER CUP (250

mL): 233 calories.

Excellent source

of niacin,

potassium,

protein and

vitamin C.

	Cookware spray	
4 lb	lean ground beef	2 kg
1	can tomato sauce (28 oz / 796 mL)	1
2	onions, chopped	2
4	cloves garlic, minced	4
½ cup	chili powder	125 mL
2 tbsp	oregano	25 mL
½ tsp	salt	2 mL
¼ cup	ground cumin	50 mL
½ tsp	hot red pepper sauce such as Tabasco	2 mL
1 tsp	cayenne pepper	5 mL
1 pint	natural ale such as Upper Canada or European-style	500 mL

1. Spray the bottom of a heavy skillet and sauté beef until no pink appears, about 15 to 20 minutes. Stir often with a wooden spoon. Drain in a colander and flush with boiling hot water to remove any remaining fat.

2. Transfer to a large kettle and add all other ingredients. Cover and simmer for 3 hours over very low heat. Mixture should just barely bubble.

3. If too thick, add a little hot water.

Yield: 1 gallon (4.5 L), the amount stipulated for chili cookoffs.

SERVING SUGGESTIONS

- Serve over fluffy white rice or a combination of white and wild rice.
- Accompany the chili with any of the following: tacos, chopped onion and lettuce, grated mild cheese, no-fat plain yogurt and salt-free whole-wheat crackers.

HOLLYWOOD MEAT LOAF

PREPARATION:

6 minutes (using

a food processor)

COOKING: *90*

minutes

FREEZING:

excellent

FREEZER LIFE:

2 months

PER PORTION:

72 calories.

Excellent source

of calcium,

niacin and

protein.

Our grandmothers made meat loaf frequently! Contrary to popular belief, a gourmet meat loaf need not contain bread crumbs to soak up fat or cholesterol-laden eggs. Our adapted recipe, now a favorite among young Hollywood actors, will make you a star in the culinary department. Don't be surprised if your family or guests claim it tastes better than Sunday's roast beef. It can also be doubled or tripled and frozen for later use in hundreds of delicious, healthy meals.

2 lb	lean ground beef	1 kg
¾ cup	chopped parsley	175 mL
¼ cup	finely chopped onion	50 mL
3 tbsp	ketchup, preferably Heinz	40 mL
1 tbsp	dried basil	15 mL
¼ cup	coarsely chopped green pepper	50 mL
½ cup	finely chopped carrot	125 mL
3	cloves garlic, minced	3
½ tsp	black pepper, freshly ground	2 mL
	Barbecue sauce (your favorite, or Gordon Sinclair Low-Cal Barbecue Sauce, page 202)	

1. In a bowl, combine all ingredients except barbecue sauce. Blend by hand and shape into an oblong loaf.
2. Place carefully upon a rack in a baking pan. All the unhealthy fat will drip into the pan.
3. Bake for 1 1/2 hours at 350°F (175°C). Half an hour before the loaf is done, using a brush, baste the part you will be serving immediately with barbecue sauce. Remove from oven and let stand for 5 minutes before slicing. Serve with fresh tomato sauce (Alfie Duncan's El Cheapo Tomato Sauce, page 195).

Yield: 1 loaf.

- You can slice the cold loaf as thinly as you wish, even with an electric knife. The slices make glorious sandwiches. Try wholewheat bread (plain or toasted), a touch of Gloria Swanson's Mayonnaise (page 185), a dab of Dijon mustard and Romaine lettuce leaves or sprouts.
- If freezing, allow loaf to cool completely. Slice and wrap each portion in plastic film before inserting in freezer bags. To use, thaw in wrappings in the refrigerator.

JEAN COCTEAU'S
MONTMARTRE MEAT LOAF

PREPARATION:
8 minutes
COOKING:
1 hour (or
microwave: 15
minutes)
FREEZING: *good*
PER SERVING:
395 calories.
Excellent source
of niacin,
potassium and
protein.

The artist and poet, the soul mate of Édith Piaf, created this quick dish so that he wouldn't have to spend too much time in the kitchen and could devote more to "intellectual pursuits." We've adapted it so you have even more time for your pursuits – intellectual or trivial.

1	can cream of mushroom soup (10 oz/284 mL)	1
1 ½ lb	lean ground beef	750 g
	or	
	1 lb (500 g) lean ground beef and ½ lb (250 g) lean ground pork	
1	small carrot, grated	1
2	cloves garlic, minced	2
1	medium onion, finely chopped	1
1 tbsp	Worcestershire sauce	15 mL
¼ tsp	black pepper, freshly ground	1 mL
4	fresh mushrooms, sliced	4
	Cookware spray	
¼ cup	skim milk	50 mL

1. Combine 1/2 cup (125 mL) soup, beef, grated carrot, garlic, onion, Worcestershire sauce and pepper. Mix well.
2. Shape into loaf and place in a slightly larger baking pan.
3. Bake at 350°F (175°C) for 1 hour. Carefully pour off fat.
4. While loaf is baking, sauté mushroom slices in sprayed skillet for 10 minutes on low heat. Set aside.
5. Heat mushrooms, remaining soup and milk in saucepan. Serve over sliced loaf.
   Yield: 5 servings.

MICROWAVE METHOD
Place loaf in microwave-safe dish. Cover with waxed paper. Microwave 15 minutes or until loaf is firm, rotating dish twice.

BAY OF FUNDY GOURMET MEAT LOAF

PREPARATION:
4 minutes
COOKING: 1
hour
FREEZING:
excellent
PER SERVING:
*416 calories.
Excellent source
of niacin,
potassium and
protein.*

You don't have to spend a bundle to come up with a winner. Just make sure the ground meat is ultra-fresh and don't add salt. The recipe doesn't include bread crumbs to soak up the fat and hike your cholesterol level.

1	envelope dry onion soup mix	1
2 lb	lean ground beef	1 kg
1	egg white	1
¾ cup	spring water	175 mL
⅓ cup	ketchup (preferably Heinz)	75 mL
	Black pepper, freshly ground	
	Barbecue sauce (your favorite, or	
	Gordon Sinclair Low-Cal Barbecue Sauce, page 202)	

1. Combine all ingredients except barbecue sauce. Form into a round loaf.
2. Place a large sheet of waxed paper in the bottom of a pie plate.
3. Put the loaf on the waxed paper and bring edges up but do not attempt to close.
4. Bake at 350°F (175°C) for 1 hour. Baste occasionally with barbecue sauce.

5. When fat accumulates, lift pie plate carefully, using oven mitts, and pour it off. (If meat is not very lean, you may have to do this several times during cooking period.)

6. Serve with a mushroom or tomato sauce.

Yield: 6 servings.

HAMBURG'S FIRST BURGER

PREPARATION:

20 minutes

COOKING: *15 to*

20 minutes

FREEZING:

excellent

(at Step 2)

PER SERVING:

326 calories.

Excellent source

of niacin,

potassium and

protein. Good

source of beta

carotene and

vitamin E.

The year was 1885 and the village was Hamburg, southwest of Buffalo, New York. It was here – or so they claim – that Frank Menches created America's first beef burger at the Hamburg County Fair. (Others credit Hamburg, Germany; the Baltic area; and even ancient Russia.) Frank had little choice; his butcher had sold out everyone's favorite pork sausages. All he had left were 10 pounds of good local beef. The rest is anticlimactic. The recipe, adapted to cut down on fat, is from one of Frank's employees.

½ cup	shredded carrot	125 mL
2 tbsp	shredded onion	25 mL
1	clove garlic, minced	1
¼ cup	wheat germ	50 mL
1 tsp	dried parsley	5 mL
½ tsp	dry mustard	2 mL
3	drops Tabasco or other red pepper sauce	3
1 lb	very lean ground beef	500 g
	Black pepper, freshly ground (optional)	
	Cookware spray (if frying)	

1. Combine all ingredients except pepper and spray and mix well.
2. Shape into 4 patties. If desired, pepper both sides.
3. Broil 1 side for 10 minutes or until well browned. Turn and broil the other side for 6 minutes. Alternatively, lightly spray a heavy skillet and cook burgers until medium or well done, turning twice. Discard fat.
4. Serve in heated wholewheat hamburger buns with favorite condiments.

Yield: 4 servings.

Camillien Houde's Mont-Royal Burgers

PREPARATION:
20 minutes
COOKING: 20
minutes
FREEZING:
excellent (after
Step 1)
PER SERVING:
290 calories.
Excellent source
of niacin,
potassium and
protein.

The ex-mayor of Montréal, imprisoned during World War II for his anti-conscription views, was guarded by none other than Private Étienne Poirier. The two became friends and, after his release, Camillien was overwhelmingly re-elected to the Hôtel de Ville by a cross-section of that great-hearted city. Camillien loved spicy foods and these were his favorite burgers.

1 ¼ lb	lean ground beef	575 g
1	small onion, grated or finely chopped	1
2	garlic cloves, minced	2
2 tbsp	tomato paste	25 mL
2 tbsp	low-fat plain yogurt	25 mL
1 tsp	cinnamon	5 mL
½ tsp	dried thyme	2 mL
¼ tsp	dried sage	1 mL
¼ tsp	black pepper, freshly ground	1 mL

SAUCE:

⅔ cup	no-fat plain yogurt	150 mL
2 tbsp	ketchup (preferably Heinz)	25 mL
2 tbsp	green onions, chopped	25 mL
¼ tsp	ground mace	1 mL

1. Combine beef with other ingredients. Shape into 5 patties.
2. Broil 1 side for 10 minutes or until well browned. Turn and broil the other side for 8 minutes.
3. Meanwhile, prepare sauce by combining ingredients. Do not heat or refrigerate. Serve at room temperature.
4. Serve burgers on heated buns and pass the sauce.
   Yield: 5 burgers.

BAYOU CAJUN BURGERS

PREPARATION:
15 minutes
COOKING: *15 to*
20 minutes
FREEZING:
excellent
(after Step 1)
PER SERVING:
197 calories.
Excellent source
of niacin,
potassium and
protein.

Bayou is from the Choctaw native word *bayuk*, meaning a small stream. The French Acadiens deported from the Atlantic region simply gallicized the word. In recent times, in Louisiana, they've also adapted the ever-popular burger to make it more pungent.

1 lb	lean ground beef	500 g
2 tbsp	finely chopped onion	25 mL
1	clove garlic, minced	1
½ tsp	dried cumin	2 mL
1 ½ tsp	oregano	7 mL
1 tsp	thyme	5 mL
½ tsp	paprika	2 mL
⅛ tsp	cayenne	0.5 mL

GARNISH:

Sliced tomatoes
Low-fat plain yogurt

1. Combine all ingredients and shape into 4 patties.
2. Broil 1 side for 10 minutes or until well browned. Turn and broil the other side for 5 to 8 minutes. Alternatively, spray a heavy skillet and brown both sides for the same lengths of time. Discard fat.
3. Serve on heated wholewheat hamburger buns. Garnish with tomatoes and yogurt.
Yield: 4 burgers.

Route 66 Hamburgers

PREPARATION:
10 minutes
COOKING: *20 to*
30 minutes
FREEZING:
excellent
(after Step 1)
PER SERVING:
296 calories.
Excellent source
of niacin,
potassium and
protein.

In *The Grapes of Wrath*, Steinbeck called Route 66 "the mother road, the road of flight." Food served in the greasy spoons along this historic route to California improves as one approaches the Pacific. In the old days, the two-lane highway carried Model As and Studebakers as mobile Americans sought the good life in California. Clark Gable and Carole Lombard spent their wedding night, March 29, 1939, in Arizona's Oatman Hotel, where these burgers were served. The Route 66 ones in our low-cal version have French panache and are glorious.

2 lb	lean ground beef	1 kg
4 tsp	black pepper, freshly ground	20 mL
	Cookware spray	
2 tbsp	brandy	25 mL
	Hot red pepper sauce (such as Tabasco) to taste	
	Worcestershire sauce to taste	
	Lemon juice to taste	
	Chopped parsley	
	Chopped chives	

1. Shape beef into 8 patties. Coat each side with pepper, pressing it into sides by hand. Let stand 30 minutes.

2. Lightly spray a heavy skillet. Add burgers and raise heat to medium. Cook until brown on one side. Turn gently. Remove burgers, pour off all fat and wipe skillet with paper towel. Put the burgers back in the skillet.

3. Add brandy and continue cooking for medium or well done. Sprinkle burgers with hot pepper sauce, Worcestershire and lemon juice to taste.

4. Serve burgers immediately, topped with sauce from skillet. Sprinkle with parsley and chives.
Yield: 8 servings.

Sloppy Joes

There is no way to determine who first invented Sloppy Joes – ground beef served with a piquant sauce. The name probably originated in the United States during the Great Depression. If you eliminate the fat, they're a good source of protein. Our favorite versions do just that. We've named our low-cal versions after locales where relatives and friends got together over the kitchen stove to experiment and invent new Sloppy Joes.

P'tit Montréal Sloppy Joes

PREPARATION:

6 minutes

COOKING: 10

minutes

FREEZING:

excellent (after

Step 3)

PER SERVING:

267 calories.

Excellent source

of iron, niacin,

potassium,

protein and

vitamin C.

2 tbsp	canola oil	25 mL
1	onion, chopped	1
1 lb	cooked meat loaf, chopped	500 g
2	cloves garlic, minced	2
2 tsp	chili powder	10 mL
1	red pepper, diced	1
1 cup	Alfie Duncan's El Cheapo Tomato Sauce (page 195)	250 mL
½ cup	ketchup (preferably Heinz)	125 mL

Cayenne and/or black pepper to taste

1. Heat oil in a frying pan. Sauté onion but do not brown.
2. Add meat loaf, garlic, chili powder, red pepper, tomato sauce and ketchup.
3. Simmer gently 10 minutes. Add cayenne and/or pepper.
4. Serve over bread or rolls. Accompany with cold, home-brewed beer or dry red wine.

Yield: 3 to 4 servings.

San Francisco Sloppy Joes

PREPARATION:

8 minutes

COOKING: *12 to*

15 minutes

FREEZING:

excellent (after

Step 3)

PER SERVING:

281 calories.

Excellent source

of iron, niacin,

potassium,

protein and

vitamin A.

2 tbsp	canola oil	25 mL
1	onion, chopped	1
1 lb	cooked meat loaf, chopped	500 g
3	cloves garlic, minced	3
¼ tsp	hot red chili flakes	1 mL
1	package frozen spinach, thawed, squeezed dry and chopped	1
	Black pepper to taste	
5	egg whites, beaten lightly	5

1. Heat oil in skillet and sauté onion until tender but not brown.
2. Add meat loaf, garlic and chili flakes. Stir well.
3. Add spinach and pepper. Simmer for 4 minutes.
4. Stir in egg whites. Cook until set. Serve with rice.

Yield: 3 to 4 servings.

VARIATIONS

- Instead of chili flakes, use cayenne or Tabasco sauce to taste.
- If you prefer moister Sloppy Joes, add 1/4 cup (50 mL) ale or stout, mixed with the egg whites.
- In season, use garden-fresh spinach and/or young dandelion leaves instead of frozen spinach.

NOTE

- Egg whites become leathery when frozen. It's best to add these when you thaw and reheat.

CHINATOWN SLOPPY JOES

PREPARATION:
6 minutes
COOKING: 18
minutes
FREEZING:
excellent (after
Step 3)
PER SERVING:
275 calories.
Excellent source
of niacin,
potassium,
protein and
vitamin C.

2 tbsp	canola oil	25 mL
1	leek or 3 green onions, chopped	1 or 3
1 lb	cooked meat loaf, chopped	500 g
1	red bell pepper, chopped	1
3	cloves garlic, minced	3
1 tbsp	fresh ginger root, chopped	15 mL
2 tbsp	soy sauce	25 mL
2 tbsp	hoisin sauce	25 mL
½ to ¾ tsp	hot Chinese chili paste	2 to 4 mL
⅔ cup	tomato sauce	150 mL
	Black pepper to taste	

GARNISH:

| 3 tbsp | fresh parsley, chopped | 40 mL |

1. Heat oil in frying pan and sauté leek or green onions until tender.
2. Add meat loaf, bell pepper, garlic, ginger, soy sauce, hoisin sauce, chili paste and tomato sauce. Stir well.
3. Simmer 10 minutes. Add pepper to taste.
4. Serve in pita bread or over rice. Sprinkle with parsley.
   Yield: 4 servings.

VARIATIONS
- Instead of parsley, use fresh cilantro.
- Instead of Chinese chili paste, use Tabasco.

Mountain Brook Sloppy Joes

PREPARATION:
6 minutes
COOKING: 15
minutes
FREEZING:
excellent
PER SERVING:
235 calories.
Excellent source
of iron, niacin,
potassium,
protein and
vitamin A.

2 tbsp	canola oil	25 mL
1	onion, chopped	1
1 lb	cooked meat loaf, chopped	500 g
¼ cup	diced celery	50 mL
3	cloves garlic, minced	3
1	tin green chilies (4 oz /110 g), diced	1
1	canned, fresh or frozen jalapeño pepper, diced	1
½ cup	taco sauce (mild or hot, your choice)	125 mL
½ cup	corn niblets, canned or frozen	125 mL
	Black pepper to taste	

1. Heat oil in a frying pan and sauté onion until tender but not brown.
2. Add meat loaf, celery, garlic, chilies and jalapeño. Cook for 3 minutes on medium heat.
3. Add taco sauce and corn. Simmer for 6 minutes. Taste and add pepper if desired. Serve in pita bread.

Yield: 4 servings.

PORK

RAYMOND MASSEY
FESTIVE PORK CHOPS

PREPARATION:
4 minutes
COOKING: 25
minutes
FREEZING:
excellent

PER SERVING: 177
calories.
Excellent source of
niacin, potassium
and protein. Good
source of vitamin C.

Hart House at the University of Toronto is named after Raymond Massey's grandfather, Hart Massey, who gave Toronto the acoustically perfect Massey Hall in 1894. The actor's British-born children, Daniel and Anna, are also well-known thespians. Anna says this delicious recipe has been in the family for generations.

6	loin pork chops, 1 inch (2.5 cm) thick	6
	Black pepper, freshly ground	
	Cookware spray	
1	large onion, chopped	1
1	clove garlic, minced	1
½ tsp	summer savory (dried)	2 mL
2 cups	chicken stock (page 24)	500 mL
1 cup	cranberries, picked over and rinsed	250 mL
1 tsp	Splenda granulated sweetener or sugar	5 mL

1. Cut away any external fat from the chops and sprinkle them with pepper.
2. Brown chops in a sprayed heavy skillet. Transfer them to a baking pan. Wash cutting board and knife in soapy water, rinse and drain.
3. Bake chops at 375°F (190°C) for 15 minutes or until cooked. Remove chops. Pour off any fat and wipe pan with a paper towel.

Add onion and sauté 5 minutes, stirring. Add garlic.

4. Add savory and chicken stock. On medium heat, reduce stock to 1 1/2 cups (375 mL). Add cranberries. Cover and simmer until they pop. Add sweetener.

If you want a smooth sauce, transfer to a blender or food processor and blend.

5. Adjust seasoning and return chops to the sauce. Simmer 2 minutes and serve.
Yield: 6 servings.

pork Chops Sensass

PREPARATION:
16 minutes
COOKING: 25 to
30 minutes
FREEZING:
excellent
PER SERVING:
228 calories.
Excellent source
of niacin,
potassium,
protein and
vitamin C.

In French, *sensass* is short for "sensational," and this award-winning entry with its medley of subtle flavors shows why the description fits. Remember to scrub the orange under warm running water before peeling.

4	thick loin pork chops	4
3 tbsp	orange peel, grated	40 mL
2 tsp	fresh or preserved ginger, minced	10 mL
1/8 tsp	ground cloves	0.5 mL
1	apple, diced	1
1	green onion, finely chopped	1
	Black pepper, freshly ground	
	Cookware spray	
1 cup	fresh orange juice	250 mL
1 cup	dry red wine	250 mL
1 tbsp	cornstarch	15 mL

1. With a sharp knife, cut off all fat from chops. Make an incision in each chop from the side.
2. Combine orange peel, ginger, cloves, diced apple and green onion. Insert some of the mixture in each chop and seal the incision with a sharp, round toothpick. Pepper to taste.
3. Spray a heavy skillet and fry chops over medium-low heat for 20 minutes, turning now and then. Remove chops and pour off any fat. Dab the skillet with a paper towel but do not scrub.
4. Into the skillet put the orange

juice, wine and cornstarch. Stir and simmer for 5 minutes or until thickened. Add chops and keep warm. Serve with mashed potatoes.

Yield: 4 servings.

INGRID BERGMAN'S ROAST PORK

PREPARATION:
10 minutes
COOKING: *2*
hours
FREEZING: *fair*
PER SERVING:
372 calories.
Excellent source
of calcium,
niacin,
potassium,
protein and
vitamin A.

An old Swedish tradition is given new life in this delicious version, a personal favorite of Humphrey Bogart's co-star in the beloved classic, *Casablanca*, one of the most "perfect" films ever made. Thanks to the prune stuffing, this dish not only looks perfect, it tastes perfect.

1	loin of Canadian pork (4 to 5 lb/2 to 2.5 kg)	1
2 cups	spring water	500 mL
22	pitted prunes	22
½ tsp	white pepper, freshly ground	2 mL
¼ tsp	ginger	1 mL

1. Have the butcher debone the roast. Ask him to cut a pocket into the centre along the full length. When you get home, remove all the fat with a sharp knife.
2. Boil water and pour over prunes. Leave for 30 minutes. Drain but reserve liquid.
3. When prunes have cooled, insert them in pocket. Season the pork with pepper and ginger.
4. With a clean string, tie the roast into a tight shape.
5. Spray a Dutch oven lightly. Brown roast on all sides. Cover and transfer to a 350°F (175°C) oven. Cook for 1 1/2 hours, basting now and then with the reserved liquid.
6. At this point, you can remove it from the oven, cool and refrigerate overnight so as to remove any fat that will rise and coagulate on the surface of the gravy. (If the roast is Canadian and typically lean, don't bother. Serve it right away.)
7. Slice roast with a sharp knife so as to retain the distinctive appearance. Place slices on warm plates and serve strained gravy in a boat.

Yield: 10 servings.

Montmagny Barbecued Spareribs

PREPARATION:
15 minutes + 24
hours
COOKING: 1 1/2
hours
FREEZING:
excellent
PER SERVING:
262 calories.
Excellent source
of niacin,
potassium and
protein.

Situated east of Québec City off the autoroute, this friendly place is replete with gourmet restaurants. Not surprisingly, since Poiriers are as numerous here as are Smiths in other cities, one of the main streets is the Boulevard des Poirier, which takes you right into the heart of things. The spareribs are outstanding.

4 lb	lean pork spareribs	2 kg
1 cup	strong ale	250 mL
¾ cup	maple syrup	175 mL
1 tbsp	ketchup (preferably Heinz)	15 mL
½ tsp	dry mustard	2 mL
1 tsp	chili powder	5 mL
1 tsp	sage	5 mL
2 tbsp	white cider vinegar	25 mL
2 tbsp	finely chopped onion	25 mL
1 tsp	Worcestershire sauce	5 mL

1. Cut spareribs into serving pieces and put them in a shallow pan. Mix remaining ingredients and pour over the ribs. Let stand in refrigerator 24 hours, turning 3 times.
2. Remove ribs from marinade. Reserve liquid.
3. Skewer and place ribs on a rack of the barbecue or broiler, about 4 inches (20 cm) from the heat.
4. Cook, turning frequently and brushing with the marinade, until brown, about 1 hour and 15 minutes.
5. Alternatively, heat oven to 350°F (175°C) and bake 1 1/2 hours or until ribs are brown and glazed. Baste often.
Yield: 4 servings.

JOHN WAYNE SWEET AND SOUR PORK

PREPARATION:
10 minutes

COOKING: 40
minutes

FREEZING:
excellent

PER SERVING:
390 calories.
Excellent source
of calcium,
niacin, potassium
and protein.

Producer Joe Pasternak claims that when smoky-voiced Marlene Dietrich spotted John Wayne lunching on this dish at the Universal Studios commissary, she exclaimed: "Momma wants him for Christmas." The pair went on to make *Seven Sinners*, *The Spoilers* and *Pittsburgh*. Marlene, a great cook in her day, then learned how to make this herself. We've adapted it for *Memory Lane*.

3 lb	cooked pork (a leftover roast is fine)	1.5 kg
	Cookware spray	
1	onion, chopped	1
2	celery stalks, chopped	2
	Black pepper, freshly ground	
¾ cup	ketchup (preferably Heinz)	175 mL
½ cup	cider vinegar	125 mL
1 tbsp	low-sodium soy sauce	15 mL
⅛ tsp	cayenne	0.5 mL
¼ cup	brown sugar or Splenda granular sweetener	50 mL

1. Heat oven to 325°F (160°C). Cut meat into cubes, discarding any fat or gristle. Set aside.
2. Spray a skillet and sauté onion and celery for 10 minutes, stirring frequently. Do not brown. Transfer to a casserole.
3. Arrange pork cubes on top.
4. Combine all other ingredients and pour over mixture. Bake 30 minutes or until heated through.

Yield: 6 servings.

RAGOÛT DE PORC SAINT-MAURE (PORK STEW)

PREPARATION:
15 minutes
COOKING: 30
minutes
FREEZING:
excellent
PER SERVING:
229 calories.
Excellent source
of niacin,
potassium,
protein and
vitamin C.

From the highest hills of Saint-Maure, New Brunswick, you can catch a glimpse of the Atlantic Ocean in the distance. Please don't try to find it. Saint-Maure is overcrowded as it is. Try this local recipe instead.

1 lb	boneless pork leg or butt, cubed	500 g
	Black pepper to taste	
2 tbsp	canola or safflower oil	25 mL
1	large onion, chopped	1
2	stalks celery, diced	2
1	carrot, sliced thinly	1
3	garlic cloves, minced	3
½ lb	mushrooms, sliced	250 g
1	can tomatoes (19 oz/540 mL), crushed	1
⅓ cup	dry red wine, ale or beef broth	75 mL
2 tbsp	tomato paste	25 mL
2 tsp	dried rosemary, crushed	10 mL
½ tsp	dried basil	2 mL
½ tsp	dried oregano, crushed	2 mL
1 tbsp	cornstarch	15 mL
	or 3 tbsp (40 mL) unbleached white flour	
2 tbsp	cold spring water	25 mL

1. Season pork with pepper. Heat oil in deep saucepan or skillet. Brown pork on all sides, stirring. Remove pork.
2. Add onion, celery and carrot to the saucepan. Sauté until barely soft, about 5 minutes. Add garlic, mushrooms, pork cubes, tomatoes, wine, tomato paste and herbs. Cover and simmer on low heat until meat is tender, about 15 minutes.

3. Make a paste of the cornstarch and water. Stir into the stew. Simmer at least 5 minutes.
4. Serve with unpeeled, steamed potatoes; steamed cabbage, cauliflower or Brussels sprouts; a combination of long-grain white and wild rice; or broad noodles.

Yield: 6 servings.

Hong Siu Chu Yuk (Chinese Red Pork Stew)

This is an easy introduction to one of the world's healthiest and oldest cuisines. The color has nothing to do with politics; it's the food that takes on a reddish tone as cooking proceeds.

PREPARATION:
15 minutes
COOKING: *100 minutes*
FREEZING: *excellent*
PER SERVING: *259 calories. Excellent source of niacin, potassium and protein.*

3 lb	lean pork butt or shoulder	1.5 kg
4 to 5 cups	spring water	1 to 1.25 L
4	slices fresh ginger root, minced	4
1/3 cup	low-sodium soy sauce	75 mL
1 tbsp	dry sherry	15 mL
3 tsp	clover honey	15 mL

1. Cut pork into 1 1/2-inch (3.5 cm) cubes and transfer to a heavy saucepan.
2. Cover with 2 to 3 cups (500 mL to 750 mL) spring water, bring rapidly to a boil and simmer for 10 minutes. Drain and rinse immediately with cold water.
3. Wash your hands, cutting board and knife in soapy water. Rinse board and knife.
4. Return pork to the saucepan, add 2 cups (500 mL) spring water and other ingredients except honey. Cover the pan and let it simmer quietly for 1 hour.
5. Add honey and stir. Simmer the mixture over low heat for another 30 minutes. Drain. Serve hot with fluffy rice, vegetables and a Chinese dipping sauce (page 200) or cold as appetizers.

Yield: 12 servings.

Sichuan Yu Xiang Pork

PREPARATION:
60 minutes
COOKING: 6
minutes
FREEZING:
excellent
PER SERVING:
274 calories.
Excellent source
of niacin,
potassium and
protein.

One of China's four great cuisines, Sichuan invariably tastes hot to uniniti-ated westerners. Served with appropriate accompaniments and lots of rice, the food is a balanced delight to the senses. The Sichuanese consider theirs to be the finest culinary delights in all of China. When one considers that they have no fewer than seven different-tasting red chili peppers and the world-famous Sichuan Culinary Institute, we admit they're probably right. Traditional Yu Xiang Pork is offered in many Chinese restaurants but the best (and most authentic) is made at home.

22	dried black wood-ear fungi and warm water for soaking	22
3	green onions	3
40	cloves garlic	40
2 inches	ginger root	5 cm
½ cup	canned bamboo shoots	125 mL
8	pickled red chilies	8
1 lb	lean pork	500 g
1 tsp	cornstarch	5 mL
2 tsp	rice wine	10 mL
3 tbsp	canola or safflower oil	40 mL
⅓ cup	dou ban chili paste	75 mL

SAUCE:

4 tsp	Splenda granular sweetener or sugar	20 mL
2 tbsp	low-sodium soy sauce	25 mL
2 tbsp	rice wine	25 mL
1 tsp	sesame oil	5 mL
2 tbsp	cornstarch	25 mL
¼ cup	beef stock (page 25)	50 mL

1. Soak fungi in warm water for 20 minutes. Combine ingredients for sauce, stir and set aside.
2. Finely chop green onions, garlic and ginger separately. Chop fungi and bamboo shoots into slivers. Remove seeds from chilies and mince until almost a paste. Set all ingredients aside in separate portions on a plate.
3. Shred pork evenly and place in a small bowl. Combine cornstarch and wine; add to pork.
4. Set wok over high heat for 30 seconds. Add oil and stir-fry pork for 1 minute or until color changes.
5. Add chilies and dou ban. Stir once.
6. Add ginger, garlic, green onions, fungi and bamboo. Stir well.
7. Stir sauce and add to wok. Stir for 20 seconds. Serve immediately with fluffy white rice. *Yield: 4 servings.*

NOTES

- Fresh or dried chilies won't work in this recipe. If the pickled ones are out of stock, use an extra tablespoon (15 mL) of dou ban.
- Wash board, hands and knife immediately after handling raw pork.

NORMAN BETHUNE'S CHOP SUEY

"My only regret is that I shall now be unable to do more," wrote Norman Bethune, the Ontario-born doctor who worked selflessly in Spain and China, in his final letter of November 13, 1939. A national hero to the Chinese, Dr. Bethune did not have time for lengthy dinners. This totally delicious recipe is an example of how to cope when you're in a hurry. The recipe is adapted from his.

PREPARATION:
15 minutes
COOKING: *8 to*
12 minutes
FREEZING: *not*
recommended
PER SERVING:
344 calories.
Excellent source
of calcium,
niacin, potassium
and protein.

2 tbsp	canola or safflower oil	25 mL
4	large celery stalks, sliced diagonally	4
1	large firm onion, thinly sliced	1
1 ½ lb	lean pork, cut into thin strips	750 g
1 cup	thinly sliced mushrooms	250 mL

1	pepper (green or red), sliced thinly	1
1	clove garlic, minced	1
1 cup	fresh, firm bean sprouts	250 mL
1 cup	low-sodium consommé or beef stock (page 25)	250 mL
1 tbsp	cornstarch	15 mL
2 tbsp	low-sodium soy sauce	25 mL
4	green onions, sliced	4
	Black pepper, freshly ground	

1. Heat oil in a cast-iron skillet or wok until it begins to smoke. Reduce heat to medium.
2. Add celery and onion. Stir and toss for 3 minutes.
3. Add pork, mushrooms and pepper. Continue stirring over medium-high heat for 3 minutes. Make sure meat is cooked through.
4. Add garlic and bean sprouts. Cook and toss for 2 minutes.
5. Combine consommé or stock, cornstarch and soy sauce. Stir well. Add to other ingredients with green onions. Stir and simmer for 2 minutes until thickened. Season with pepper. Serve over fluffy white rice. *Yield: 6 servings.*

DELHI CURRIED PORK

Delhi is in Ontario, where we first tasted this spicy and very satisfying "Indian" dish. The original recipe was brought back from Bombay in 1935. We've adapted it to cut down on fat. Use any leftover cooked pork.

	Cookware spray	
3	large onions, chopped	3
2	stalks celery, chopped	2
1	large carrot, sliced	1
2 tbsp	cornstarch	25 mL
2 cups	chicken stock (page 24)	500 mL
2 cups or more	lean, cooked pork cubes	500 mL
2	garlic cloves, minced	2

PREPARATION:

20 minutes

COOKING: 35 to

45 minutes

FREEZING:

excellent

PER PORTION:

200 calories.

Excellent source

of calcium,

niacin, potassium

and vitamin A.

1	green pepper, coarsely chopped	1
1 ½ tsp	curry powder	7 mL
⅛ tsp	cayenne	0.5 mL
1	apple, cored and cubed	1
1 ½ tbsp	raisins	20 mL
1 tbsp	pine nuts or chopped walnuts	15 mL
1	tomato, quartered	1
2 tbsp	low-fat yogurt or evaporated skim milk	25 mL

1. Spray the bottom of a Dutch oven. In it, sauté onions, celery and carrot over low heat for 5 minutes. Cover and let simmer 15 minutes.
2. Make a paste of the cornstarch and a little stock. Add this and all other ingredients except yogurt, cover and continue simmering a further 20 minutes. Do not overcook.
3. There should be enough liquid to cover the pork and vegetables. If liquid is too thin, add a little more cornstarch mixed with cold spring water. (Note: Cool and freeze, if desired. Thaw, warm, and proceed with Step 4.)
4. Just before serving, add yogurt or skim milk. Serve with rice. *Yield: 4 to 6 servings.*

JAMBALAYA ACADIEN

This dish originated with the Acajuns of Louisiana, descendants of the Acadian citizens deported from the Maritimes in 1755. The Créole influence is reflected in the choice of spices. Serve with cold home-brewed beer and Roch Voisine. Try to save some for next day when things quiet down. Reheated in the oven, this dish tastes even more sensational than the first time round.

2 tbsp	canola or safflower oil	25 mL
4 cups	chopped onion	1 L
¾ cup	chopped green pepper	175 mL
⅓ cup	chopped green onion	75 mL
2 tbsp	finely chopped parsley	25 mL

Preparation:
30 minutes

Cooking: 65
minutes

Freezing:
excellent

Per portion:
360 calories.
Excellent source
of calcium,
folate, niacin,
potassium and
protein.

1 lb	lean pork, cubed	500 g
1 cup	chopped smoked ham	250 mL
6	smoked sausages sliced ¼ inch (1 cm) thick (Polish kielbasa or other)	6
1 tbsp	minced garlic	15 mL
⅓ tsp	pepper, freshly ground	1 mL
¼ tsp	cayenne	1 mL
½ tsp	chili powder	2 mL
2	bay leaves	2
¼ tsp	thyme	1 mL
⅛ tsp	ground cloves	0.5 mL
1 ½ cups	long-grain white rice	375 mL
	or	
	1 ¼ cups (300 mL) white rice and	
	¼ cup (50 mL) cooked wild rice	
3 cups	beef stock (page 25)	750 mL

1. In a heavy saucepan over low heat, put oil, onion, green pepper, green onion, parsley, pork and ham and simmer gently, stirring constantly, for 15 minutes. Cover and set aside.

2. In a heavy skillet, gently fry sausage slices to remove some of the fat, about 15 minutes. Drain on paper towels and dispose of fat.

3. Add sausage, garlic, pepper, cayenne, chili powder, bay leaves, thyme and cloves to mixture in saucepan. Cook for 5 minutes, stirring occasionally.

4. Add rice (including cooked wild rice, if used) and beef stock. Mix well and bring to a boil. Cover, reduce heat to minimum and simmer for 35 minutes, stirring occasionally.

5. Uncover, remove bay leaves, stir, raise heat to medium and cook a further 10 minutes or until rice is fluffy and relatively dry.

Yield: 4 servings.

WLMK'S Pork and Apple Pie

PREPARATION:
12 minutes

BAKING: *55 to 65 minutes*

FREEZING: *excellent*

PER SERVING: *297 calories. Excellent source of calcium, niacin, potassium, protein and vitamin A.*

William Lyon Mackenzie King was not only a mystic prime minister (1921–26, 1926–30, 1935–48) but a connoisseur of "good, old-fashioned food." It's unlikely he obtained this recipe from his departed mother (via a séance) but he did insist on it being served at least twice a month. Pork is nutritious and, these days, exceptionally lean.

	Cookware spray	
1 ½ lb	lean pork, cubed	750 g
1	onion, chopped	1
1 tbsp	canola oil	15 mL
2	cloves garlic, minced	2
1 ½ tsp	sage	7 mL
¼ tsp	black pepper, freshly ground	1 mL
10 oz	condensed chicken stock (homemade or canned)	284 mL
2	sour apples, unpeeled, washed and chopped	2
2 tbsp	unbleached white flour	25 mL
4	medium potatoes, steamed	4
3 tbsp	low-fat margarine	40 mL
½ cup	skim milk	125 mL
	Dash of paprika	

1. Spray frying pan with cookware spray and sauté pork 20 minutes on low heat, stirring frequently.
2. Remove pork, rinse pan in hot water and wipe dry with paper towels. Rub paper towel over pork cubes to remove any fat.
3. Sauté onion in 1 tbsp oil until golden, about 4 minutes.
4. Add pork cubes, garlic, sage, pepper and chicken stock. Cover and simmer until pork is tender (about 15 minutes for cubed pork shoulder and 20 for cubed loin chops).
5. In a bag or covered bowl, toss apple slices with flour. Add them to the pork mixture and stir.
6. Cover and simmer until apples are tender. Spoon into a shallow casserole.

7. Mash cooked potatoes with margarine and milk. Beat until fluffy.

8. Top the pork mixture with the mashed potatoes. Sprinkle with paprika. Bake at 400°F (200°C) for 15 minutes. Turn on broiler and continue cooking until top is golden brown.

Yield: 8 servings.

LUPE VELEZ CHILI VERDE

Not all chili begins with ripe red tomatoes. In Mexico, the traditional dish is made with *tomatillos* – green tomatoes. And we believe you'll agree with Lupe Velez, the silent screen star known as the Mexican Spitfire, that they make a delectable difference. Our version uses green tomatoes from the garden – something to keep in mind in the fall when you wonder what to do with that hefty surplus.

PREPARATION:
14 minutes
COOKING: 65
minutes
FREEZING:
excellent
PER CUP (250
mL): 252 calories.
Excellent source
of niacin,
potassium,
protein and
vitamins
A and C.

	Cookware spray	
2 lb	lean pork shoulder	1 kg
2	cloves garlic, minced	2
1	jalapeño pepper, minced, or ½ tsp (2 mL) cayenne	1
2	large onions, chopped	2
1	green pepper, seeded and chopped	1
6	large green tomatoes, chopped	6
¼ cup	orange juice	50 mL
¼ cup	lemon juice	50 mL
1 tsp	Splenda granulated sweetener or sugar	5 mL
½ tsp	ground coriander	2 mL
⅛ tsp	black pepper, freshly ground	0.5 mL
	Spring water	

1. Spray the bottom of a heavy saucepan.

2. Remove any fat from the pork and cut the meat into 1-inch (2.5 cm) cubes. Brown on all sides for 5 minutes. Remove pork with a slotted spoon and wipe saucepan with a paper towel.

3. Add all ingredients except

spring water to saucepan and simmer for 60 minutes. Stir now and then. Add water only if necessary. Serve with rice or steamed potatoes.

Yield: 10 servings.

VARIATION

- A first-class Mexican green chili calls for pork but you can substitute chicken or lamb.

TOURTIÈRE RENÉ LÉVESQUE

PREPARATION:
16 minutes
COOKING: *85*
minutes
FREEZING:
excellent
PER SERVING:
215 calories.
Excellent source
of niacin,
potassium,
protein and
vitamin A.

When the French first came to Québec, they found the native Montagnais using *tourtes*, a kind of wild pigeon, in many of their savory dishes. The unpolluted skies were full of these birds. The collision of the European and native Indian cultures produced the first *tourtières*. As more Europeans arrived, the *tourtes* became extinct and the descendants of the first Francophones were forced to use other ingredients. Here is a modern, tasty version for two pies (one can be frozen and baked later). We've named it in honor of René Lévesque, the late premier of Québec and an outstanding democrat, who feared that les Québécois were in danger of becoming as extinct as the *tourtes*.

Low-cal pastry for two 2-crust pies (page 267)

FILLING:

1 lb	lean pork (neck or shoulder)	500 g
1 lb	lean veal (neck or shoulder)	500 g
2	slices lean back bacon (fat removed)	2
1	clove garlic	1
1	onion	1
¼ cup	spring water	50 mL
½ to ¾ tsp	black pepper	2 to 4 mL
	Pinches of cumin, thyme, sage, savory and ground allspice	
1	medium baking potato, peeled and grated	1
¼ cup	grated carrot	50 mL

3 tbsp	chopped fresh or frozen parsley	40 mL
	or	
½ tsp	dried parsley	2 mL

1. Prepare and chill pastry.
2. Grind pork, veal, bacon, garlic and onion. Sauté for 10 minutes. Add water, spices and herbs. Cover and simmer gently for 25 minutes. Add grated potato and carrot. Simmer another 5 minutes. Add parsley and let cool.
3. Heat oven to 400°F (200°C). Roll pastry and line two 9-inch (22 cm) pie plates. Fill with cooled mixture and cover with pastry. Brush tops with water. Cut slits in tops to allow steam to escape. (At this point, pies can be frozen.)
4. Bake 15 minutes, lower heat to 325°F (160°C) and bake another 30 minutes or until pastry is golden brown.
   Yield: 2 pies.

CÉLINA FOURNIER'S AMQUI TOURTIÈRE

PREPARATION:
30 minutes
COOKING: 55
minutes
FREEZING:
excellent
FREEZER LIFE:
6 months
PER SERVING:
316 calories.
Excellent source
of calcium,
niacin, potassium
and protein.

This was the recipe that won my grandfather Victor's heart at a New Year's *réveillon* in Balmoral in 1868. Célina learned it from her mother, of course, before they left Amqui in the backwoods of Québec to settle in the backwoods of New Brunswick. This branch of the Fourniers and Poiriers has Montagnais native Indian blood, which may explain the choice of meat. If you can't get it, use lean ground beef, pork and veal or turkey.

2 lb	ground venison or moose meat	1 kg
1 ½ lb	ground lean pork	750 g
1 ½ lb	ground lean veal or turkey	750 g
3	cloves garlic, minced	3
2	firm onions, chopped	2
5 tbsp	chopped fresh or frozen parsley	65 mL
1 ½ tsp	dry savory	7 mL

1 ½ tsp	cinnamon	7 mL
1 ½ tsp	powdered cloves	7 mL
	Black pepper, freshly ground	
1 cup	spring water	250 mL

Pastry for two 8-inch (20 cm) pie shells and tops (page 266)

1. Put ground meats, garlic, onions, seasonings and the water in a large pot with a heavy bottom. Simmer, stirring occasionally, for 10 minutes. Do not overcook.

2. Remove from heat, remove excess fat by refrigeration or using paper towels, and prepare 2 pie shells. Stir meat mixture well and spoon mixture into shells. Set oven at 425°F (220°C).

3. After pie shells are filled, cover the tops with the rest of the pastry and slit to allow escape of steam. Seal edges.

4. At this point, you can freeze one of the pies for later use. If so, wrap tightly in plastic, label and date.

5. Bake for 20 minutes, then reduce oven to 350°F (180°C) and continue baking for another 25 minutes or until golden brown.

6. Remove and let stand a few minutes before slicing. Serve with a homemade chili sauce or Mon Oncle Jules's Relish (page 234).
Yield: 2 pies.

Tourtière Variations

Père Godin's Tourtière: Use 2 lb (1 kg) ground pork, 1 chopped onion, 2 tbsp (25 mL) poultry seasoning, 1 tsp (5 mL) ground allspice, 1 cup (250 mL) warm water, 2/3 (150 mL) cup milk, 1 1/2-oz (12 g) package butter-flavor granules, 1 cup (250 mL) instant potato flakes. Use about 2 tsp (10 mL) milk to brush pastry prior to baking. Proceed as in Tourtière René Lévesque (page 89). Combine water, milk and butter-flavor granules in a bowl. Add potato flakes and mix well. Fold this mixture into cooked pork and stir. Makes 2 pies.

Thérèse Pitre's Tourtière: Follow the above recipe but instead of potato flakes, use 3 cups (750 mL) fine wholewheat breadcrumbs. Add 1 tsp (5 mL) ground nutmeg to the seasonings. Proceed as in Tourtière René Lévesque (page 89).

CANADIAN BRASS GLAZED HAM

PREPARATION:

20 minutes

COOKING: 2

hours

FREEZING:

excellent

FREEZER LIFE:

1 month

PER SERVING:

272 calories.

Excellent source

of niacin,

potassium,

protein and

vitamin C.

The new pork is ultra-lean! For dieters and others who are wary of fat and cholesterol, see the discussion on pages 17–18. This festive dish was served at a gala reception following a riveting performance by the world-acclaimed brass quartet with the Brantford Symphony Orchestra. A ham this size is often sold at a very low price per pound, so use the outstanding recipe for any large party. Leftovers can always be frozen and are terrific for snacks and high-protein breakfasts. Try it with our new low-cal Farm-Fresh Egg Substitute (page 12).

8 lb	semi-boneless cooked ham	4 kg
16	cloves	16
2 cups	orange juice	500 mL
1 cup	dry white wine	250 mL
1	orange rind, washed, dried and grated	1
2 tbsp	clover honey	25 mL
1 tsp	ground ginger	5 mL
1 tsp	dry mustard	5 mL

1. Trim ham, removing fat with a sharp knife. Leave a paper-thin layer.
2. Insert cloves into fat side. Place ham in roasting pan, fat side up. Bake at 350°F (175°C) for 40 minutes. Remove ham and discard fat. Wipe pan with paper towel. Return ham to pan.
3. Combine orange juice, wine and orange rind; set 1/2 cup (125 mL) of the mixture aside and pour remainder over ham.
4. Roast at 325°F (160°C) for 50 minutes, basting now and then.
5. Into reserved liquid stir honey, ginger and mustard. Pour over ham and continue baking for 30 minutes. Baste now and then, using a pastry brush.

Yield: 22 servings.

FREEZING

- Cut in thick slices. Put greaseproof paper between each slice. Overwrap in one or more freezer bags from which air has been removed by drawing on a straw. Seal, date and label.

FAST-AND-SPEEDY NIAGARA FALLS HAM

PREPARATION: 4 minutes

COOKING: 12 minutes

FREEZING: excellent

PER SERVING: 269 calories. Excellent source of niacin, potassium, protein and vitamins A and C.

This traditional dish is still served in restaurants on both the Canadian and U.S. sides of the falls. You can rekindle honeymoon memories in just 16 minutes.

1 cup	canned or frozen peaches	250 mL
2 tbsp	clover honey	25 mL
2 tbsp	lemon juice	25 mL
¼ tsp	ground cinnamon	1 mL
⅛ tsp	cumin	0.5 mL
2 lb	boneless cooked ham slice, 1 ½ inches (3.5 cm) thick	1 kg

1. Drain peaches. In blender or food processor, combine peaches with honey, lemon juice, cinnamon and cumin. Blend until smooth.

2. Place ham in microwavable dish. Cover with waxed paper. Microwave at high (100%) for 5 minutes. Turn ham and brush with peach mixture. Continue at high another 5 minutes. Remove and set aside.

3. Pour rest of the mixture into a 2-cup (500 mL) Pyrex measure. Microwave, uncovered, on high for 2 minutes until hot. Stir. Slice ham into serving pieces. Spoon glaze over ham.

Yield: 6 servings.

FREDERICTON HAM CASSEROLE

PREPARATION:
*30 minutes +
overnight
refrigeration*
BAKING: *1 hour*
FREEZING:
excellent
PER SERVING:
*390 calories.
Excellent source
of calcium, iron,
niacin,
potassium,
protein and
vitamin A.*

With new health guidelines finally acknowledging that breads and pasta are good for you, try this easy version of an old New Brunswick favorite. Use lean ham and, if you prefer, low-fat sharp cheese. If you're having guests, prepare it the night before so you won't be lost in the kitchen while your visitors try to keep the conversation going. Serve with a green salad and marinated tomatoes (page 178).

	Cookware spray	
12	slices wholewheat bread	12
6	slices cooked lean ham	6
6	slices old Cheddar cheese	6
6	egg whites	6
2 ½ cups	skim milk, fresh or reconstituted	625 mL
¼ cup	finely chopped onion	50 mL
1	clove garlic, minced	1
½ cup	finely chopped green pepper	125 mL
¾ tsp	dry mustard	4 mL
2 tsp	Worcestershire sauce	10 mL
¼ tsp	black pepper, freshly ground	1 mL
⅛ tsp	cayenne	0.5 mL
½ cup	evaporated skim milk	125 mL
	Dry wholewheat bread crumbs	

1. Lightly spray a 13-by-9-inch (3.5 L) casserole and layer with 6 slices of bread. Place a slice of ham on each. Top with cheese and another slice of bread.

2. Beat egg whites, then add 2 1/2 cups (625 mL) milk, onion, garlic, green pepper, mustard, Worcestershire sauce, pepper and cayenne. Pour over casserole layers.

3. Cover casserole and refrigerate overnight.

4. About an hour before serving, pour 1/2 cup (125 mL) milk over the casserole and top with a layer of bread crumbs. Bake at 350°F (175°C) for 1 hour or

until puffy and golden. Remove
and let stand for 5 minutes
before cutting.

Yield: 6 servings.

KLONDIKE STRATA

PREPARATION:
10 minutes
BAKING: *60*
minutes
FREEZING: *poor*
PER SERVING:
336 calories.
Excellent source
of calcium,
niacin,
potassium,
protein and
vitamin A.

Here's one of the tastiest recipes ever to emerge from the historic days of the Klondike Gold Rush. The boys needed all the sustenance they could get, and Klondike Molly (née Molly Maguire in Seattle) was more than willing to accommodate – for a price. Not surprisingly, she became Queen of the Stratas, dishing out 10,000 in a single month. Our low-cal version is as satisfying as Molly's.

12	slices not-quite-stale wholewheat bread	12
6	slices lean cooked ham	6
6	slices low-fat Swiss cheese	6
3 cups	chopped asparagus (about 12 stalks), fresh or thawed	750 mL
1	medium onion, minced	1
2 tbsp	chopped fresh parsley	25 mL
4	egg whites	4
2 cups	skim milk	500 mL
1 tsp	Dijon mustard, preferably Aristocrate	5 mL
1 tsp	Worcestershire sauce	5 mL
1	clove garlic, minced	1
	Dash of paprika	
	Pepper or cayenne (optional)	

TOPPING:

1 cup	crushed bran flakes	250 mL
2 tbsp	canola or safflower oil	25 mL

1. Grease a large 13-by-9-inch (3.5 L) dish. Place 6 slices of bread on bottom. Cover with ham and top with cheese slices.

2. Steam asparagus until tender-crisp. Rinse with cold water and add to dish. (Thawed asparagus should simply be drained and chopped; do not cook.)

3. Add onion, parsley and the rest of the bread in alternate layers.

4. Whisk egg whites, milk, mustard, Worcestershire sauce, minced garlic, paprika and, if you wish, a dash of pepper or cayenne. Pour over bread strata. Cover and refrigerate for 12 hours.

5. Next day, remove from refrigerator and bring to room temperature. Combine bran flakes and oil; sprinkle over strata.

6. Bake in a 325°F (160°C) oven for 1 hour until puffy and brown. Remove and let stand for 15 minutes before slicing. *Yield: 6 servings.*

POULTRY

Africville Chicken

PREPARATION:

12 minutes

COOKING: *16 to*

20 minutes

FREEZING:

excellent

PER SERVING:

350 calories.

Excellent source

of niacin,

potassium,

protein and

vitamin A.

This is a fantastic barbecue recipe but it's also delicious grilled in the oven. The Arawak Indians who inhabited Jamaica cooked whole animals over a wood fire. Holes were jabbed in the carcass and stuffed with spices. Serve this adapted and updated version with Caribana Rice and Peas (page 162).

1 tbsp	allspice, ground	15 mL
1 tbsp	thyme	15 mL
1 ½ tsp	chili flakes	7 mL
1 ½ tsp	black pepper, freshly ground	7 mL
1 ½ tsp	sage	7 mL
¾ tsp	nutmeg	4 mL
¾ tsp	cinnamon	4 mL
2 tbsp	garlic powder	25 mL
¼ cup	canola oil	50 mL
¼ cup	soy sauce	50 mL
¾ cup	vinegar	175 mL
½ cup	orange juice	125 mL
	Juice of 1 lime or lemon	
1	scotch bonnet pepper, seeded, chopped	1
1 cup	chopped onion	250 mL
3	green onions, chopped	3
6	single chicken breasts, skinned and deboned	6

1. To make the marinade, combine all the dry flavorings, then stir in the remaining ingredients except the chicken. Stir well.
2. Pour the marinade over the chicken and refrigerate for 4 to 6 hours.
3. Grill chicken for 8 minutes on each side over medium heat, basting with marinade every now and then.
4. Boil the remaining marinade to serve with the chicken.

Yield: 5 servings.

NOTE
Scotch bonnet pepper is available in farmers' markets and most greengrocers.

JUDY GARLAND RAINBOW CHICKEN

PREPARATION:
15 minutes
COOKING: 75 minutes
FREEZING: excellent
PER SERVING:
347 calories.
Excellent source of calcium,
niacin,
potassium,
protein and
vitamin A.

This comforting and delectable dish was served just before the cast trooped in to see the last rushes of *The Wizard of Oz*. Judy insisted on the recipe, which we've adapted. You don't have to be a busy showbiz star to enjoy this low-cal tasty dinner. It can be prepared the day before and reheated while the guests settle down with the cocktails.

3 ½ lb	fresh chicken pieces	1.5 kg
	Cookware spray	
¼ cup	unbleached white flour	50 mL
2 cups	whole small onions (or 1 cup/250 mL chopped)	500 mL
1 cup	fresh mushrooms, sliced	250 mL
1	medium red pepper, chopped	1
2	cloves garlic, minced	2
½ cup	shredded low-salt, low-fat Cheddar cheese	125 mL
⅔ cup	evaporated skim milk	150 mL
1	can cream of mushroom soup (10 oz/284 mL)	1
⅓ tsp	black pepper, freshly ground	1.5 mL
¼ tsp	paprika	1 mL

1. Remove fat and skin from chicken.
2. Spray a baking dish large enough to lay the pieces in a single layer. Coat the chicken pieces with flour and lay them in the dish. Bake for 30 minutes at 425°F (220°C). Turn pieces over and continue baking another 20 minutes. Remove from oven. Pour off any fat and wipe with paper towels.
3. In a sprayed skilled, sauté onions, mushrooms and red pepper for 5 minutes and set aside.
4. Lower oven temperature to 325°F (160°C). Combine all other ingredients except paprika with the onion mixture and pour over chicken. Cover and bake 25 minutes. Serve with fluffy rice and sprinkle chicken with paprika.

Yield: 8 servings.

MAE WEST "COME-UP-AND-SEE-ME-SOMETIME" CHICKEN

We don't know if this is what the forever-youthful star served Cary Grant when he took her up on the famous invitation. Mae wasn't talking but she did provide the recipe to Craig Russell, the Canadian performer who impersonated her on stage and became a close personal confidant in her golden years.

PREPARATION:
10 minutes
COOKING: 35 minutes
FREEZING: excellent
PER SERVING:
359 calories.
Excellent source of calcium, potassium, protein and vitamin A.

3 lb	chicken pieces	1.5 kg
½ cup	unbleached white flour	125 mL
	Black pepper, freshly ground	
	Cookware spray	
5	green onions, chopped	5
3	cloves garlic, chopped	3
1	green pepper, chopped	1
12	mushrooms, sliced	12
2 tbsp	tomato paste	25 mL
½ cup	dry white wine	125 mL

2	tomatoes, unpeeled, chopped	2
⅔ cup	chicken stock	150 mL
¼ cup	brandy	50 mL
1	bay leaf	1
3 tbsp	chopped fresh parsley	40 mL

1. Remove skin and fat from chicken pieces. Place flour and pepper in a clean plastic bag and shake chicken pieces in it.
2. Spray the bottom of a Dutch oven and fry chicken for 5 minutes on each side. Add all other ingredients, cover and simmer over low heat for 25 minutes or until chicken is tender.
3. Add more pepper if desired and serve with rice or noodles.
Yield: 8 servings.

MARC FOISY DES FORGES'S COQ AU VIN

PREPARATION:
35 minutes
COOKING: *60 to*
70 minutes
FREEZING:
excellent
PER SERVING:
350 calories.
Excellent source
of calcium,
potassium and
protein.

The classic *vin* for this dish is Chambertin, but a hearty dry red wine will do (as will a Beaujolais or Chianti). Some would even use a dry white, but Monsieur Foisy des Forges – manager of the Lindsay, Ontario, Business Improvement Area office – nixes that heresy. This low-fat version retains all the flavor and the rich, mahogany-colored sauce of the traditional French dish. To maintain tradition, serve with steamed potatoes and a green salad.

3 lb	chicken parts, cut into serving pieces	1.5 kg
	Cookware spray	
3	medium onions, chopped	3
3	cloves garlic, minced	3
¼ lb	lean Canadian bacon or smoked pork chop, diced	125 g
	Spring water and dry vermouth, 1 tbsp (15 mL) of each	
2 tbsp	cognac or brandy	25 mL
2 cups	dry red wine	500 mL

BOUQUET GARNI *(tied in cheesecloth):*

1	celery stalk with leaves	1
1	carrot, cut into strips	1
5	sprigs parsley	5
1	leek or 3 large green onions, coarsely chopped	1
1	small bay leaf	1
¼ tsp	each, thyme and basil	1 mL
1 tbsp	fresh chervil or marjoram	15 mL
8	black or green peppercorns, crushed	8
24	pearl onions	24
½ lb	fresh mushrooms	250 g
½ tbsp	tomato paste	7 mL
2 tsp	cornstarch	10 mL

GARNISH:

Cooked mushrooms, pearl onions and fresh parsley

1. In a large pot, boil sufficient water to cover chicken. Add chicken parts and boil for 5 minutes. Drain. Remove fat and skin under cold running water and discard.
2. Return chicken parts to pot.
3. Spray a frying pan or electric skillet. Cover and sauté onions, garlic and bacon until onions are translucent. Add water and vermouth as needed to maintain moisture.
4. Add cognac to chicken and ignite, shuffling the pot until flames subside.
5. Add wine, bouquet garni and enough water to cover chicken.

Cover and simmer for 40 minutes or until chicken is fork-tender. Meanwhile, in a sprayed skillet, sauté pearl onions and mushrooms to glaze them. If necessary, add some of the liquid from the chicken.

6. Remove chicken parts from pot and keep warm.
7. Skim fat from sauce and bring to a boil. Continue cooking until sauce is reduced to one-third. Correct seasonings.
8. Blend tomato paste with cornstarch and some of the cooking liquid to form a paste. Beat the mixture into the sauce until it thickens.

9. Return chicken to the sauce and surround with glazed onions and mushrooms. Toss chicken parts gently to cover with sauce. Heat for 3 minutes and serve immediately, garnished with cooked mushrooms, glazed onions and parsley.

Yield: 6 servings.

VARIATIONS
- Add 12 stuffed olives, cut in half.
- Add a couple of sliced carrots halfway through the cooking process.

WHITE HOUSE HOT OR COLD CHICKEN

PREPARATION:
20 minutes
COOKING: *90 minutes*
FREEZING: *excellent*
PER SERVING:
285 calories. Excellent source of potassium and protein. Good source of calcium.

A new chef at the White House, a proponent of light cuisine, has banned heavy cream and butter-based dishes. President Clinton and the First Lady favor healthier, low-cholesterol meals made with fish and poultry. "This should result in a slimmer, healthier president and a healthier nutritional example for Americans," said the *New York Times*. A tasty recipe we would recommend is this double-duty one, which can be served hot or cold.

3 lb	chicken pieces (breast and legs)	2.5 kg
	Cookware spray	
2 tbsp	dry vermouth	25 mL
2 cups	dry white wine	500 mL
2 tbsp	lime juice	25 mL
3	garlic cloves, minced	3
2 tbsp	white vinegar	25 mL
2	bay leaves	2
12	6 black and 6 green peppercorns	12
5	juniper berries	5

GARNISH:

Orange or lemon slices

1. Remove fat from chicken pieces. Spray a large skillet, dip chicken pieces in cold water and brown on medium heat with the vermouth.
2. In a saucepan, combine all other ingredients except orange slices. Simmer the marinade over low heat for 10 minutes.
3. Spray the bottom of a deep casserole. Transfer chicken pieces from skillet to the casserole. Pour marinade over chicken pieces. Cover tightly and bake at 350°F (175°C) for 1 hour or until tender. Garnish and serve.

Yield: 4 servings.

NOTE
- Allow casserole to cool, then chill, covered, overnight in the refrigerator. The sauce will form a delightful aspic.

POULET HENRI IV

This is best done in a pressure cooker, a far better investment for the average home than a microwave oven. Our version of the classic French recipe greatly reduces the number of calories.

PREPARATION: 20 minutes
COOKING: 30 or 40 minutes
FREEZING: excellent
PER PORTION: 231 calories. Excellent source of potassium and protein. Good source of niacin and vitamin C.

1	utility-grade chicken (about 3 lb)	1.5 kg
1	bay leaf	1
3 to 4 cups	chicken stock (page 24)	750 mL to 1 L
	Black pepper, freshly ground	
1 lb	unpeeled carrots, scrubbed	500 g
1 lb	young turnips, peeled	500 g
1 lb	medium unpeeled potatoes, scrubbed	500 g
1	small cabbage, trimmed and quartered	1

SAUCE:

2 tbsp	low-cal butter-flavored margarine such as Country Crock or Lactantia	25 mL
¼ cup	unbleached white flour	50 mL
2	garlic cloves, crushed	2

3 tbsp	evaporated skim milk	40 mL
	Black pepper, freshly ground	

1. Allow 10 minutes per pound (20 minutes per kilogram) cooking time in the pressure cooker. Remove skin and external fat. (If frozen, chicken should be thawed overnight in the refrigerator.)

2. Place chicken in pressure cooker with bay leaf and enough stock to half fill the base. Add pepper to taste. Attach lid, lock and bring to high (15 lb/7 kg) pressure.

3. Four minutes before end of cooking time, place cooker in cold water to reduce pressure. Add carrots, turnips and potatoes. Bring to a boil and add cabbage. Put on lid and bring to high (15 lb/7 kg) pressure. Cook 4 minutes.

4. Reduce pressure again in cold water. Transfer chicken to a warm serving platter with vegetables. Keep hot. Strain stock.

5. Melt margarine in a pan, stir in flour and cook gently for 1 minute. Blend in garlic and 2 1/2 cups (625 mL) of the stock. Simmer for 3 minutes, stirring. Add milk and pepper to taste. Do not reboil.

Yield: 4 servings.

Tugboat Annie Chicken with Brandied Pears

The house of the beloved movie star Marie Dressler is still maintained in Cobourg, Ontario, just as it was when "Tugboat Annie" was a little girl there. You can even enjoy a wonderful meal while indulging in a bit of nostalgia. The place is now a gourmet haven. If you can't make it to beautiful Cobourg, try this fragrant dish at home. Because the alcohol evaporates, the entrée is low-fat. The pears, of course, should be firm but ripe.

6	chicken breast halves (1 ½ lb/750 g), skinned and deboned	6
3 tbsp	low-sodium soy sauce	40 mL

PREPARATION: 6
minutes
COOKING: 25
minutes
FREEZING:
excellent
PER SERVING:
240 calories.
Excellent source
of potassium and
protein. Good
source of calcium
and niacin.

4 tsp	cornstarch	20 mL
1 cup	brandy	250 mL
2	pears	2

GARNISH:

3 tbsp	chopped parsley	40 mL
	Lemon or lime wedges	

1. Place breasts in a baking pan. Drizzle them evenly with soy sauce. Bake, uncovered, at 450°F (230°C) for 20 minutes, basting now and then using a pastry brush.
2. In a saucepan, stir cornstarch and brandy together.
3. Scrub but do not peel pears. Core and slice thinly. Add pears to the pan and bring to the boil, stirring. Reduce heat, cover and simmer for 5 minutes.
4. Turn chicken pieces over. Add pear mixture and stir gently to combine. Turn oven off and serve within 5 minutes with fluffy white and wild rice (see Little Current Wild Rice Pilaf, page 143). Garnish with parsley and offer guests lemon or lime wedges.

Yield: 6 servings.

RED FLAG CHICKEN STIR-FRY

A serving of this culinary delight is more easily digested than a Mao poem. You decide which is the more enjoyable. Based on an ancient recipe, our low-cal version is economical, quick and easy to prepare – with or without the poetry.

1	whole broccoli	1
1	cooked chicken, deboned and skin removed	1
2 tbsp	peanut oil	25 mL
1 tbsp	fresh or preserved ginger root, minced	15 mL
4	green onions, chopped	4
3	cloves garlic, minced	3

PREPARATION:
10 minutes + 30
minutes' soaking
time
COOKING: *11 to*
12 minutes
FREEZING:
excellent
PER SERVING:
268 calories.
Excellent source
of calcium,
folate, potassium,
protein and
vitamin A.

½ cup	chicken stock (page 24)	125 mL
2 tbsp	soy sauce	25 mL
2 tbsp	hoisin sauce	25 mL
1 tbsp	rice wine	15 mL
2 tsp	cornstarch	10 mL
1 tbsp	spring water	15 mL

GARNISH:

Sliced almonds

1. Cut off tough ends of stems, discard, and soak broccoli in cold water for 30 minutes. While broccoli is soaking, prepare chicken if you haven't yet removed the bones and skin. Cut meat into 1-inch (2.5 cm) cubes.

2. After 30 minutes, run cold water over broccoli and drain. Cut tops into florets and stems into thick medallions.

3. Put peanut oil into wok or skillet and heat. Stir-fry ginger and green onion 1 minute. Add garlic.

4. Add broccoli medallions, chicken stock, soy sauce, hoisin sauce and rice wine. Cover and cook for 3 minutes. Add broccoli florets, stir, cover and cook for 3 minutes.

5. Add chicken cubes. Stir. Cover again and cook another 3 minutes or long enough to heat chicken.

6. Mix cornstarch with 1 tbsp spring water. Stir into pan and cook for 1 minute.

7. Transfer to serving plates and sprinkle with almonds.
Yield: 4 servings.

POULET DE GRAND PRÉ

This is an exotic (and quick to prepare) Acadien dish. In summer, use your own fresh garden tomatoes, blanched and peeled or left as is. Don't forget there's a difference between peeling vegetables and peeling poultry. Chicken skin is where the fat is. Vegetable peelings contain most of the vitamins.

PREPARATION:

20 minutes

COOKING: 50

minutes

FREEZING:

excellent

PER SERVING:

260 calories.

Excellent source

of potassium and

protein. Good

source of

calcium, niacin

and vitamin C.

1 ½ tsp	canola or safflower oil	7 mL
4 to 6	chicken legs with backs attached, skinned	4 to 6
½ cup	sliced celery	125 mL
¼ cup	chopped onion	50 mL
1	green bell pepper, seeded and chopped	1
2	cloves fresh garlic, minced	2
2 cups	canned, fresh or frozen tomatoes	500 mL
½ lb	mushrooms, sliced	250 g
1 tsp	dried tarragon, crushed	5 mL
½ tsp	fresh black pepper	2 mL
⅛ tsp	cayenne pepper or Tabasco sauce	0.5 mL
2 tsp	red wine vinegar	10 mL
⅓ cup	minced fresh parsley	75 mL

1. In a heavy saucepan, heat half the oil and over low or medium heat, fry chicken in batches until almost brown. Keep turning or chicken will stick. Set the fried chicken on a flat pizza pan.
2. Pour out the fat and oil. Wipe edge of saucepan with paper towel leaving a film of oil on the bottom of the pan.
3. Set heat at medium, add remaining oil, celery, onion and green pepper. Sauté for 5 minutes.
4. Stir in garlic, tomatoes, mushrooms, tarragon, pepper and cayenne. Cover and simmer on low heat for 25 minutes.
5. Stir in chicken pieces and red wine vinegar. Simmer for 5 minutes. Add fresh parsley.
6. Serve over pasta or rice.
   Yield: 4 to 6 servings.

VARIATIONS

- Use 4 boneless, skinless chicken breast halves cut into chunks.
- Instead of celery, use green olives with pimientos, sliced, but remember that bottled olives are very salty and thus not good for your heart. (This is outrageously good, so make plenty and freeze in TV dinner trays for future use.)
- Substitute balsamic vinegar for the red wine one.
- Virgin olive oil can be substituted for canola or safflower. In areas where it's used, heart disease is practically unknown.

Point Pelée Birders' Pie

PREPARATION:
25 minutes
+ overnight
defatting
COOKING: 90
minutes
FREEZING: good
PER SERVING:
365 calories.
Excellent source
of potassium and
protein. Good
source of calcium
and niacin.

Point Pelée, Canada's smallest national park, is 30 miles (50 km) southeast of Detroit and Windsor and draws birders from all over the world. From early to mid-May, you can easily spot 100 different species. And with 12 miles (19 km) of beautiful beach, strolling is a must. Bird watching can work up an appetite for lunch, and this low-cal pie, developed by an Atlanta Annie Poirier Committee for local birders heading north, is delicious hot or cold. Carry it in a cooler with ice.

1	chicken (about 3 ½ lb)	1.6 kg
2 lb	lean pork shoulder, cubed	1 kg
½ tsp	salt	2 mL
1	small onion, chopped	1
2	cloves garlic, minced	2
¼ tsp	black pepper, freshly ground	1 mL
¼ tsp	turmeric (optional)	1 mL

CRUST:

¼ cup	polyunsaturated margarine	50 mL
4	egg whites	4
½ tsp	each ground nutmeg, cinnamon and salt	2 mL
½ cup	clover honey	125 mL
5 cups	farina	1.25 L
1 tbsp	cornstarch	15 mL
1 tsp	baking powder	5 mL
	Cookware spray	

1. Remove skin and fat from chicken.
2. Place whole chicken and pork cubes in a large saucepan. Add 1/2 tsp salt. Cover with water and simmer 1 hour. Remove and drain liquid into a bowl. Put meat in another bowl, cover both bowls and refrigerate overnight.
3. Next day, remove any fat from the liquid. Debone chicken and

cut meat into bite-sized cubes.

4. Make the pastry, starting by melting the margarine. Whisk egg whites for 2 minutes until foamy. Combine with nutmeg, cinnamon, salt and honey.

5. Combine farina, cornstarch and baking powder. Mix well. Add to the egg mixture and blend to form a dough. Cut the dough into 2 sections, divided roughly two-thirds and one-third.

6. Heat oven to 350°F (175°C). Spray a casserole. Using two-thirds of the dough, form a

1-inch (2.5 cm) thick shell on bottom and sides. Fill with cooked meat, onion, garlic, pepper, turmeric and 1 1/2 cups (375 mL) of the reserved liquid. Set aside 1/2 cup (125 mL) of the liquid.

7. Top with rest of dough and make small slits with a sharp paring knife. Bake 1 1/2 hours, basting the topping now and then with reserved liquid. Serve hot or cold.

Yield: 8 servings.

James Cagney Turkey Rolls

The Little Caesar of moviedom fame was a caring host who knew the value of high-protein, low-cal gourmet cuisine like these turkey rolls. "If ya wanna be active and stay in shape, learn to cook," he admonished close friends. Each serving of this award winner delivers only 6 g of fat but 27 g of protein as well as vitamins A and C, niacin, folate, magnesium and zinc.

PREPARATION:
12 minutes
COOKING: *30 to*
35 minutes
FREEZING: *not*
recommended
PER SERVING:
175 calories.
Excellent source
of niacin,
potassium,
protein and
vitamins A
and C.

2	beefsteak tomatoes, unpeeled	2
1	red pepper, chopped	1
½ cup	chopped onion	125 mL
2	cloves garlic, minced	2
2 tbsp	chopped fresh parsley	25 mL
¼ tsp	dried tarragon leaves	1 mL
¼ tsp	cayenne or hot pepper flakes	1 mL
½ cup	spring water	125 mL
1 ½ tbsp each	cider vinegar and clover honey	20 mL each

14 oz	skinless turkey breast, chilled	400 g
12	large fresh spinach leaves, washed, dried and stemmed	12
	Black pepper, freshly ground	
8	fresh shrimp, peeled, deveined and nicked with a sharp knife	8
2 tbsp	unbleached white flour	25 mL
	Cookware spray	

1. Wash and chop tomatoes. In a saucepan, combine tomatoes with red pepper, onion, garlic, parsley, tarragon, cayenne, spring water, vinegar and honey. Simmer, partially covered, for 20 to 25 minutes. Cool. Transfer to a blender or food processor and blend until smooth. Pour into the top of a double boiler to keep the sauce warm.

2. With a sharp knife, cut the turkey into 4 slices. Place each slice between sheets of waxed paper and pound with a mallet until cutlets are flat. Wash hands and mallet.

3. Steam spinach leaves for 2 min-utes to blanch. Spread the spinach on the cutlets. Season with pepper to taste. Put 2 shrimp on each cutlet; roll the cutlet and filling and fasten with toothpicks. Coat the roll lightly with flour. Wash hands.

4. Spray a skillet and brown rolls on all sides over medium-high heat. Transfer the rolls to a baking sheet and cook at 375°F (190°C) for 20 minutes. Dispose of waxed paper and wash hands.

5. Remove toothpicks, let stand for 5 minutes and slice rolls.

6. Spoon hot sauce onto warm plates and place turkey slices on top.
   Yield: 4 servings.

OCEAN LIMITED TURKEY

The Ocean Limited, which began running between Montréal and Halifax in the early 1920s, was as enchanting in its day as the Orient Express. In fact, there was more space, and accommodations were far more luxurious, offering observation cars, sleepers, dining and lounge cars. Passengers had to reserve their places in the elegant mahogany-panelled dining car, gen-

PREPARATION:
6 minutes
COOKING: 21
minutes
FREEZING:
excellent
PER SERVING:
320 calories.
Excellent source
of calcium,
potassium and
protein. Good
source of niacin
and vitamin C.

tlemen had to wear a shirt and tie, and murders were not *de rigueur*. Every place setting (nothing but pure crystal and European porcelain, thank you) included a fresh, bright red Rose d'Anjou. There were no paper napkins – only reusable, pure white Irish linen. And there were uniformed porters at major stops. Waiters spoke English and French, and the wines were elegantly decanted. This dish was popular on the Ocean Limited menu. "Ladies and gentlemen, this way, please."

1	orange, well-scrubbed	1
1 tbsp	canola oil	25 mL
1	onion, chopped	1
1 cup	long-grain rice	250 mL
½ cup	chopped celery	125 mL
¼ cup	minced parsley	50 mL
3 cups	cubed roast turkey	750 mL
1 ½ cups	chicken stock (page 24)	375 mL
½ cup	orange juice	125 mL
¼ cup	slivered almonds or pine nuts	50 mL
¼ cup	raisins	50 mL
1 tbsp	slivered fresh or preserved ginger	15 mL
1 tsp	cumin	5 mL

Black pepper, freshly ground, to taste

1. Grate the orange rind. Set the orange aside.
2. Mix oil, onion and rice in a casserole. Microwave uncovered at high (100%) for 3 minutes. Stir once during this time.
3. Add the rind and remaining ingredients, except orange.

Cover and microwave at high for 18 minutes. Stir twice during this time.

4. When the liquid is absorbed and rice is tender, remove and serve. Slice the orange and use for garnish.

Yield: 4 servings.

FISH AND OTHER SEAFOOD

You simply cannot buy fresh ocean fish in places like Montréal or Toronto. If your lot in life is to be an inlander, your best bet for freshness is canned or frozen fish. Once you understand the different and – to some inlanders – confusing varieties of canned salmon, you'll be able to turn out these old-fashioned culinary triumphs.

The canned varieties are usually sockeye, keta, coho, spring and pink. Canned pink salmon is low in oil, fine-textured and pink-fleshed – good for the calorie-conscious and for dishes where color is important.

Deep-red sockeye salmon is more fattening than pink. The flesh is firm and the deep-red tint unmistakable but so are the calories. Restigouche salmon, king of the North Atlantic, is a species in danger of total extinction.

Sole Duglère de Percé

PREPARATION:
15 minutes
COOKING: 40
minutes
FREEZING:
excellent
PER SERVING:
219 calories.
Excellent source
of calcium,
potassium,
protein and
vitamin A. Good
source of
vitamin C.

A French classic, this is the most impressive fish dish ever created but think twice before ordering it in even the fanciest restaurant. It has to be made at home with tender loving care. In a Percé restaurant, don't miss the local periwinkles *(bigorneaux)* – an appetizer and treat found nowhere else on Earth.

	Cookware spray	
1 tbsp	butter-flavored margarine	15 mL
2 tbsp	finely chopped onion	25 mL
1	small clove garlic, minced	1
½ cup	fish stock or clam juice	125 mL
½ cup	dry white wine	125 mL
4 to 6	sole fillets, frozen	4 to 6
2 tbsp	minced parsley	25 mL
½ cup	canned plum tomatoes, drained and chopped	125 mL
⅛ tsp	freshly ground black pepper	0.5 mL

1. Spray a skillet, add margarine and sauté onion over medium heat until transparent.
2. Transfer onion to a wide lasagna dish. Add garlic, fish stock and wine. Place fillets on top.
3. Sprinkle fillets with parsley and top with tomatoes. Bake at 425°F (220°C) for 40 minutes or until fish flakes when tested with a fork.
4. Remove fillets gently to a serving dish and keep warm. Stir sauce, add pepper and reduce sauce over high heat to 1 cup (250 mL).
5. Pour sauce over fillets.
   Yield: 4 servings.

Notes
- If using fresh sole (not recommended except in coastal areas), reduce oven to 350°F (175°C) and bake 10 to 12 minutes. If you can find any, cod may be substituted for sole.
- Powdered fish stock is sold in bulk food and health stores.

Viking Trail Fillets

PREPARATION:
10 minutes
BAKING: *15*
minutes
FREEZING: *not*
recommended
PER SERVING:
268 calories.
Excellent source
of calcium,
potassium and
protein. Fair
source of
vitamin A.

Forget Christopher Columbus and Jacques Cartier. The Vikings got here first. Newfoundland's l'Anse aux Meadows is where you'll discover the Norsemen's sod houses built a thousand years ago. The Viking Trail is a 267-mile (430 km) highway that connects two UNESCO World Heritage Sites. Despite overfishing by foreigners, you can still enjoy Newfie hospitality, terrific scenery and the traditional nutritious cuisine of this spectacular island.

1	package of frozen fish fillets (12 oz/280 g)	1
1	carrot, scrubbed and cut into matchstick-sized pieces	1
1	green onion, finely chopped	1
3 or 4	mushrooms, sliced	3 or 4
1	clove garlic, minced	1
1 inch	fresh or preserved ginger root	2.5 cm
2 tsp	lemon juice	10 mL
1 tbsp	butter-flavored margarine	15 mL
	Black pepper, freshly ground	

1. Heat oven to 450°F (230°C). Grease two shallow dishes, each measuring 15 x 12 inches (38 x 30 cm).
2. Place half the fillets in each dish. Top with remaining ingredients. Sprinkle with pepper to taste. Cover loosely with parchment paper.
3. Bake 15 minutes or until fish flakes with a fork.
   Yield: 2 servings.

Benny Hill Plat du Jour

The British comedian did his own cooking in the tiny apartment he maintained near the TV studios in London. He had a weight problem and this was one of his favorite low-cal seafood recipes. It's based on a traditional one prepared in British homes for centuries.

PREPARATION:

10 minutes
+ overnight
thawing

COOKING: 35
minutes

FREEZING:
excellent

PER SERVING:
268 calories.
Excellent source
of calcium and
potassium. Good
source of
vitamins A
and C.

1	package frozen sole or cod (14 oz/400 g)	1
	Cookware spray	
1	can tomatoes (14 oz/398 mL)	1
1	onion, chopped	1
1	clove garlic, minced	1
1	stalk celery, chopped	1
1	medium green pepper, chopped	1
2 tbsp	lemon juice	25 mL
½ tsp	dried thyme	2 mL
	Dash of cayenne	
½ cup	grated Cheddar cheese	125 mL
1	can shrimp (6 ½ oz /184 g)	1

GARNISH:

Chopped fresh parsley

1. Thaw fish overnight in refrigerator.
2. If using fillets, separate them and place in the bottom of a sprayed casserole dish.
3. Combine remaining ingredients except cheese and shrimp; spoon the mixture over fish.
4. Bake at 400°F (200°C) for 20 minutes. Combine grated cheese with shrimp and spread over fish. Cook another 10 to 15 minutes or until fish flakes with a fork. Serve with garnish.
Yield: 3 servings.

ALFRED HITCHCOCK'S SALMON LOAF

PREPARATION:

12 minutes

BAKING: *1 hour*

FREEZING:

excellent

PER SERVING:

240 calories.

Excellent source

of calcium and

protein. Good

source of

potassium and

vitamin C.

The master of horror was also a master of culinary delights. This old-fashioned "comfort food" is loaded with minerals and vitamins. Hitchcock used to moan about the tepid-tasting loaf served in the film studio commissary. Whenever he had the time, this one was made for him at home.

2	cans salmon (each can 7 oz/220 g)	2
3	egg whites	3
½ cup	skim milk, fresh or reconstituted	125 mL
1 ½ cups	unsalted soda biscuits, crumbled	375 mL
1 cup	cooked mashed potatoes	250 mL
3 tbsp	lemon juice	40 mL
⅛ tsp	black pepper, freshly ground	0.5 mL
1	small onion, chopped	1
1	clove garlic, minced	1
½ cup	chopped celery	125 mL
1 tbsp	chopped fresh parsley	15 mL
1 tsp	tarragon	5 mL
	Cookware spray	

1. Put salmon and liquid in a bowl. Flake with a fork and crush bones.
2. Beat egg whites briefly. Add them and all other ingredients except cookware spray to the salmon. Mix well.
3. Lightly spray a 6-cup (1.5 L) loaf pan and pack it with the salmon mixture. (If you wish, use a fish mold.)
4. Cover the pan and set in another pan of water. Bake at 350°F (175°C) for 1 hour or until set.
5. Serve cold with curried mayonnaise or hot with lemon sauce. *Yield: 6 servings.*

JOHN LENNON SALMON CAKES

PREPARATION:

10 minutes

COOKING: *16*

minutes

FREEZING:

excellent

PER SERVING:

247 calories.

Excellent source

of calcium and

potassium. Good

source of

vitamins A

and D.

The British enjoy their seafood and Lennon traced his love of salmon back to the early days in Liverpool. The bones and skin are rich in calcium and vitamin D, essential for strong bones and teeth. You'll need four bowls to do this right.

2 cups	mashed unpeeled potatoes	500 mL
1	small carrot, scrubbed and steamed	1
1 tsp	polyunsaturated margarine	5 mL
1 tbsp	finely chopped onion	15 mL
1	can pink salmon (7 oz/220 g)	1
1 tsp	fresh lemon juice	5 mL
2 tbsp	skim milk, fresh or reconstituted	25 mL
2	sprigs parsley, chopped	2
	Black pepper, freshly ground	
2	egg whites, beaten	2
¼ cup	wholewheat bread crumbs	50 mL
¼ cup	unbleached white flour	50 mL
	Cookware spray	

1. Mash the potatoes and carrot together with the margarine and onion.
2. Flake the salmon and add to the potato mixture. Add lemon juice, milk, parsley and pepper to taste. Mix well and form into four patties.
3. Roll each patty in the beaten egg whites, then in bread crumbs, then in the flour. Set aside for 5 minutes.
4. Spray a skillet and fry patties over medium to low heat until nicely browned, about 16 minutes. Serve with lemon wedges and Emmie Wilkins's Tartar Sauce (page 205).

Yield: 4 servings.

- Use canned tuna instead of salmon.
- Use any leftover cooked fish such as cod, halibut or sole. For a pleasing exotic touch, season with 1/4 tsp (1 mL) ground ginger.

JUNEAU SALMON NOODLE CASSEROLE

PREPARATION:
10 minutes
COOKING: *25 to*
40 minutes
FREEZING: *not*
recommended
PER SERVING:
273 calories.
Excellent source
of calcium and
potassium. Good
source of
vitamins A
and D.

Despite a devastating oil spill, salmon farming is still an important industry for Alaska and British Columbia. This nostalgic dish, easy to prepare, is a perennial hit at bridge parties and luncheons. And skim milk cuts down on calories while maintaining nutrition and sensational taste.

1	can salmon (15 ½ oz/480 g)	1
3 tbsp	polyunsaturated margarine	40 mL
2 tbsp	unbleached white flour	25 mL
½ tsp	dry mustard	2 mL
1 ½ cups	evaporated skim milk	375 mL
1	package frozen mixed vegetables (10 oz/300 g), thawed and drained	1
3 cups	broad noodles, cooked "al dente"	750 mL
1 ½ cups	low-fat Cheddar cheese, shredded	375 mL
2 tbsp	chopped fresh parsley	25 mL
	Cookware spray	

1. Drain the salmon and break into chunks.
2. In a saucepan, melt margarine and stir in flour and mustard. Gradually add milk, stirring until somewhat thickened.
3. Add vegetables, cooked noodles, 1 cup (250 mL) cheese and parsley. Fold in salmon.
4. Pour into lightly sprayed 2-quart (2 L) baking dish. Cover and bake at 350°F (175°C) for 25 minutes.
5. Sprinkle with remaining cheese. Bake uncovered 5 minutes or until cheese melts.

Yield: 5 servings.

Cliff Barlow's Smoked Fish Dinner

PREPARATION: 12
minutes
COOKING: 15 to
20 minutes
FREEZING:
excellent
PER PORTION:
330 calories for
cod, 346 for
haddock.
Excellent source
of potassium,
protein and
vitamin A. Good
source of folate
and niacin.

Annie Poirier's son-in-law, Cliff Barlow, got this appetizing and nutritious recipe from his mother and she from hers. It's ideal for inlanders since smoked fish is available everywhere. Our method removes the salt. When shopping, pick a thick middle portion and avoid the tail-ends. In New York, San Francisco, Toronto and other cities, the best selection is on Wednesday.

1 lb	smoked cod or haddock	500 g
1 quart	spring water	1 L
2 cups	skim milk	500 mL
3 tbsp	cornstarch	40 mL
1	small onion, chopped	1
1	garlic clove, chopped	1
3 tbsp	chopped parsley	40 mL
½ cup	chopped celery	125 mL
⅛ tsp	freshly ground black pepper	0.5 mL
1 tsp	canola oil	5 mL

GARNISH:

Sweet paprika
Garlic-flavored, unsalted croutons

1. In a saucepan, cover fish with water and simmer over medium heat for 15 minutes. Do not overcook. Drain.

2. In a cup, combine some of the milk with the cornstarch. Add to the rest of the milk and stir.

3. Pour the milk mixture over the fish. Add all other ingredients and simmer over low heat for 10 minutes. Garnish and serve with steamed potatoes and vegetables.
Yield: 2 to 3 servings.

Tourtière Chéticamp

PREPARATION:
20 minutes
BAKING: *25 to 30*
minutes
COOKING:
excellent
PER SERVING:
180 calories.
Excellent source
of calcium,
potassium,
protein and
vitamin A.

Chéticamp, Nova Scotia, is a picturesque village on the ocean, where everyone is French speaking and a culinary artist. This Chéticamp favorite uses neither *tourtes* nor meats. Nothing goes in this dish but the bounty of the land and the still relatively unpolluted harvest of the oceans. It was created some three centuries ago by the native Micmacs and the French-speaking Acadiens, prior to their deportation to Louisiana. This is the modern version.

1 lb	frozen fish (cod, sole, bluefish or other)	500 g
1	bay leaf	1
1 tbsp	lemon juice	15 mL
1 cup	spring water	250 mL
2 tsp	minced garlic	10 mL
2 tbsp	chopped onion	25 mL
1/4 cup	diced celery	50 mL
1/3 cup	canola oil	75 mL
1/3 cup	unbleached white flour	75 mL
1/4 tsp	dry mustard	1 mL
1/2 tsp	chopped parsley	2 mL
1/4 tsp	thyme	1 mL
1/4 tsp	tarragon	1 mL
	Pepper to taste	
1 cup	liquid from poached fish	250 mL
2 tbsp	chopped nuts	25 mL
2 tbsp	sweet red pepper or pimiento, chopped	25 mL
	Pastry for a 2-crust 9-inch (23 cm) pie (page 266)	

1. Heat oven to 400°F (200°C). Put fish in a saucepan and add bay leaf, lemon juice and water.

2. Bring to a boil, reduce heat to minimum, cover and simmer 6 to 8 minutes or until fish flakes. Drain well, reserving 1 cup (250 mL) liquid. Discard bay leaf.

3. Sauté garlic, onion and celery in oil for 5 minutes. Do not brown.

4. Blend in flour, mustard, parsley, thyme, tarragon and pepper. Add milk and poaching liquid.

Cook on low heat, stirring constantly, until thickened.

5. Remove from heat. Stir in nuts, red pepper and fish.

6. Mix well and pour into pastry-lined 9-inch (23 cm or 1 L) pie plate; cover with top crust, trim with sharp knife, seal edges and flute with a fork. With tip of sharp knife, make steam vents in top crust.

7. Bake for 25 to 30 minutes. Let stand 15 minutes before cutting. *Yield: 6 servings.*

TOURTIÈRE MARCO POLO

The Italian merchant with the itchy feet and canvas sails wrote about his travels in Asia and excited his 13th-century compatriots with some newly acquired culinary tastes. Some restaurateurs claim Marco picked up this traditional recipe from tuna fishermen. Our low-cal version tastes even better.

PREPARATION:
20 minutes
BAKING: *40 minutes*
FREEZING: *excellent*
PER SERVING: *320 calories. Excellent source of calcium, potassium, protein and vitamin A.*

	Unbaked 9-inch (23 cm) pie shell (page 266)	1
1	jar marinated artichoke hearts (6 oz/170 mL)	1
	Cookware spray	
1 cup	sliced fresh mushrooms	250 mL
½ cup	sliced green onion	125 mL
1	clove garlic, minced	1
½ tsp	tarragon, crumbled	2 mL
1 tsp	Dijon mustard	5 mL
⅛ tsp	white pepper, freshly ground	0.5 mL
3	egg whites, beaten	3
1	egg, beaten	1

1 ½ cups	evaporated skim milk	375 mL
1	can white tuna (3 ½ oz/100 g)	1
1 cup	processed Swiss cheese, grated	250 mL

GARNISH:

| 1 | small carrot, cut into curls | 1 |
| 1 tsp | fresh parsley, chopped | 5 mL |

1. Line pie plate with pastry and flute the edges.
2. Drain artichokes, reserving marinade.
3. In a sprayed skillet, sauté mushrooms, onion, garlic and tarragon for 5 minutes. Set aside.
4. Combine mustard, pepper, egg whites and egg, milk and some or all of the artichoke marinade (according to taste). Drain tuna.
5. Add flaked tuna and cheese. Turn into lined pie plate.
6. Reserve two artichokes for garnish. Arrange the rest on top of the egg mixture (cut larger artichokes in half). Bake at 425°F (220°C) for 10 minutes. Lower heat to 350°F (175°C) and bake another 30 minutes or until set. Let stand 10 minutes before cutting. Garnish with artichokes, carrot curls and fresh parsley. *Yield: 5 servings.*

VARIATIONS

- Use canned salmon or small shrimp instead of tuna. Drain before using.

Vancouver Ouzeri

(Prawns with Feta and Wine)

Preparation: 12
minutes
Cooking: 10
minutes
Freezing:
excellent
Per serving:
280 calories.
Excellent source
of calcium,
potassium and
protein. Good
source of
vitamin C.

This simple dish will tempt even the most jaded appetites. It was developed by West Coast Greek Canadians from a traditional recipe. Go easy on the Tabasco or use freshly ground black pepper.

2 tbsp	canola oil	25 mL
3	cloves garlic, minced	3
¼ cup	chopped fresh basil	50 mL
¼ cup	chopped celery leaves	50 mL
½ cup	chopped leeks or green onions	125 mL
1 lb	jumbo shrimp, deveined and peeled	500 g
20	mushroom caps, washed and dried	20
1 cup	diced fresh tomato	250 mL
½ cup	dry white wine	125 mL
	Dash of hot pepper sauce (Tabasco)	
5 tbsp	feta cheese, crumbled	65 mL

1. In a wok over moderate heat, combine oil, garlic, basil, celery and leeks. Stir-fry for 3 to 4 minutes.
2. Add shrimp and mushrooms. Sauté until shrimp are pink – about 3 to 4 minutes.
3. Add tomato, wine and hot pepper sauce. Stir-fry for 1 to 2 minutes. Add feta cheese and stir-fry for another 3 minutes. Serve immediately with rice.
   Yield: 4 servings.

PASTA AND RICE

THE LOW-CAL TRUTH ABOUT PASTA

The new Canadian and U.S. food guides recommend five to twelve servings per day from the grain products category, which includes pasta. One cup (250 mL) qualifies as a serving and accounts for only 164 calories, thus demolishing the old myth that macaroni and spaghetti are fattening. Like wholewheat bread, pasta is a great source of essential nutrients, including the B vitamins thiamin, riboflavin and niacin, as well as iron. It's also a terrific way to add fiber to your diet.

Is pasta fattening? Not if you follow the Memory Lane recipes. It's what you put *on top* of fettuccine or spaghetti that's often rich in calories and fat, not what's *inside* the pasta. All our pasta recipes have been adapted and triple-tested to make sure they equal or exceed the traditional ones in eye appeal, taste and texture while drastically falling short of the calorie count. A bonus – pasta contains absolutely no cholesterol.

No one knows for sure when the Italians first made pasta. The Chinese invented noodles in the first century A.D. The earliest documentary evidence of macaroni in Italy is dated 1279, and spaghetti and other pasta forms came later. In those early days, Italians did not yet have tomatoes.

The Asiatic noodles were made from rice, the European from wheat, usually durum semolina, the kind preferred by most North Americans. Centuries before their lands were confiscated by the European Christians, native Indians had developed their own pasta varieties, using corn and wheat. Even today, Indian corn soup and stews are embellished with hand-made pastas.

Don't be misled by the "virtues" of fresh pasta. Refrigerated for days under fluorescent lighting, "fresh pasta" at the supermarket can be off-color and often rancid to the point that it actually smells bad. Unlike dry pasta, fresh pasta contains eggs and excess gluten, giving it a short "shelf life."

According to our Chinese and Italian friends, the world's finest dry pasta today is made right here in Canada, thanks to the wheat-growing Prairies, the northern air and the still relatively clean water. It takes longer to cook but it doesn't stick together. Our friends mail packages of Canadian pasta to their relatives overseas every Christmas and New Year. American and Canadian dry pasta are in every sense as fresh as fresh can be.

With the exception of certain noodles, dry pasta contains no wretched eggs to hike your cholesterol level.* It's a fantastic source of carbohydrates which, after you've indulged, convert into glucose, the fuel your body actually craves. Don't let anyone tell you pasta is fattening. Your body needs it.

*As of May 1994 all U.S. processed foods must carry new nutrition labels listing key ingredients in terms of "daily values," the percentage of each nutrient recommended for a balanced, 2000-calorie diet. Included in the list are calories per serving, total fat, saturated fat, cholesterol, sodium, sugars and actual nutrients. Unique in the modern world, this brave initiative took years of research, an act of Congress and resistance to food industry pressure. The new labels help people compare different foods to see how they fit into an overall diet. The Foundation and Institute hope that all other countries, including Canada, will follow suit.

CALIFORNIA BROCCOLI FETTUCCINE

PREPARATION: 8
minutes
COOKING: 20
minutes
FREEZING:
excellent
PER SERVING:
260 calories.
Excellent source
of calcium,
folate, potassium
and vitamin A.

Science is finally catching up with Grandma, who told you to eat your vegetables. Broccoli is a member of the Cruciferae family (along with cabbage, cauliflower, Brussels sprouts and kale) and contains sulforaphane, a powerful cancer-fighting agent and detoxifier. It boosts the body's natural enzyme defences against chemicals that cause cancer, say researchers at Johns Hopkins University in Baltimore. We should enjoy broccoli and other cruciferous vegetables every day. For starters, try our tantalizing new version of an old classic. Even the garlic is good for you!

3	cloves garlic, chopped	3
1	green onion, chopped	1
4 tbsp	canola oil	50 mL
	Pinch of dried basil	
	Pinch of cayenne	
1	fresh tomato, chopped (or canned, if you prefer)	1
½ cup	chicken stock (page 24)	125 mL
1 cup	broccoli, washed and chopped	250 g
8 oz	fettuccine	250 g
	Grated Parmesan cheese	

GARNISH:

Soy bacon bits

1. In a saucepan, sauté garlic and onion in 2 tbsp (25 mL) oil for 5 minutes. In another saucepan, bring water to the boil for the pasta.

2. Add basil, cayenne, tomato, stock and broccoli to the garlic and onion mixture. Simmer uncovered for 15 minutes. Stir lightly.

3. Cook pasta for 7 minutes or until al dente. Toss immediately with remaining oil and Parmesan cheese.

4. Serve topped with sauce and soy bacon bits.
   Yield: 3 servings.

Fettuccine Toronto

PREPARATION: 4
minutes
COOKING: 9 to
10 minutes
FREEZING: not
recommended
PER SERVING:
292 calories.
Excellent source
of calcium,
potassium and
vitamin A. Good
source of niacin
and protein.

This improved, low-fat version of the traditional recipe is named after the city that's the center of Italian life in Canada and has welcomed Sophia Loren, Gina Lollobrigida and Pope John Paul II with open arms. The original recipe, created in 1914 by Rome restaurateur Alfredo Di Lelio for his pregnant wife, who had lost her appetite, was heavy on butter and cream and delivered a whopping 755 calories per cup (250 mL)! Our low-cal version is smooth and creamy.

2	slices cooked lean ham, chopped	2
2	cloves garlic, minced	2
1 tbsp	canola oil	15 mL
	Black pepper, freshly ground	
8 oz	fettuccine	250 g
2 tbsp	low-fat cream cheese at room temperature	25 mL
3 tbsp	freshly grated Parmesan cheese	40 mL
¾ cup	evaporated skim milk	175 mL
	Low-fat margarine	

GARNISH:

	Freshly grated Parmesan cheese	
3 tbsp	chopped fresh parsley	40 mL

1. In a heavy pot, sauté ham and garlic in oil for 2 minutes. Add black pepper to taste.
2. Prepare pasta according to directions but do not overcook. It should be al dente. If using fresh noodles, 3 to 4 minutes will do just fine.
3. Add cream cheese and Parmesan cheese to the ham and garlic. Stir and add milk. Simmer for 2 minutes. Stir and set aside.
4. Drain pasta and add it to the other pot. Mix lightly.
5. If necessary, add low-fat margarine and toss lightly.
6. Serve immediately, garnished with Parmesan cheese and chopped parsley.
   Yield: 2 servings.

VARIATIONS

- Instead of cream cheese and milk, use 1/2 cup (125 mL) low-calorie sour cream and 1/2 cup (125 mL) low-fat plain yogurt. Combine well and follow Step 3.
- Pasta may be cooked in low-sodium chicken stock. Drain and reserve stock for soup.

ALICE MARCOTTE SAINTE-CROIX LINGUINE WITH CHICKEN

PREPARATION:
25 minutes
COOKING: 12
minutes
FREEZING:
excellent
PER SERVING:
269 calories.
Excellent source
of niacin,
potassium and
protein. Good
source of
vitamin C.

One of Étienne Poirier's five sisters, Alice, and her husband, Georges, lived in a large, historic house in Sainte-Croix-de-Lotbinière, near the city of Québec. She knew how to entertain. Her guests often raved about this particular dish, picked up by Alice on a trip to Rome, where she had an audience with Pope Pius XII. Apart from free-range chicken, a major ingredient is the tomato sauce. For jaded taste buds, it really should be home-made. (If you haven't canned or frozen any, see page 195.)

2	chicken breasts, boned, skinned and cut into strips	2
3 tbsp	olive oil	40 mL
½ cup	tomato sauce	125 mL
1 lb	linguine (green and white for color)	500 g
1 cup	tomato sauce	250 mL
1 tsp	butter-flavored granules	5 mL
1 tsp	chopped fresh basil (or ½ tsp/2 mL dried)	5 mL
	Black pepper, freshly ground, to taste	
	Pinch of cumin	

GARNISH:

Chopped fresh parsley

1. After preparing the chicken, be sure to wash your hands, the knife and anything else the chicken has touched.
2. Fry chicken in the olive oil over medium heat until golden. Remove chicken and set aside.
3. Drain oil from the pan and wipe with paper towels. Pour in 1/2 cup (125 mL) tomato sauce but do not heat until ready to serve.
4. Cook linguine in boiling water 7 minutes or so. Do not overcook – it should not be mushy. Drain.
5. In a separate pot, heat 1 cup (250 mL) of tomato sauce. Add butter-flavored granules. Simmer until they dissolve. Add linguine, chicken and seasonings (except parsley). Cook no more than 2 minutes, stirring thoroughly.
6. Heap onto warm plates, garnish with chopped parsley and serve with additional heated tomato sauce in a gravy bowl. Some folks like a touch of shredded Cheddar or even Romano cheese with this.

Yield: 4 servings.

LINGUINE CHARLO

PREPARATION:

15 minutes

COOKING: *28 minutes*

FREEZING: *not recommended*

PER SERVING:

282 calories.

Excellent source of calcium, potassium and vitamin A. Good source of niacin.

This wonderful recipe originated with Giuseppe DeMelo, an irrepressible Jaguar mechanic who married an Acadienne from New Brunswick's North Shore. He claims that the clams dug out by the Micmac natives at Eel River Bar near Charlo are the tastiest and meatiest in the world. If you can't get to Charlo, any fresh clams will do.

½ tsp	polyunsaturated margarine	2 mL
1 tbsp	olive oil	15 mL
2 tbsp	chopped green onion	25 mL
2 tsp	minced parsley	10 mL
1 tbsp	unbleached white flour	15 mL
2 tbsp	cold spring water	25 mL
¼ cup	dry white wine	50 mL
1 ½ cups	chicken or fish stock (pages 24 or 26)	375 mL

2 tsp	minced garlic	10 mL
12	fresh clams	12
½ tsp	olive oil	2 mL
	Black pepper, freshly ground	
6 oz	linguine or fettuccine	170 g

1. In frying pan, melt margarine, add olive oil, and sauté the green onions. Avoid browning. Add parsley and simmer on low heat for 2 minutes.
2. In a small cup, stir flour and water together and mix to a smooth paste. Pour into frying pan, stirring. Reduce to lowest heat.
3. Add wine and stock, stirring constantly, until sauce is reduced to a smooth consistency. Add garlic.
4. Place fresh clams on sauce and cover tightly. Simmer for 6 minutes or until they open. (Discard any that do not open.) Remove clams and keep hot.
5. Add remaining olive oil and reduce sauce over medium heat until it thickens. Add pepper and reduce heat immediately.
6. Add pasta to a large pot of boiling water. Cook for 7 minutes. Drain and toss in colander. Combine with sauce and mix well.
7. Place pasta on two plates, top with clams, and serve immediately.

Yield: 2 servings.

VARIATIONS

- Garnish with freshly chopped parsley.
- Provide a bowl of finely powdered Romano cheese.
- If using canned clams, drain after opening and add juice to make up 1 1/2 cups (375 mL) stock. When sauce is thickened, add clams, heat gently but do not boil or they will harden. Serve immediately.

WOODSTOCK BALSAMIC PENNE

PREPARATION:
6 minutes
COOKING: 12
minutes
FREEZING:
excellent
PER SERVING:
274 calories.
Excellent source
of potassium and
vitamin C.

We've come a long way since Grandma's comforting macaroni and cheese dishes. Except for Mediterranean countries, balsamic vinegar was unknown in the Americas until recent times. However, we know this yuppie creation would receive her approval since it's based on Grandma's common sense and flair for good food.

3	green onions	3
½ cup	virgin olive oil	125 mL
2	sprigs fresh rosemary (or 2½ tsp/12 mL dried)	2
5	garlic cloves, minced	5
2	cans plum tomatoes (each can 28 oz/796 mL)	2
	Black pepper, freshly ground	
3 tbsp	chopped parsley	50 mL
1 lb	pasta (penne or tubular)	500 g
2 tsp	balsamic vinegar	10 mL

1. Chop green onions and sauté in oil on medium heat.
2. Add fresh rosemary and garlic. Sauté 1 minute only. Add tomatoes and pepper. Simmer 10 minutes. Add parsley and turn off heat.
3. Cook pasta until tender but still firm, drain and transfer immediately to pan containing sauce.
4. Over low heat, toss for 1 minute.
5. Add vinegar and toss. Serve immediately.
   Yield: 4 servings.

JANETVILLE PASTA WITH FIDDLEHEADS

PREPARATION:
10 minutes
COOKING: 20
minutes
(Microwave:
12 minutes)
FREEZING: not
recommended
PER SERVING:
282 calories.
Excellent source
of calcium,
potassium and
vitamin A.

Fiddleheads (fern heads) appear in cool marshy areas as one of the first harbingers of spring. The delicacy was discovered by natives 40,000 years ago. Our low-cal recipe is from Janetville, Ontario, where fiddleheads grow in abundance. If you buy yours in a local market and the tips of the stems have darkened, simply clip them off with a small knife or scissors. Flash-frozen, they're now available worldwide throughout the year.

½ lb	fiddleheads	250 g
12 oz	penne or rotini pasta	340 g
1 ½ cups	skim milk, fresh or reconstituted	375 mL
2 tbsp	unbleached white flour	30 mL
1 tbsp	polyunsaturated margarine	15 mL
5	green onions, chopped	5
¼ tsp	black pepper, freshly ground	1 mL
1 ½ cups	Parmesan cheese, freshly grated	375 mL
	Dash of cayenne (optional)	

1. Fresh fiddleheads are usually clean and insect-free, but wash them under running water and drain anyway. Cut off any stems longer than 3 inches (7.5 cm). Steam 6 minutes until tender-crisp. Cover and set aside.
2. Cook pasta according to directions or about 8 minutes for al dente.
3. Blend a little milk with the flour to make a paste. Add to the rest of the milk, preferably in top of double boiler. Add all other ingredients except pasta and fiddleheads. Stir well and simmer, stirring, until cheese melts and mixture thickens.
4. Drain pasta. Transfer to a warm serving bowl and toss with fiddleheads and cheese sauce. *Yield: 4 servings.*

Microwave Method

1. Clean fresh fiddleheads as described above. Cook pasta on stove top in the ordinary way.

2. In a microwavable bowl, combine margarine and onions. Microwave, uncovered, at high (100%) for 2 minutes.

3. Blend in flour and pepper, and microwave at high for 2 minutes. Whisk in milk gradually until smooth. Microwave, uncovered, at high for 4 to 6 minutes until mixture boils and thickens.

4. Stir in cheese. Microwave at medium for 30 seconds or so. Set aside and keep warm.

5. Combine fiddleheads and 2 tbsp water in a microwavable dish. Cover and microwave at high (100%) for 3 minutes until tender-crisp. Follow Step 4

Variation

- Instead of fiddleheads, use fresh asparagus or broccoli.

Étienne's World-Famous Spaghetti Sauce

This is my favorite recipe – I've made it for 40 years – and it still has 'em raving in the cities where I lived, worked and had my being: London, Paris, Hamburg, Rome, Montréal, Toronto and New York. My flat in Chelsea, London – where I worked in public relations for Pan American World Airways – was always open to hard-working show-biz celebrities, day or night. Cary Grant asked me to freeze some of this sauce for him; Greta Garbo – a superb actress but a lousy cook – demanded the recipe, Mae West insisted it made her feel "just right" and Tallulah Bankhead would always thank me via a very wet kiss.

I think the secret is that it's chunky. Don't use the food processor or you'll end up with a gooey, nondescript mess. And unless you want a figure like Shelley Winters or Liz Taylor (in her "eat-everything" phases), forget everything you've been taught about how to make spaghetti sauce Bolognese and follow these directions. Before the guests arrive, sip a dry

PREPARATION: 12
to 15 minutes
COOKING: 95
minutes
FREEZING:
excellent
FREEZER LIFE:
1 year
PER SERVING:
360 calories.
Excellent source
of calcium,
potassium and
vitamin A. Good
source of niacin
and vitamin C.

martini; after they're ensconced, bring out the chilled white wine (to be followed by red Chianti when the hot plates are served).

8 oz	fresh white mushrooms	250 g
1	large onion, chopped	1
1	medium green pepper or ½ large one, seeded and chopped	1
1 tbsp	olive oil	15 mL
1 lb	roast meat loaf	500 g
1	can plum tomatoes (28 oz/796 mL)	1
4	large cloves garlic, chopped	4
2	slices prosciutto, chopped	2
3 tbsp	corn syrup or light molasses	40 mL
1	can tomato paste (6 oz/156 mL)	1
½ cup	chopped fresh parsley	125 mL
2	bay leaves	2
	Pinch of cumin	
	Pinch of thyme	
½ cup	finely chopped carrot	125 mL
1 cup	clear chicken stock (page 24)	250 mL
	(or 1 cube of chicken bouillon dissolved in hot water)	
¼ tsp	black pepper, freshly ground	1 mL
	Cayenne to taste	
½ tsp	each basil and oregano	2 mL

1. Wash the mushrooms. Dry them and slice into halves or quarters.
2. In a saucepan, sauté onion, green pepper and mushrooms in olive oil. Cover and simmer for 20 minutes. Do not drain.
3. Chop or cube the meat loaf. Run a sharp knife through the tomatoes before emptying the can but do not mash. Add with all other ingredients except the basil and oregano.
4. Simmer uncovered until sauce thickens – about 1 hour.
5. Add basil and oregano. Simmer another 15 minutes. Remove bay leaves.
6. Taste and adjust seasonings. Serve over cooked spaghetti and pass freshly ground Romano cheese. A simple green salad and garlic bread are called for but not always required (depending on the exuberance of guests).

Yield: 6 delizioso servings.

FOUNDATION'S $100 SEAFOOD PASTA SAUCE

PREPARATION: 5
minutes
COOKING: 20
minutes
FREEZING:
excellent
PER SERVING:
400 calories.
Excellent source
of calcium,
potassium,
protein and
vitamin A. Good
source of
vitamin C.

Just because this is so simple and quick to prepare doesn't mean it isn't a gourmet delight. It is. The dish was first served at a $100-a-plate fundraising dinner for the Annie & Etienne Poirier Foundation. Almost all the guests demanded copies of the recipe. It is now a staple at fundraising dinners across the country.

2 tbsp	canola oil	25 mL
1	large onion, chopped	1
1	bay leaf	1
2	cloves garlic, minced	2
1	can plum tomatoes (28 oz/796 mL), mashed	1
4	sprigs fresh parsley, chopped	4
1 ½ lb	raw shrimp, shelled and chopped	750 g
¼ tsp	oregano	1 mL
¼ tsp	basil	1 mL
	Touch of cayenne	
	Black pepper, freshly ground	
	Tomato juice	

1. In the oil, sauté the onion until transparent. Add bay leaf, garlic, tomatoes and parsley. Simmer uncovered for 15 minutes.
2. Add shrimp, oregano, basil and cayenne. Simmer for 5 minutes.

Add pepper to taste and, if sauce is too thick, a little tomato juice.

3. Serve over hot fettuccine or spaghetti and pass the Romano cheese.

VARIATIONS

- For 2 servings, cut the recipe in half and in place of the raw shrimp use 6.5 oz/184 g canned, drained salad shrimp or flaked light tuna. Simply heat. Do not simmer more than 1 minute.
- Rather than shrimp, use 2 cups (500 mL) of any of the following: raw clams minus juice; raw oysters, chopped; crab or lobster, chopped; baby squid, sliced thin.

SPAGHETTI ALLA PUTANESCA

If you include chili flakes, this superb traditional vegetarian dish has plenty of bite and fire. Serve with a green salad and chilled dry white wine or home-brewed lager.

PREPARATION:
20 minutes
COOKING: 15
minutes
FREEZING:
excellent
PER SERVING:
228 calories.
Excellent source
of vitamin C.
Good source of
niacin, potassium
and vitamin A.

4	plum tomatoes (fresh, canned or frozen)	4
1	clove garlic, minced	1
3	green onions, chopped	3
2 tbsp	virgin olive oil	25 mL
¼ cup	finely chopped sun-dried tomatoes	50 mL
¼ cup	finely chopped black olives	50 mL
¼ cup	chopped artichoke hearts	50 mL
¼ cup	dry white wine	50 mL
¼ tsp	chili flakes (optional)	1 mL
	Black pepper, freshly ground	
½ lb	spaghetti	250 g
	Parmesan or Romano cheese, freshly grated	

1. Purée or mash tomatoes and set aside.
2. In frying pan, sauté garlic and onions in oil for 2 minutes.
3. Add sun-dried tomatoes, olives and artichokes and continue cooking on low heat for 5 minutes.

4. Add wine, puréed tomatoes, chili flakes (if using) and pepper to taste. Stir and simmer on low for 5 minutes. Remove from heat.

5. Cook spaghetti according to package directions for no more than 7 minutes or until al dente. Drain and toss.

6. Reheat sauce and add spaghetti. Heat through for 2 minutes, blending carefully to combine ingredients. Serve immediately with grated Parmesan or Romano cheese.

Yield: 4 servings.

EVANGELINE HEALTH LUNCHEON

She was the bereft lover in Longfellow's famous poem. This Acadien recipe uses fresh tomatoes and is loaded with protein. The beans are easily digestible because they complement the rice. More than 200 varieties of chili peppers – most of 'em hot – are now grown. The word *chili* is the Nahautl native name. After Columbus took some back to Europe, they became a culinary hit and spread to Africa, Ethiopia, Hungary, India, Thailand, Indonesia and even China's Sichuan province. Chalk it up as one more native contribution to world cuisines.

PREPARATION:
10 minutes
COOKING: 12 to
15 minutes
FREEZING:
excellent
PER SERVING:
400 calories.
Excellent source
of calcium,
potassium,
protein and
vitamin A. Good
source of niacin
and vitamin C.

1 cup	long-grain or wild rice, cooked	250 mL
2	cans black beans (each can 19 oz/540 mL), cooked	2
2	cans crushed tomatoes (each can 19 oz/540 mL)	2
1	can chopped green chilies (4 oz/114 mL),	1
¼ cup	barbecue sauce (page 202)	50 mL
¼ tsp	dried basil	1 mL
½ tsp	cumin	2 mL
3	cloves garlic, minced	3
2 ½ cups	(12 oz/350 g) frozen vegetables such as corn or macédoine	625 mL
	Black pepper, freshly ground	

1. If using cold cooked rice, reheat in oven at 350°F (175°C) for 10 minutes. If very dry, add 3 tbsp (40 mL) cold spring water.

2. Rinse and drain beans. In a saucepan, combine beans, tomatoes, chilies, barbecue sauce, basil, cumin and garlic. Simmer for 10 minutes. Add frozen vegetables.

3. Add pepper to taste. Simmer another few minutes until vegetables are crispy-tender. Serve over rice.

Yield: 4 servings.

Cajun Beans and Rice

When first deported from Canada, the Acadien settlers found themselves in a strange land but one with rich soil producing an abundance of good food. Inexpensive and totally delicious, this recipe is a now Louisiana tradition. It's also very nutritious. Serve on beds of fluffy white rice.

PREPARATION:
15 minutes +
treatment of
beans
COOKING: 2 1/2
hours
FREEZING:
excellent
PER SERVING:
282 calories.
Excellent source
of calcium,
folate, niacin,
potassium and
protein.

2 ½ cups	dried red kidney beans	625 mL
1 lb	smoked pork sausage	500 g
8 cups	vegetable stock or spring water	2 L
½ cup	beef stock (page 25)	125 mL
2 tbsp	canola or safflower oil	25 mL
2	onions, chopped	2
4	cloves garlic, minced	4
1	green pepper, chopped	1
2	stalks celery, chopped	2
½ lb	lean cooked ham, diced	250 g
3	bay leaves	3
3	sprigs fresh parsley	3
¼ tsp	cayenne	1 mL
¼ tsp	black pepper, freshly ground	1 mL

GARNISH:

Green onion and/or fresh parsley, chopped

1. Wash and drain beans. Soak overnight or use quick method (page 147).
2. In a large heavy pot, sauté sausages for 30 minutes, pricking now and then with a fork. Remove sausages to paper towels and dab until traces of fat are removed. Rinse pot in hot water and dry with paper towels.
3. Add vegetable stock and beef stock. Add all other ingredients except garnish. Bring to boiling point, cover, reduce heat and simmer 1 1/2 hours. Uncover and simmer another 30 minutes.
4. At this point, you may remove 1 cup (250 mL) of the beans and purée in a food processor but this is not absolutely necessary.
5. Discard bay leaves. Taste and add more cayenne if you like it "hot."
6. Serve over mounds of fluffy white or brown rice and add garnish.
   Yield: 6 servings.

JOSÉPHINE SAVOIE CAJUN JAMBALAYA

A grandchild of *Acadiens* deported from Nova Scotia, Joséphine Savoie was not only a great beauty but a creative gourmet cook. With borrowed funds, she opened one of the first Cajun restaurants in la Nouvelle-Orléans. Intrigued by Créole cooking, she developed the first jambalayas. The word *jambalaia* is Provençal French for a chicken and rice stew. The Louisiana town of Gonzales is now the jambalaya capital of the world.

PREPARATION:
22 minutes
COOKING: *75 to 85 minutes*
FREEZING: *excellent*
PER SERVING:
290 calories.
Excellent source of calcium, niacin, potassium and vitamins A and C.

4 cups	chopped onion	1L
2 tbsp	canola or safflower oil	25 mL
2 cups	sliced mushrooms	500 mL
1 cup	diced cooked chicken	250 mL
	or fresh shrimp, peeled and deveined	
1 cup	cooked, diced, very lean ham	250 mL
12	small pork sausages, cut in pieces, fried and defatted	12
1 ½ cups	chopped celery	375 mL

1 ½ cups	chopped green pepper	375 mL
3	cloves garlic, minced	3
1 tsp each	cayenne, cumin, dried basil,	5 mL each
	dried thyme and freshly ground black pepper	
1 lb	cooked beef or meat loaf, cubed	500 g
2 ½ cups	canned tomatoes, undrained	625 mL
2 cups	long-grain rice	500 mL
1 ½ cups	chicken broth	375 mL
3 tbsp	chopped parsley	40 mL
2	bay leaves	2

1. In a large heavy ovenproof pot, sauté onions in oil for 5 minutes until dark brown but not burned. Stir frequently.
2. Stir in mushrooms and continue cooking for 4 minutes. Stir.
3. Add chicken, ham and sausages. Cook for 5 minutes.
4. Add all other ingredients except shrimp, if using. Stir well and cover. Bake at 350°F (175°C) for 45 minutes or until rice is tender.
5. If using shrimp (or any other seafood), stir in, cover and bake a further 15 minutes. Stir well. Discard bay leaves. Cover again and let stand 10 minutes before serving.

Yield: 8 servings.

VARIATION

- Instead of canned tomatoes, add another 2 1/2 cups (625 mL) chicken stock (page 24).

Ava Gardner's Paella Valenciana

PREPARATION:

25 minutes

COOKING: *45 to*

60 minutes

FREEZING:

excellent

PER SERVING:

390 calories.

Excellent source

of calcium,

potassium,

protein and

vitamin A. Good

source of niacin.

The fun-loving actress learned to cook the traditional Spanish rice dish, now enjoyed throughout the world, in Spain itself, where she lived for many years. Ingredients vary somewhat from region to region. Spaniards inland tend to favor meat, chicken and vegetables. Others use seafood, poultry and chorizo, the spicy sausage now sold in farmers' markets everywhere. The word *paella* means a large, heavy frying pan. Spain's most famous and imaginative dish is intended for entertaining appreciative guests. Make it a signature event by adding your own favorite items and deleting others.

1 ½ lb	lobster or 10 small tails, fresh or frozen	750 g
12	or more clams, mussels or oysters	12
5 cups	chicken or beef broth	1.25 L
	or reconstituted canned consommé	
	Cookware spray	
1	chorizo or hot pepperoni, sliced	1
2 ½ lb	chicken, defatted, skinned	1.25 kg
	and cut into pieces	
2	cloves garlic, peeled and skewered with toothpicks	2
1	onion, chopped	1
2 tbsp	chopped fresh parsley	25 mL
2 oz	Canadian peameal bacon	50 g
½ cup	squid, fresh or frozen,	125 mL
	cut into ½-inch (1 cm) strips or rings	
1 lb	medium shrimp, shelled and deveined	500 g
2 tsp	capers	10 mL
¼ tsp	crushed coriander	1 mL
1	green pepper, seeded and chopped	1
1 tsp	oregano	5 mL
2	peppercorns	2
1	bay leaf	1
½ tsp	saffron or turmeric	2 mL

1 tsp	white vinegar	5 mL
3 tbsp	tomato sauce	40 mL
1 ½ cups	shelled green peas (8 oz/250 g)	375 mL
3 cups	long-grain rice	750 mL
¼ tsp	red pepper sauce (Tabasco or other)	1 mL
1 tbsp	dry sherry	15 mL
3	sprigs of parsley, washed and chopped	3
1	lemon, quartered	1
1	can pimiento, drained and chopped	1

GARNISH:

	Lemon wedges	
	Clams, mussels and/or oysters	
3 sprigs	parsley, washed and chopped	3 sprigs
1 tbsp	dry sherry	15 mL
1	can pimiento, heated, drained and chopped	1

1. Remove meat from lobster. Scrub clams or mussels.
2. Bring broth to a boil. Reduce heat and simmer.
3. Spray a large but shallow heat-proof casserole. Diameter should be at least 16 inches (40 cm).
4. Fry sliced chorizo on very low heat until fat is exuded. Remove chorizo and set aside. Discard fat and wipe pan with a paper towel.
5. Dip chicken pieces in cold water and drain but do not pat dry. Sauté garlic (skewered on toothpicks to make removal easier) and half the chopped onions until translucent. Increase heat to medium high, add chicken pieces and brown both sides, adding a few tablespoons of the broth as necessary to prevent burning. Add chorizo and remaining onion, parsley and additional hot broth as necessary and cook, stirring, for 5 minutes. Remove and reserve garlic. Discard toothpicks.
6. Add 1 cup (250 mL) of broth, reduce heat to medium low. Add bacon and squid. Cook for 1 minute, stirring. Add shrimp and cook for 5 minutes or until shrimp turn pink. Add capers, coriander, green pepper, oregano and peppercorns.
7. Add bay leaf and 2 cups (500 mL) hot broth. Allow to boil. Meanwhile, crush saffron with

reserved garlic, blend with 1 tablespoon (15 mL) of hot broth and vinegar and add to mixture.

8. Add tomato sauce, peas and rice and cook for 15 minutes.

9. Add hot pepper sauce and additional broth as required and cook for 5 minutes, stirring. At this point, you may remove the dish from the heat and set it aside if you plan to continue

cooking later.

10. Steam clams, mussels and/or oysters in a little water until shells open. Use these as a garnish, sprinkled with sherry and parsley, along with lemon wedges and pimientos.

11. If rice appears to be dry, add a little stock or hot water. Serve with your favorite Sangria.
 Yield: 10 servings.

Little Current Wild Rice Pilaf

PREPARATION:
20 minutes +
soaking
COOKING: *45*
minutes
FREEZING:
excellent
PER SERVING:
160 calories.
Excellent source
of calcium,
potassium and
vitamin A.

Little Current is one of the prettiest spots on Manitoulin Island – the largest fresh water island in the world – and has been home to the native Ojibwes for thousands of years. Once prepared, this textured native dish is sometimes mixed with equal quantities of cooked brown or white rice. The wild rice is really not expensive because a little goes a long way.

½ cup	native wild rice	125 mL
1 ½ cups	boiling chicken stock (page 24)	375 mL
	Cookware spray	
½ cup	chopped green onions	125 mL
2	cloves garlic, minced	2
½ cup	chopped sweet red bell peppers	125 mL
2	bay leaves	2
⅛ tsp	cayenne	0.5 mL
3 tbsp	chopped fresh parsley	40 mL

1. Rinse the rice and cover with the boiling stock. Simmer for 5 minutes. Remove from heat and let stand, covered, for 1 hour.
2. Spray a heavy saucepan and sauté onions, garlic and chopped pepper for 5 minutes over medium heat, stirring.
3. Add rice and stock to the onions along with the other ingredients, making sure bay leaves are at the bottom.
4. Cover and simmer for 45 minutes or until rice is tender. Remove bay leaves, stir and serve.

Yield: 4 servings.

NOTE

After removing bay leaves, you can add any other cooked rice, in equal proportions or to taste. If freezing, allow to cool completely, then seal and label. Thaw overnight in the refrigerator, transfer to an ovenproof dish, cover and reheat in the oven.

RISOTTO DE FLORENCE

The Italians love their risotto and many have it as a first course every day. This traditional Florentine version is easy to master.

1	medium onion, chopped	1
1 tbsp	olive oil	15 mL
3 tbsp each	finely chopped fresh basil, rosemary, sage and thyme (or 2 tsp/10 mL each dried)	40 mL each
⅓ cup	chopped fresh parsley	75 mL
1	clove garlic, minced	1
1 cup	Arborio rice	250 mL
3 cups	chicken broth	750 mL
	Black pepper, freshly ground	
	Parmesan cheese	

PREPARATION: 12 minutes
COOKING: 30 minutes
(Microwave: 16 minutes)
FREEZING: excellent
PER SERVING: 218 calories.
Excellent source of calcium, potassium and vitamin A.

1. In a large heavy saucepan, sauté onion in oil.
2. Add half the herbs, garlic and the rice. Stir. Cook for 3 minutes.
3. Add chicken broth, stirring. Simmer gently until broth is absorbed, about 20 minutes.

Add more broth, if necessary, until rice loses its chalky center.
4. Remove from heat. Add pepper and remaining herbs. Sprinkle with grated cheese. Serve at once.
   Yield: 3 servings or 6 side dishes.

MICROWAVE METHOD

1. Heat oil in an 8-by-8-inch (2 L) shallow uncovered microwavable dish uncovered at high (100% power) for 2 minutes. Add onion. Stir. Cook uncovered at high for 1 minute.
2. Stir in rice, garlic and half the herbs. Cook uncovered at high for 4 minutes.
3. Add broth, stir, and cook uncovered at high for 9 minutes.
4. Remove from oven and let stand uncovered for about 5 minutes until all liquid is absorbed. Stir in pepper and remaining herbs. Stir in grated cheese. If desired, drizzle with additional olive oil.

BEANS AND VEGETABLES

WHY TEMPT FATE? CUT THE CANCER RISK!

We've known it for a long time but the verdict is now clear: some foods do help prevent the development of cancerous cells in the human body. Chief among these is garlic followed by members of the cabbage family (cauliflower, Brussels sprouts and broccoli).

Featured in many of our recipes, garlic is the all-star, as most Europeans have known for centuries. Farther to the east, it's called "Russian penicillin." It contains calcium, potassium, phosphorus, protein and vitamins B and C.

Studies in laboratory mice showed garlic compounds helped inhibit the growth of lung tumors blamed on tobacco smoke. They also protect the liver from damage caused by the painkiller acetaminophen.

Modern research also indicates that garlic helps reduce blood pressure in hypertensive patients. It also lowers cholesterol and cleanses the blood of excess glucose. (Blood sugar is also a causative factor in arteriosclerosis and heart attacks.) Others report that it alleviates grippe, sore throat and bronchial congestion. Garlic contains the natural antibiotic *allicin*, which destroys disease germs without sweeping away the friendly bacteria!

ALL YOU NEED TO KNOW ABOUT COOKING DRIED BEANS

Sort and rinse beans in clear running water before using. To replace the water lost in drying, soak each cup (250 mL) of beans in 3 cups (750 mL) of water. Before cooking, choose one of the soaking methods below:

Soaking Methods

Quick Method
Bring to a boil, cover and simmer for 2 minutes. Remove from heat and let stand 1 hour. Drain.

Overnight Method
Let stand overnight in refrigerator. Drain. This method requires less cooking time and the beans retain their shape better.

Microwave Method
Combine 3 cups (750 mL) hot water and 1 cup (250 mL) of dry beans in a 4-quart (4.5 L) microwavable casserole. Cover and microwave at high (100%) power for 15 minutes or until boiling. Let stand 1 hour. Drain.

Various Cooking Methods
Baked beans are best cooked at low heat in an oven but there are other methods. Soak the beans first according to one of the methods listed above.

Conventional Range-top
Bring to a boil, reduce heat and simmer until fork tender, about 70 minutes.

Microwave
Cover and microwave at high (100%) power for 10 to 15 minutes or until boiling. Stir and microwave at medium (50%) power for 35 minutes, stirring every 15 minutes or until fork tender.

Crockery
Place beans in crockery cooker and add 6 cups (1.5 L) water per 1 lb (500 g) beans. Cook on low for 8 to 12 hours.

Pressure Cooker
Place soaked beans and enough spring water to cover them in pressure cooker. To allow for expansion, fill no more than one-third of cooker. Add 1 tsp (15 mL) oil to reduce foaming. Cover and cook at 10 lb (4.5 kg) pressure about 20 minutes.

FÈVES AU LARD LAURENTIENNES (LAURENTIAN BAKED BEANS)

Similar to Boston Baked Beans, the Laurentian version was usually made with maple syrup, a method the French settlers learned from the native Indians. In these health-conscious times, beans are making a comeback. To get the maximum benefit from the protein, eat beans with cereal-grain bread. Beans contain no cholesterol whatsoever and each cup (250 mL) delivers 1061 g of potassium!

To really go back in time, serve this hearty dish with native bannock (page 212) or sourdough biscuits (page 216).

PREPARATION:
30 minutes +
soaking
BAKING: 8 hours
FREEZING:
excellent
PER SERVING:
265 calories.
Excellent source
of calcium, folate
and potassium.
Good source of
fiber and protein.

1 lb	white pea beans, washed and soaked overnight	500 g
5 cups	spring water	1.25 mL
½ lb	lean salt pork	250 g
1	large onion, chopped	1
½	green pepper, chopped	1/2
6 oz	ketchup (preferably Heinz)	170 mL
⅓ cup	Splenda granular sweetener or brown sugar	75 mL
¼ cup	maple syrup, corn syrup or molasses	50 mL
1 tsp	dry mustard	5 mL
2	cloves garlic, minced	2
	Pinch of thyme	
	Pinch of cumin	

1. Soak beans overnight in spring water or use quick method (page 147).
2. Simmer salt pork for 30 minutes. Drain, rinse under cold water and cube.
3. Combine all ingredients in a 6-qt (7 L) casserole.
4. Bake covered at 225°F (110°C) for 8 hours or until tender. Add more water if required.
   Yield: 8 servings.

Rudolph Valentino
Baked Lima Beans

PREPARATION:

*12 minutes + 1
hour soaking
time*

BAKING: *2 1/2
hours*

FREEZING: *good*

PER SERVING:

*250 calories.
Excellent source
of calcium,
potassium and
protein.*

The male sex symbol starred in *The Sheik*, the 1921 classic silent movie that sent women's hearts spinning and their husbands sputtering. Someone gave the suave actor the idea that lima beans are an aphrodisiac. There's truth to this because they're supremely nutritious and a good source of protein. We've named this tasty dish in his honor.

1 lb	dried lima beans	500 g
2 quarts	spring water	2 L
1	large onion, chopped	1
½ lb	lean cooked ham, diced	250 g
2	garlic cloves, minced	2
2	stalks celery, chopped	2
¼ cup	brown sugar or Splenda granular sweetener	50 mL
2 tbsp	Dijon mustard	25 mL
1 tbsp	Worcestershire sauce	15 mL
¼ cup	molasses	50 mL
¼ cup	Heinz ketchup	50 mL
⅛ tsp	ground cloves	0.5 mL
⅛ tsp	black pepper, freshly ground	0.5 mL

1. Wash and rinse beans. Transfer to saucepan and cover with 2 quarts (2 L) water.
2. Bring to a boil and simmer for 3 minutes. Remove from heat and let stand 1 hour.
3. Add onion. Bring to a boil and reduce heat to lowest setting. Simmer 1 hour until tender.
4. Drain beans, reserving liquid.

Transfer to a ceramic casserole (such as Corning Ware) with diced ham and other ingredients.

5. Bake at 300°F (150°C) for 1 1/2 hours. Add reserved liquid as required to prevent drying out. Serve with fresh whole-wheat buns.

Yield: 6 servings.

Truman Capote
4-Alarm Tex-Mex Chili

A fanatic about chili powder, which may explain his raffish personality, Truman Capote insisted on making his own with ground hot peppers, cumin, garlic, oregano, cloves and allspice. There is no single official recipe for the powder. Store varieties are often quite mild so you might want to spike yours with cayenne. Avoid skin contact and don't rub your eyes after handling any dried or fresh hot peppers. Our adapted version freezes well and flavors improve.

PREPARATION:
20 minutes +
overnight soaking
COOKING: 2
hours, 40 minutes
FREEZING:
excellent
FREEZER LIFE: 3
months
PER SERVING:
290 calories.
Excellent source
of calcium,
potassium and
protein. Good
source of
vitamin C.

1 ½ lb	pinto and/or red kidney beans	750 g
2 ½ lb	lean stewing beef, cubed	1.25 kg
1 tbsp	canola oil	15 mL
2	large onions, coarsely chopped	2
1	can crushed tomatoes (28 oz / 796 mL)	1
	or crush your own with a potato masher	
1	can plum tomatoes (28 oz / 796 mL), chopped	1
1 tbsp	jalapeño peppers, minced (optional)	15 mL
3 tbsp	crushed fresh garlic	40 mL
¾ tsp	oregano	4 mL
⅓ tsp	cumin	1.5 mL
1 tbsp	chili powder	15 mL
1 tbsp	cayenne	15 mL
¼ tsp	salt	1 mL
1 ½ tsp	black pepper, freshly ground	7 mL

GARNISH:

Chopped green onions, low-fat sour cream and grated Cheddar cheese

1. Soak beans for 8 to 12 hours in water. Simmer for 20 minutes. Drain and reserve liquid.
2. In a heavy Dutch oven, sauté beef cubes, browning on all sides in oil. Add onions and cook another 5 minutes on low heat.
3. Add tomatoes and other ingredients except reserved bean stock.
4. Simmer uncovered for 2 hours. If mixture becomes too thick, dilute with some of the bean stock.
5. Ladle into bowls and serve the green onions, grated cheese and cream in a dish on the side. *Yield: 6 to 8 servings.*

NOTE
- This one is very hot so you may want to eliminate the jalapeño peppers and cut down on chili powder and cayenne; they can be added halfway through the long simmering.

VARIATIONS
- For a more intriguing flavor, add 1/8 tsp (0.5 mL) allspice and 1/4 tsp (1 mL) coriander.
- Add 1 stalk celery and 2 green peppers, coarsely chopped, and 1 cup (250 mL) corn kernels (frozen, fresh or canned).

KEDGWICK VEGETARIAN CHILI

This award-winner was first served by Annie Poirier Committee volunteers at a fundraising event in the pleasant village of Kedgwick, New Brunswick. Easy to make, it also goes easy on the calories and gives you enough protein to kick up your heels and dance the night away.

1	large onion, chopped	1
1 tbsp	canola oil	15 mL
1	can plum tomatoes (28 oz/796 mL)	1
1	can kidney or pinto beans (20 oz/620 mL)	1
4 tbsp	tomato paste	50 mL

PREPARATION:	½ cup	frozen corn kernels	125 mL
15 minutes	1 cup	frozen, seasoned tofu (see page 170)	250 mL
COOKING: 70	1	large carrot, diced and cubed	1
minutes	1	stalk celery, diced	1
FREEZING:	1	small green pepper, diced	1
excellent	4 tbsp	chopped parsley	50 mL
PER SERVING:	1 tbsp	corn syrup	15 mL
240 calories.	¼ cup	dry red wine	50 mL
Excellent source	1 tbsp	lemon juice	15 mL
of calcium,	½ tsp	Tabasco sauce	2 mL
potassium and		or	
protein. Good	¼ tsp	cayenne pepper	1 mL
source of	1 ½ tsp	chili powder	7 mL
vitamins A	¼ tsp	cumin	1 mL
and C.		Black pepper, freshly ground, to taste	
	3	cloves garlic, minced	3

GARNISH:

Grated Cheddar cheese, chopped green onions and low-fat sour cream

1. In a large pot, sauté onion in oil for a few minutes until translucent.

2. Break up tomatoes with a fork or knife and add to the pot with juice.

3. Strain beans and reserve liquid. Add beans to pot along with all other ingredients, except garlic and garnishes.

4. Simmer over low heat for 40 minutes, stirring now and then.

5. Add garlic and simmer another 10 minutes. If mixture is too thick, dilute with bean liquid.

6. Garnish and serve with grilled garlic bread. Keeps in the fridge for a week and freezes well.
   Yield: 5 servings.

Vegetable Dishes

Green Beans

Wash garden-fresh green beans but do not cut or shuck (this will only accelerate leaching of valuable minerals and vitamins). (On a balding, overpopulated planet, we need all the minerals and vitamins we can get.) Steam 10 minutes until crisp-tender or as you like them. Allow them to cool slightly. You may now remove ends and strings and cut into short lengths or strips. Serve with melted, polyunsaturated, butter-flavored margarine. If you must reheat, simply spray a skillet and toss the beans in it for a minute. *Merveilleux!*

Freezing String Beans

Pick from the garden while they are young and thin so they will be tender and stringless. Wash, trim the ends and blanch for 1 to 2 minutes in boiling water. Cool under running cold water, drain, dry and pack in plastic bags. You can also spread them out on trays and freeze, then pack into bags. Each time you need some, shake out the amount needed.

Recommended freezer life: 1 year.

To use, steam until tender-crisp, about 3 minutes.

GREEN BEANS, BALMORAL STYLE

PREPARATION: 3 minutes
COOKING: 5 to 10 minutes
FREEZING: excellent
PER SERVING: 85 calories.

This was a favorite with Queen Mary, the fabulous lady who did so much for a war-weary world, and the Balmoral we refer to, of course, is the royal refuge in Scotland.

3 cups	cold, cooked green beans (see above)	750 mL
1	can whole mushrooms (10 oz/284 mL)	1
	Cookware spray	
½ cup	light sour cream	125 mL
	Black pepper, freshly ground	

1. Prepare the beans and set aside. Drain the mushrooms, rinse in cold water to remove the salt and drain again. (You may, of course, use fresh, thoroughly washed mushrooms but sauté them for 10 minutes on low heat in a sprayed skillet.)

2. In a sprayed saucepan, uncovered, sauté the canned, drained mushrooms for 5 minutes on low heat.

3. Cut the beans French-style into strips. Add beans, pepper and sour cream to mushrooms. Stir and warm over medium heat. Do not boil!

Yield: 6 servings.

Green Beans à la Gaspésienne

This dish was created by a Gaspé teacher, Mademoiselle Yvette Mazerolle, who hated ordinary food and came up with this tantalizing blend of flavors. It calls for tomatoes, a native of the Americas, and is based on an old Micmac recipe.

½ cup	canola or safflower oil	125 mL
1	onion, thinly sliced	1
1 cup	plum tomatoes, canned or fresh	250 mL
½	green pepper, diced	½
½ cup	chopped celery	125 mL
1	clove garlic, minced	1
¼ cup	spring water	50 mL
¼ tsp	freshly ground black pepper	1 mL
2	cloves	2
1	bay leaf	1
7	sprigs parsley	7
½ tsp	dried chervil	2 mL
	Cheesecloth and string	
1 lb	fresh green beans, steamed until tender-crisp	500 g

1. Heat the oil in a saucepan. Add onion and sauté until golden. Add tomatoes, green pepper, celery, garlic, water and pepper.
2. Tie cloves, bay leaf, parsley and chervil in cheesecloth. Add to vegetables.
3. Simmer, uncovered, for 25 minutes. Add beans, reduce heat and simmer until heated through. Remove bag and serve. *Yield: 5 servings.*

Pennsylvania German Carrot~ Parsnip Casserole

PREPARATION: 6 minutes
COOKING: 40 minutes
FREEZING: excellent
PER SERVING: 140 calories. Excellent source of potassium and vitamin A. Good source of calcium, folate and vitamins C and E.

Serve this intriguing combination with roast turkey and be prepared for compliments. Our recipe comes from Pennsylvania Dutch country and descendants of 17th-century German and Swiss immigrants. The term "Pennsylvania Dutch" is misleading because "Dutch" is a rendering of "Deutsch," meaning German.

3 cups	chopped carrots	750 mL
3 cups	chopped parsnips	750 mL
¼ cup	polyunsaturated margarine or safflower oil	50 mL
¼ cup	skim or 2% milk	50 mL
	Pinch of dried cumin	
	Black pepper, freshly ground, to taste	

GARNISH:

¼ cup	chopped parsley	50 mL

1. Steam carrots for 15 minutes. Add parsnips and continue cooking until tender. Remove and mash.
2. Add margarine, milk, cumin and pepper. Garnish with parsley. If desired, prepare ahead and reheat at serving time. *Yield: 5 servings.*

CAROLE LOMBARD HOLLYWOOD PURÉE

PREPARATION:
10 minutes
COOKING: *30*
minutes
MAXIMUM
REFRIGERATOR
LIFE: *2 days*
FREEZING:
excellent
PER SERVING:
70 calories.
Excellent source
of calcium,
potassium and
vitamins A and
E. Good source
of folate and
vitamin C.

The love of Clark Gable's life came into the world at 2:41 p.m. and astrologers who practise Horary believe that folks born between 12 p.m. and 6 p.m. feel they have a mission in life.

One of Ms Lombard's missions was to promote war bonds during World War II. Another was to serve her male guest "down-to-earth good food." This gourmet recipe, adapted by our chefs, is high in vitamins and low in price.

1 lb	carrots, scrubbed	500 g
1 lb	yellow rutabaga, peeled and cubed	500 g
1	hard (unripe) pear, cored and cubed (unpeeled)	1
3 tbsp	polyunsaturated margarine	40 mL
¾ cup	evaporated skim milk	175 mL
½ tsp	ground ginger	2 mL
	Black pepper, freshly ground	
1 tsp	fresh nutmeg, grated	5 mL
	or ⅛ tsp (0.5 mL) ground*	

1. Steam vegetables and pear until tender, about 30 minutes.
2. Purée in a food processor. Add margarine, milk and ginger. Pulse.
3. Season to taste with pepper.
4. Transfer to a serving dish and sprinkle with nutmeg.
5. If preparing for next day, cool, cover and refrigerate. Prior to serving, bake at 350°F (180°C) until hot, about 20 minutes.
Yield: 8 servings.

Ground nutmeg turns rancid after 2 months.
Fresh nutmeg can be purchased in health-food stores or farmers' markets.

BERKSHIRE HILLS SIDE DISH

PREPARATION:
8 minutes
COOKING: 14
minutes
FREEZING:
excellent
PER SERVING:
70 calories.
Excellent source
of folate and
potassium. Good
source of
calcium and
vitamins A
and C.

While most winter cauliflower originates in California and Florida, this tempting dish comes from the range of hills and mountains in western Massachusetts. The tomato, a berry unknown to Europeans prior to Columbus, shows the native aboriginal influence.

1	small onion, chopped	1
1	clove garlic, minced	1
1	stalk celery, finely chopped	1
1	large tomato, chopped	1
¼ lb	green beans, trimmed and chopped	125 g
1 ½ lb	cauliflower, cut or broken into florets	750 g
	Juice of ½ lemon	
⅓ cup	chicken stock (page 24)	75 mL
	Black pepper, freshly ground	
	Butter-flavor buds	

1. In a saucepan, sauté onion over medium heat for 4 minutes. Add garlic, celery, tomato, beans, cauliflower, lemon juice and stock. Cover and simmer gently for 10 minutes. (Cauliflower should not be mushy.)
2. Add more stock if too dry. Season with pepper and butter buds to taste.
   Yield: 4 servings.

VARIATION
• Add soy bacon bits just before serving.

THE LESSON OF THE LONGHOUSE

The native longhouse is still part of the landscape, however blighted this may be by the pollution of "progress." Mohawk farmer Lehman Gibson explains: "The longhouse is about the planting, the seasons, the sun and the moon.... Each individual has a song – the one he or she sings when planting. Then we form a circle and sing the different songs. It expresses our happiness to be alive and to be able to plant."

And well might they sing! The European invasion and the advent of chemical agriculture struck dual blows to a civilization in full bloom. Today's native farmers are once again growing rare vegetables without the use of fertilizers or pesticides. These include 8 traditional squashes and 60 different beans with names like Wild Goose, Hummingbird, Wampum, Kahnawake Mohawk Nap Pole, Jacob's Cattle Dry Bush and Trout Dry Bush. Many vegetable varieties have vanished forever, but native connoisseurs are collecting rare seeds from elders in Canada and the United States.

A few ancient Iroquois squash varieties – Crooked Neck, Sugar Pumpkin and White Paddy – are, thankfully, still available from commercial seed suppliers. There is also an endangered variety of potato called The Horn, a purple-colored delight for jaded tastebuds. By seeking out these rare and endangered plants – whether we're gardeners or cooks – we can help to preserve these varieties of vegetables for future generations.

A TRUE NATIVE: CORN

If natives hadn't come to the rescue with donations of corn, the first English settlers would have starved because their wheat crop had failed. Had the natives known how overpopulated North America would become, they might not have been so kind-hearted.

Pre-Columbian native agriculture centered on corn, beans and squash.

The earliest corn originated in Mexico, Guatemala and Honduras some 8,000 years ago. Two Spaniards dispatched by Columbus found native corn in central Cuba in 1492, and he introduced it with fanfare to Europe. This, however, was only the beginning of a sad story.

Over time, laboratory corn developed by large agricultural companies put a damper on native agriculture. The new hybrids created a dependency on suppliers by farmers. The latter were discouraged from growing their own seed. Chemical companies supplied not only seed but pesticides and fertilizers for mono-agriculture. Growing one or two varieties was very profitable and farmers became a captive market. Corn is now used in more than 2,000 products (alcohol, candy, cereals, colas, medicines, oil, paper and even whiskey).

This same "cult of progress" – spurred by the population explosion – not only put native and small farmers out of business but created the potential for genetic shrinkage and crop blights. Within the next few decades, the world could lose 250,000 plant species. Every commercial crop in Canada and the United States now has a very narrow genetic base. The potentially disastrous situation should give everyone cause for concern.

North American First Nations are, however, beginning to fight back. Over the centuries, the Six Nations peoples domesticated wild plant varieties and produced more than 20 kinds of corn, 8 squashes and 60 different beans. Seeds of traditional native crops are being preserved in high-tech cold-storage facilities. The possibilities for organic Iroquois horticulture are immense and should be actively encouraged by anyone interested in good food – anyone with brains and tastebuds.

If you're ever near a First Nations community when the corn is being harvested, try to purchase organically grown Mohawk Long Ears and Mohawk Round Nose (two species of white corn), Wampum Flint (purple-blue with a sprinkling of white), Tonawanda Seneca Flint (pinkish-purple). There is even a distinctive Indian popcorn. These rare seeds have been passed from generation to generation. (After the American revolution, the Iroquois migrated to Ontario and took the rare seeds with them. In the United States, this priceless heritage was eradicated by agribusiness and its bankers.)

CORN ON THE COB

PREPARATION:
1 minute
COOKING:
5 minutes
FREEZING: *not*
appropriate
PER EAR: *83*
calories.
Excellent source
of folate and
potassium. Good
source of
vitamins A
and C.

6   ears of corn   6
Boiling unsalted water

1. Bring enough water to the boil to cover corn.
2. Remove husks and silk. Drop corn in boiling water. Cover.
3. Salt promotes toughness so don't add any.
4. Serve immediately with butter-flavored margarine and a pepper mill.
5. If corn is overcooked, it will be tough.

HOW TO BARBECUE FRESH CORN

1. Carefully pull back husks. Rub with margarine. Push back the husks to original positions. Secure ends with twine to prevent them opening up.
2. Soak in water 20 minutes. Drain.
3. Place 4 inches (10 cm) above hot coals and cook 10 to 15 minutes, turning frequently. Do not use aluminum foil, a probable cause of Alzheimer's disease.

MICROWAVED CORN ON THE COB

1. Leave 4 to 6 corn cobs in their own jackets. If more than a day old, soak in cold water 10 minutes.
2. Trim ends to fit oven.
3. Arrange in spoke fashion with thicker pieces near the edges.
4. Microwave at high (100%) 2 minutes per cob, or until tender but still resistant when pressed with fingers.
5. Depending on size of oven, corn may have to be turned and rearranged to ensure even cooking.
6. Let stand 10 minutes to further tenderize. Remove husk and silk. Serve immediately.

Chéticamp Garden~Fresh Corn

PREPARATION:
2 minutes
COOKING: 8
minutes
FREEZING:
excellent
PER SERVING:
140 calories.
Excellent source
of folate and
potassium. Good
source of
vitamins A
and C.

Garlic's reputation as a health aid is well deserved. It keeps the blood and heart healthy and is believed to cure many other ailments. The use of garlic in this delicious recipe from Chéticamp helps explain why the Acadiens of this Nova Scotian village live such long and useful lives.

6	ears corn, freshly picked after water boils	6
3	cloves garlic	3
2 tbsp	canola oil	25 mL
¼ cup	chopped chives or green onions	50 mL
	Black pepper, freshly ground	

1. Bring a large pot of water to the boil. Add corn and cook for 6 minutes.
2. Drain. Cut niblets from cobs with a sharp knife and place in a bowl.
3. When ready to serve, add garlic to heated oil in a skillet. Sauté for 2 minutes but do not brown. Add corn and toss.
4. Add chives and pepper to taste. *Yield: 4 servings.*

VARIATION:
- Add soy bacon bits, chopped red pepper and/or butter buds. Heat thoroughly and serve.

Lancaster County Corn Pie

Lancaster, Pennsylvania, is the largest Mennonite community in the world. The Mennonites are a branch of the Anabaptists, founded in Zurich around 1525. Persecuted, they fled to the Americas. They cling to the old ways, live off the land and are renowned for their sustaining and delicious plain food, like this amazing corn pie.

PREPARATION:

6 minutes

BAKING: 40

minutes

FREEZING:

excellent

PER SERVING:

300 calories.

Excellent source

of potassium.

Good source of

folate, protein

and vitamins A

and C.

Low-cal pastry for two-crust pie (page 267)

4 cups	corn kernels (fresh, frozen or canned)	1 L
2 tbsp	polyunsaturated margarine	25 mL
½ cup	skim milk, fresh or reconstituted	125 mL
	Black pepper, freshly ground	

1. Line deep pie dish or casserole with pastry.
2. Combine other ingredients and pepper to taste. The milk should just moisten the corn.
3. Transfer to pie shell. Cover with pastry.
4. Bake at 400°C (200°C) for 40 minutes or until crust is golden brown. Let stand for 5 minutes before cutting.

Yield: 6 servings.

CARIBANA RICE AND PEAS

PREPARATION:

4 minutes

COOKING: 25

minutes

FREEZING:

excellent

PER SERVING:

200 calories.

Excellent source

of calcium,

potassium and

vitamin A. Good

source of iron,

folate, protein

and vitamin C.

Toronto's fabulous summer celebration gives visitors an opportunity to savor traditional Caribbean cuisine. This recipe is outrageously good with Africville Chicken (page 97).

2 tbsp	canola oil	25 mL
1	clove garlic, minced	1
1	small onion, chopped	1
1	small green pepper, chopped	1
1	hot green pepper, seeded and chopped	1
2 cups	long-grain rice	500 mL
4 cups	chicken or beef stock (pages 24 & 25)	1 L
1	small tomato, unpeeled, chopped	1
1	can pigeon peas (15 oz/454 mL), rinsed and drained	1

1. Put oil in a saucepan, add garlic, onion and peppers and sauté, covered, over medium heat for 5 minutes. Stir frequently.
2. Add rice, stock, tomato and pigeon peas. Stir and cook, covered, over low heat until rice is tender and liquid absorbed, about 20 minutes.
3. Fluff and serve.
Yield: 5 servings.

LOUIS ARAGON BAKED POTATOES WITH YOGURT

PREPARATION:
4 minutes + 20 minutes in freezer
BAKING: *50 to 55 minutes*
FREEZING: *not recommended*
PER SERVING:
235 calories. Excellent source of potassium and vitamin A.

For the partisans fighting the Nazi federalists in World War II, Aragon composed *Les Yeux d'Elsa* in which Love was identified with Liberty. Full of lyrical tenderness, Elsa became France. Under the occupation, the lack of butter, cream and fat reduced heart disease by a quarter. As this delicious low-cal version proves, *le bon goût* and love remained unchallenged.

6	baking potatoes, unpeeled	6
1 cup	no-fat yogurt	250 mL
2 tbsp	chopped fresh chives	25 mL
2 tbsp	chopped fresh basil	25 mL
2 tbsp	chopped fresh mint	25 mL
½ tsp	black pepper, freshly ground	2 mL

1. Scrub potatoes under running water. Rinse, dry and prick in three spots with a sharp knife. Place in freezer for 20 minutes (this makes them more floury).
2. Place potatoes on middle rack of a 400°F (200°C) oven and bake for 50 to 55 minutes or until tender when pierced with a fork. Do not oil or wrap them in foil.
3. Meanwhile, combine yogurt with herbs and pepper and stir well.
4. To serve, cut open each potato with a sharp knife. Place a dollop of herbed yogurt on each half and offer guests extra helpings from a chilled bowl.
Yield: 6 servings.

VARIATIONS

- Use other herbs such as parsley, dill, cilantro, summer savor, or green onions.
- In winter, use dried herbs but reduce the amounts by three-quarters.

GREEN GABLES SCALLOPED POTATOES

PREPARATION:
12 minutes
COOKING: *60 minutes*
FREEZING: *excellent*
PER SERVING:
298 calories.
Excellent source of potassium.
Good source of calcium, folate, protein and vitamin C.

Spud country is, of course, Prince Edward Island, home of Anne and her creator, Lucy Maud Montgomery. Needless to point out, "Spud Islanders," as they proudly call themselves, also raise chickens. This hearty dish is a break from the usual recipe using milk. With chicken stock, the results are very tasty, indeed.

	Cookware spray	
4	large baking potatoes, unpeeled, thinly sliced	4
½ cup	unbleached white flour	125 mL
	Fresh pepper to taste	
1 tbsp	fresh thyme leaves	15 mL
	or 1 tsp (5 mL) dried thyme	
	Pinch of paprika	
2	large onions, thinly sliced	2
1 ½ cups	chicken stock (page 24)	375 mL
2 tbsp	canola oil	25 mL
2 tbsp	butter-flavor buds	25 mL

1. Spray an oblong casserole.
2. In a plastic bag, shake potato slices – a few at a time – with flour, pepper, thyme and paprika.
3. Stand slices up in casserole, alternating with onion slices.
4. When casserole is filled, pour in chicken stock at one end so as not to dislodge seasoned flour. Sprinkle top with oil and butter-flavor buds.

5. Bake at 400°F (200°C) until top is lightly browned – about 1 hour.

6. If reheating next day, add a little milk.
Yield: 5 servings.

FLIN FLON BAKED POTATOES

With a little imagination, the lowly potato becomes a gourmet delight, as shown by this creative recipe from Flin Flon, the northwestern Manitoba town. Aged white Cheddar cheese gives it a real lift.

PREPARATION:
20 minutes
BAKING: 65
minutes
FREEZING: *not*
recommended
PER SERVING:
295 calories.
Excellent source
of potassium.
Good source of
calcium, folate,
niacin, protein
and vitamin C.

4	baking potatoes, unpeeled, scrubbed and washed	4
	Cookware spray	
3 tbsp	melted polyunsaturated margarine or canola oil	40 mL
3 tbsp	chopped mixed fresh herbs (parsley, thyme and/or sage)	40 mL
2 tsp	dried herbs (basil, thyme, oregano or other favorites)	10 mL
¼ cup	grated old Cheddar cheese	50 mL
1 ½ tsp	grated Parmesan cheese	7 mL

1. With a sharp knife, remove any blemishes from the potatoes.
2. Place each potato on a board, the squat side at the bottom.
3. With a sharp knife, make thin slices two-thirds of the way through the potato. Be careful not to cut right through to the bottom.
4. Place potatoes in a sprayed baking dish. Fan slices carefully.
5. Drizzle with margarine or oil and sprinkle with herbs.
6. Bake at 425°F (220°C) for 50 minutes.
7. Remove and sprinkle with cheeses.
8. Return to oven for another 15 minutes or until lightly browned.
Yield: 4 servings.

VARIATIONS
• Instead of herbs, use 1 tsp (5 mL) caraway seeds, powdered in a coffee or spice mill.

MICROWAVE METHOD

Follow Steps 1 to 5 and place in a microwave-safe dish. Microwave at high power (100%) for 10 minutes (rearrange them after 5 minutes). Let rest for 5 minutes. Sprinkle with cheeses and microwave another 6 minutes at high (100%) until cheeses are melted.

RICHARD HATFIELD POTATO PIE

PREPARATION:
15 minutes
COOKING: 90
minutes
FREEZING:
excellent
PER SERVING:

223 calories.
Excellent source
of potassium.
Good source of
calcium, folate
and vitamins A,
C and E.

This is one traditional recipe which should be revived in these diet-conscious days. Potatoes are non-fattening – it's often what we serve with them that ups the calorie count. The New Brunswick premier brought one of these pies with him when he presented Annie Poirier with a plaque for her community work. His 1870 Hatfield Heritage House, near the world's longest covered bridge in Hartland, is now a restaurant and bed and breakfast.

6	large baking potatoes (2 ¾ lb/1.35 kg)	6
	Cookware spray	
½ cup	chopped sweet red pepper	125 mL
2 cups	chopped onions	500 mL
2 tbsp	canola oil	25 mL
3	garlic cloves, minced	3
¼ tsp	dried thyme	1 mL
2 tbsp	chopped fresh parsley	25 mL
	cubed cooked lean ham	175 mL
1	egg white, lightly beaten with a fork	1
¾ cup	evaporated skim milk	175 mL
¼ tsp	black pepper, freshly ground	1 mL
	Low-cal pastry for 9-inch pie (page 266)	

GLAZE:

1	egg white	1
1 tbsp	evaporated skim milk	15 mL

1. Wash but do not peel potatoes. Steam whole until they are almost done, about 40 to 50 minutes.
2. In a sprayed skillet, sauté red pepper and onions for 10 minutes. Do not brown.
3. Mash or rice potatoes. Add all other ingredients except pastry and combine well.
4. Prepare pastry. Line bottom of 9-inch (23 cm) pan. Spoon in the filling, mounding slightly in the center. Cover the top with the crust. Trim excess pastry and cut 5 steam vents in the top.
5. Make the glaze by mixing the egg white and milk. Apply it with a brush and bake the pie at 425°F (220°C) for 10 minutes. Reduce heat to 350°F (175°C) and continue baking for 30 minutes or until pastry is puffed. *Yield: 10 servings.*

Klondike Kate's Turnip and Apples

Preparation:
6 minutes
Cooking: 40 to
60 minutes
Freezing:
excellent
Per serving:
248 calories.
Excellent source
of potassium.
Good source of
calcium and
vitamins A
and C.

If you think the lowly rutabaga can't become gourmet fare, you haven't heard of Klondike Kate. She was a dazzling dancer at the Savoy Hotel in Dawson during the gold rush – and an excellent cook, judging by this recipe. Where she got the apples in the frozen north is anyone's guess – perhaps they were shipped in for after-dinner "favors." She married John Matson, a miner, who says the turnip and apples did it.

1	rutabaga	1
½ cup	brown sugar or Splenda granular sweetener	125 mL
1 tsp	cinnamon	5 mL
	Pinch of cumin	
4	tart green apples, unpeeled and sliced	4
3 tbsp	unbleached white flour	40 mL
3 tbsp	canola oil	40 mL
	Black pepper, freshly ground, to taste	

1. Peel and cube rutabaga.
2. Steam until tender.
3. Mix half the sugar with cinnamon and cumin. Toss with apples.
4. In a small bowl, mix flour and the rest of the sugar. Add 2 tbsp (25 mL) oil and mix well.
5. Mash rutabaga with remaining oil. Spread one-third in an oiled casserole. Spread half the apple mixture on top. Repeat layers. Dot with flour mixture.
6. Bake at 350°F (175°C) for 30 to 40 minutes until top is golden. Season with pepper to taste.

Yield: 6 servings.

Saskatoon Vegetarian Chili

PREPARATION: 8 minutes
COOKING: 45 minutes
FREEZING: excellent
PER SERVING: 242 calories. Excellent source of calcium, folate, potassium and vitamin C. Good source of iron, niacin, protein and vitamin A.

You'll find the patties in health-food stores. High in protein and other nutrients, they make a nutritious substitute for meat. If using canned beans, do not drain. This zippy dish originated with a health-food club in the western city. Chilis are almost as old as the hills, and creative cooks are forever inventing new versions. Ours is definitely low-cal.

1	medium onion, chopped	1
2 tbsp	canola or safflower oil	25 mL
1 ½ tsp	chili powder	7 mL
4	veggie burger patties	4
¾ cup	vegetable stock	175 mL
1	can tomatoes (19 oz/540 mL), chopped	1
1	can red kidney beans (14 oz/398 mL)	1
2	jalapeño peppers or cayenne to taste	2
2	garlic cloves, minced	2
	Black pepper, freshly ground	

GARNISH:

Grated sharp Cheddar cheese, shredded lettuce and no-fat yogurt

1. In a saucepan, sauté onion in oil for 5 minutes.
2. Add chili powder, burgers (crumbled), stock and tomatoes.
3. Cover and simmer for 20 minutes. Stir now and then.
4. Add all other ingredients. Cover and simmer for 15 minutes. Garnish with grated cheese, lettuce and yogurt.

Yield: 4 servings.

RED RIVER VEGETARIAN LOAF

The classic Red River cart, first built at Pembina, Saskatchewan, looked like a huge basket between two large wheels. By 1845, they were used to transport food supplies and furs south to St. Paul, Minnesota, a fur trade center. The longest train had over 500 carts and oxen! If you love a tasty meat loaf, enjoy this one and give the cattle ranch a rest.

PREPARATION:
10 minutes
COOKING: *55 to*
65 minutes
FREEZING:
excellent
PER SERVING:
250 calories.
Excellent source
of calcium,
potassium,
protein and
vitamin A. Good
source of
calcium, folate,
niacin and
vitamin C.

2 tbsp	canola oil	25 mL
1 cup	finely chopped onions	250 mL
3	cloves garlic, minced or crushed	3
1 cup	finely diced celery	250 mL
1 lb	mushrooms, sliced	500 g
1 cup	ground roasted peanuts or cashews (unsalted)	250 mL
1 cup	ground walnuts	250 mL
1 cup	bread crumbs	250 mL
1 tbsp	brewer's yeast (optional)	15 mL
1 tbsp	chopped parsley	15 mL
	Grated rind of 1/3 lemon	
1 tsp	thyme	5 mL
1/2 tsp	marjoram	2 mL
1/2 tsp	freshly ground pepper	2 mL
1/2 tsp	ground coriander	2 mL
1/4 tsp	ground nutmeg	1 mL
1/8 tsp	cumin	0.5 mL
1 cup	grated Cheddar cheese	250 mL
3 or 4	eggs, lightly beaten	3 or 4

| 2 tbsp | tamari or soy sauce | 25 mL |

Paprika and grated Cheddar cheese for topping

1. Heat oven to 350°F (175°C). Heat oil in frying pan and sauté onions. Do not brown. Add garlic and celery. Lower heat. Sauté for 10 minutes, stirring occasionally.
2. Bake mushrooms on sheet in oven for 15 minutes. Drain off liquid.
3. Combine nuts, bread crumbs, brewer's yeast, parsley and lemon rind. Stir in seasonings. Mix well. Add cheese and beat-en eggs. Add mixture from frying pan. Add tamari and blend well.
4. Transfer mixture to lightly oiled loaf pan or ovenproof dish. Bake 30 to 40 minutes.
5. Sprinkle with grated Cheddar and paprika. Bake a further 5 minutes.
6. Let stand for 10 minutes and serve with vegetables.
   Yield: 12 slices.

MISHIMA'S TOFU "GROUND BEEF"

The distinguished and exceptionally creative Japanese novelist lamented the passing of "the old traditions." He extolled tofu as a terrific source of protein. It has no fat to clog your pristine arteries. The trick is to know what to do with it. This mixture, which uses tofu made from soybean, can replace ground beef just about anywhere – in enchiladas, lasagna, cabbage rolls, chili con carne or spaghetti sauce.

16 oz	tofu	500 g
½ cup	mushrooms	125 mL
1 tbsp	canola or safflower oil	15 mL
1 tbsp	low-sodium soy sauce	15 mL
1 tsp	cider or wine vinegar	5 mL
3	cloves garlic, peeled and minced	3
1 tsp	Dijon-type mustard	5 mL
½ tsp	fancy Barbados molasses	2 mL

PREPARATION: 8

minutes

COOKING: 20

minutes +

(depending on

type of tofu)

REFRIGERATOR

LIFE: *16 days*

FREEZING: *excel-*

lent and highly

recommended

PER 1/2 CUP (125

mL): *157 calories.*

Excellent source

of calcium and

potassium. Good

source of folate,

niacin and

protein.

| ½ tsp | dried thyme, rubbed | 2 mL |
| ½ tsp | dried sage, rubbed | 2 mL |

1. Drain the tofu and rinse with cold water. Drain again.
2. Crumble or chop into small cubes and drop in *ungreased* skillet. Turn heat to medium.
3. Wash mushrooms under running water, remove dirt with fingers, rinse, drain and chop. Add to skillet. (Don't fall for that old canard about using a damp cloth. A bacteria-laden cloth *cannot* clean anything, least of all mushrooms grown in black dirt and sheep dung!)
4. Add all other ingredients and stir well.
5. Reduce heat to low and continue simmering until tofu has exuded all its whey and is quite dry. Stir now and then. This will take about 20 minutes.
6. Dry, tofu will be half its original size. Remove from heat and cool.
7. Refrigerate or, to achieve the chewy texture of ground beef, freeze overnight in small plastic bags. Use within 2 months.
   Yield: 1 1/2 cups (375 mL) seasoned tofu.

TOKYO TOFU BURGERS

Known in East Asia for more than 2,000 years, tofu is natural and inexpensive. It is prepared in more than 40,000 shops in Japan alone. Given the world population explosion, more farmers will be planting soybeans from which tofu is made. Soybeans yield far more usable protein per acre than other crops. These delicious burgers will convince even the most skeptical.

2 lb	tofu, mashed with a fork	1 kg
2 cups	fine wholewheat bread crumbs	500 mL
1 tbsp	low-sodium soy sauce	15 mL
1 tsp	garlic powder	5 mL
½ tsp	black pepper, freshly ground	2 mL
½ cup	finely chopped celery	125 mL

PREPARATION:
12 minutes
COOKING: 15
minutes
FREEZING:
excellent
PER SERVING:
176 calories.
Excellent source
of calcium and
potassium. Good
source of folate,
iron, niacin,
protein and
vitamin A.

2 tsp	onion powder	10 mL
½ cup	cornmeal	125 mL
¼ cup	unbleached white flour	50 mL
	Cookware spray	
1 tsp	finely chopped fresh parsley	5 mL
1 tsp	Worcestershire sauce	5 mL

1. Combine first seven ingredients and form into 10 patties.
2. Combine cornmeal and flour.
3. Roll patties in flour mixture. Coat well.
4. Spray a heavy skillet. In it, brown patties on each side for about 15 minutes on low to medium heat.
5. Drain on paper towels. Put a drop or two of Worcestershire sauce on each and sprinkle with parsley.
6. Serve on hot buns with garnishes (sliced tomatoes, onion rings, green relish, Dijon mustard) or plain.

Yield: 10 burgers.

Salads and Salad Dressings

Santa Monica Caesar Salad

PREPARATION:

22 minutes

PER SERVING:

130 calories.
Excellent source
of potassium.
Good source of
calcium and
vitamin A.

California is the land of sunshine, fresh winter vegetables and physical fitness buffs. This low-cal version of an old favorite comes from Santa Monica where some of the modern world's most talented chefs invent and re-invent fine cuisine with dazzling aplomb.

1	large clove garlic, peeled and cut in half	1
4	anchovy fillets	4
¼ cup	Gloria Swanson's Mayonnaise (page 185)	50 mL
	or	
¼ cup	Hollywood Tofu Mayonnaise (page 186)	50 mL
1 tbsp	lemon juice	15 mL
	Tabasco sauce to taste	
2 tbsp	canola or safflower oil	25 mL
1	head romaine lettuce	1
1	tbsp grated Parmesan cheese	15 mL

GARNISH:

3 tbsp	soy bacon bits	45 mL
	Croutons	

1. Rub bottom of a large salad bowl with the garlic. Discard garlic.
2. Add anchovies and mash with a fork. Add mayonnaise, lemon juice, Tabasco and oil. Stir with a wooden spoon.
3. Wash the romaine and spin-dry.

Tear leaves into pieces. Add to salad bowl. Stir gently to coat. Sprinkle with Parmesan cheese.
4. Transfer to serving plates and sprinkle with soy bacon bits and croutons.

Yield: 5 servings.

Notes

Some culinary "artists" mash the garlic with the anchovies and a tablespoon of oil, spread the mixture on slices of French bread and toast in a cool oven at 300°F (150°C) for 30 minutes or until crisp. Once cooled, these replace the croutons. Some people also add a partially boiled (60 seconds) egg to make sure no one lives to a ripe old age. The more fiendish even toss in coarse salt and fried bacon! We recommend none of these procedures.

The original Caesar was created at the San Diego race track by chef Alexander Cardini in honor of his brother, Caesar, also a chef – not in Rome but in the United Kingdom. Both died very young of heart disease.

AUTHENTIC AMSTERDAM COLESLAW

The name coleslaw comes from the Dutch words *kool sla* – they and not the Americans or Canadians invented cabbage salad. Any fresh cabbage will do, including green, red, Savoy or Chinese.

PREPARATION:
15 minutes
PER SERVING:
193 calories.
Excellent source
of potassium
and vitamin C.
Good source of
calcium, folate
and vitamin A.

1 ½ lb	cabbage, cored and finely shredded	750 g
½ cup	canned or cooked corn kernels	125 mL
3 tbsp	cider, malt or white vinegar	40 mL
1	small onion, finely chopped	1
1	medium carrot, grated	1
⅔ cup	Gloria Swanson's Mayonnaise (page 185)	150 mL
½ tsp	Splenda granular sweetener or sugar (optional)	2 mL

1. Scrub cabbage under running lukewarm water and remove any scarred leaves before shredding. If possible, use a food processor for the shredding.
2. Transfer shredded cabbage to a mixing bowl. In the food processor, pulse corn kernels a few times to cut them.
3. Combine all ingredients and toss well. Let stand 30 minutes. For limp coleslaw, cover and refrigerate.

Yield: 4 servings.

VARIATIONS

- Substitute a little no-fat yogurt for some of the mayonnaise.
- Add walnut pieces or sliced apples sprinkled with lemon juice.
- Add diced green or red pepper, shredded celery and/or caraway seeds.

HINT

An electric meat slicer prepares shredded cabbage in a jiffy.

JOHN G. TAMES CLASSIC GREEK SALAD

PREPARATION:

15 minutes + marinating

PER SERVING:

264 calories. Excellent source of calcium, folate, potassium and vitamin A. Good source of iron and protein.

The founder of Toronto's bustling Communica ad agency once attributed his success in the world's most competitive business to two factors: beautiful women and gorgeous Greek salads. "Both," declared he, "are good for the heart." Coming from Athenian ancestry, he should know. We approve of the tofu for the high, no-fat protein in this low-cal version of a true classic from ancient times.

1 tsp	basil	5 mL
½ cup	olive oil (preferably Greek virgin)	125 mL
½ tsp	oregano	2 mL
½ tsp	black pepper, freshly ground	2 mL
½ tsp	salt (optional and not recommended)	2 mL
¼ cup	red wine vinegar	50 mL
1 lb	firm tofu, drained and cubed	500 g

3	beefsteak tomatoes	3
3	cucumbers (the kind with seeds)	3
½	large Spanish onion, chopped	½
1 cup	Greek olives (the blacker, the better)	250 mL
	Romaine lettuce	

1. Combine basil, oil, oregano, pepper, salt (if using) and vinegar. Pour over tofu cubes and marinate for 2 hours, covered, in the refrigerator. Stir twice.
2. Wash and cut tomatoes into wedges. Scrub, wash and slice cucumbers thinly. Do not peel. Add to marinated tofu.
3. Add chopped onion and olives, sliced or whole.
4. Wash lettuce and dry thoroughly in a spinner. Tear into pieces.
5. Toss marinated dressing and lettuce.

Yield: 6 servings.

Magnificent Snowbirds Moose Jaw Rice Salad

PREPARATION:

15 minutes +

chilling

COOKING: *40*

minutes

PER SERVING:

207 calories.

Excellent source

of calcium,

potassium,

protein and

vitamins A and

C. Good source

of niacin.

We don't know how a major in the world's finest team of aviation aerobats finds time to cook since the members work 12-hour days. One who does submitted this award-winning classic recipe. "If you don't eat right, you can't fly right," he wrote. We agree. This salad might not get you airborne but it's guaranteed to have you flying back to the buffet for seconds and even thirds.

½ cup	native wild rice	125 mL
¾ cup	Gloria Swanson's Mayonnaise (page 185)	175 mL
2 tbsp	chopped green onion	25 mL
1 tsp	curry powder	5 mL
½ tsp	dry mustard	2 mL
⅛ tsp	hot pepper sauce such as Tabasco	0.5 mL
2 cups	low-sodium chicken stock (page 24)	500 mL

1 cup	long-grain rice	250 mL
2 cups	cooked, lean ham, cut in julienne strips	500 mL
1 cup	sliced raw cauliflower	250 mL
1 cup	frozen peas, cooked and chilled	250 mL
½ cup	chopped celery	125 mL
½ cup	thinly sliced radishes	125 mL
1	ripe but firm melon, chilled	1

1. Soak wild rice in cold water. While preparing other ingredients, rinse the rice and soak it several times until water runs clear. Drain.
2. As the wild rice soaks, combine mayonnaise, onion, curry, mustard and hot pepper sauce. Cover and chill.
3. Add wild rice to boiling stock. Reduce heat, cover and simmer for 20 minutes. Add long-grain rice. Cover again and continue simmering on low heat for 20 minutes or until cooked and fluffy. Cool at room temperature.
4. Toss rice with salad dressing. Cover and chill for 3 hours.
5. Combine both mixtures, add ham and vegetables and toss.
6. Peel melon, cut in half and remove seeds. Cut into rings. Place one ring on each plate and mound with salad.

Yield: 6 servings.

SHOAL LAKE RICE SALAD

At a 1992 meeting of indigenous peoples from around the world, native chefs compared culinary notes and came up with this healthy no-cholesterol winner. They named it after the First Nations community of Shoal Lake in Ontario. Wild rice has twice the protein of white rice, as well as vitamin B, iron and manganese. Kiwi fruit is rich in vitamin C. And everyone knows what an apple a day does.

½ cup	native wild rice	125 mL
1 ½ cups	boiling spring water	375 mL
½ cup	brown rice	125 mL

PREPARATION:

10 minutes +

cooking and

chilling

PER SERVING:

113 calories.

Excellent source

of iron,

manganese,

potassium and

vitamins B and

C. Good source

of calcium,

folate and

niacin.

1	clove garlic, minced	1
3 cups	cold spring water	1.25 L
2	New Zealand kiwi fruit, sliced and halved	2
1	Ontario McIntosh apple, cored and cubed	1
½ cup	diced celery	125 mL
½ cup	red pepper strips	125 mL
¼ cup	toasted walnut pieces	50 mL
¼ cup	chopped green onions	50 mL
2 tbsp	chopped celery	25 mL
3 tbsp	sherry vinegar	40 mL
1 tbsp	canola or safflower oil	15 mL

1. Rinse wild rice and cover with the boiling water. Simmer for 5 minutes. Remove from heat and let stand, covered, for 1 hour.
2. Rinse brown rice in a sieve and discard any pebbles. Add garlic and 1 1/2 cups (375 mL) cold water. Cover and simmer on low heat for 45 minutes or until tender.
3. Drain wild rice. Add 1 1/2 cups (375 mL) water and simmer for 30 minutes or until very tender.
4. Combine the rices in a bowl.
5. Add all ingredients except vinegar and oil. Toss well.
6. Shake vinegar and oil together and dribble over salad. Cover and refrigerate for 2 hours. *Yield: 6 servings.*

NAVAJO MARINATED TOMATOES

Natives in what is now Arizona, Mexico and Utah cultivated tomatoes for thousands of years. The berry was unknown in Asia and Europe until the European invasions of the so-called New World. Juicy red tomatoes are now cherished in gardens worldwide. This is an update of an old native treat. Arrange the tomatoes on large plates and let guests help themselves. Basil, the royal herb, imparts a touch of sweetness and softens the vinegar.

PREPARATION: 5
minutes
CHILLING: 1
hour
PER SERVING:
23 calories.
Excellent source
of potassium
and vitamin A.
Good source of
calcium and
vitamin C.

6	vine-ripened tomatoes	6
1 tbsp	red wine vinegar	15 mL
½ tsp	dried sweet basil	2 mL
2	green onions, chopped	2
	Black pepper, freshly ground	

GARNISH:

Fresh parsley sprigs

1. Wash tomatoes but do not peel. Slice and arrange on 1 or 2 large plates or 6 individual salad plates.
2. Sprinkle lightly with red wine vinegar.
3. Rub basil in the palm of the hand until it is powdered. Sprinkle over slices.
4. Add green onions and pepper to taste. Cover and chill.
5. When serving, garnish with parsley, stems removed.
   Yield: 6 servings.

VARIATIONS

- If red wine vinegar is unavailable, a mild malt or white wine vinegar will do nicely.
- Add a few drops of canola or safflower oil.
- Use fresh basil leaves, finely chopped.
- Add freshly grated Parmesan cheese. Pine nuts puréed in a blender can be combined with the cheese for crunch and flavor. Add a clove of garlic for even more zing!

GATES MARINATED VEGETABLE SALAD

PREPARATION:

20 minutes

COOKING: 5

minutes

PER SERVING:

90 calories.

Excellent source

of potassium

and vitamin A.

Good source of

calcium, folate

and vitamin C.

John G. Gates invented the V-belt in 1917 in Denver, Colorado, and the rest is automotive history. Fiercely committed to quality above all, Gates companies throughout the world manufacture belts, hoses and a host of other specialized products. This low-cal salad was served at a 1979 employee celebration in Brantford, Ontario, site of two busy Gates plants. It's loaded with minerals and vitamins the body craves.

⅔ cup	fresh carrot juice	150 mL
3 tbsp	lemon juice	40 mL
1	garlic clove, minced	1
2 tbsp	canola oil	25 mL
¼ cup	chopped green onions	50 mL
½ tsp	Splenda granular sweetener or sugar	2 mL
1 tsp	grated lemon peel	5 mL
⅛ tsp	black pepper, freshly ground	0.5 mL
1 cup	carrot slices, julienned to ¼-inch (0.5 cm)	250 mL
2 cups	broccoli florets	500 mL
1 cup	green beans, cut in 1-inch (2.5 cm) pieces	250 mL
1	sweet red pepper, seeded and sliced in ¼-inch (0.5 cm) pieces	1
2 cups	zucchini, cut into ½-inch (1 cm) pieces	500 mL

1. Combine carrot and lemon juices, garlic, oil, onion, sweetener, lemon peel and pepper in a bowl.

2. Steam carrots, broccoli, green beans, red pepper and zucchini for no more than 5 minutes. They should remain crisp.

3. Transfer immediately to a serving bowl. Toss with dressing. Cover and chill for 3 hours.
Yield: 5 servings.

Saint John's United Church Salad

PREPARATION:

12 minutes

PER SERVING:

*110 calories.
Excellent source
of folate,
potassium and
vitamin C.
Good source of
calcium, dietary
fiber and
vitamin A.*

This was a delightful hit at a fundraising event catered by the ladies of Saint John's United Church in Dalhousie, New Brunswick. And since the health-conscious were aware of dietary restrictions, it's definitely low-cal and nutritious. Try serving it with John Barrymore's Honey-Lime Dressing (page 184).

6 cups	Romaine lettuce, washed, dried and torn into bite-sized bits	1.5 L
1 cup	honeydew melon balls	250 mL
1 cup	pineapple cubes	250 mL
1 cup	navel orange sections, white pith removed	250 mL
1 cup	raspberries or strawberries	250 mL
½ cup	wild blueberries	125 mL

1. Arrange lettuce in salad bowl.
2. Put the other ingredients over the lettuce, arranging them attractively.
3. Sprinkle with favorite dressing (see above).

   Yield: 5 servings.

Fort Edmonton Ginger Beef Salad

Easy to make and low in calories, this recipe wins raves the first time round – and every other time. Don't let the olive oil scare you – people in countries that produce and consume large quantities of it have remarkably low cholesterol counts and practically no heart disease. Alberta's Fort Edmonton was built in 1795 as a trading post, where a version of the salad originated in 1921. We've adapted it.

PREPARATION:

20 minutes

+ overnight

marination

COOKING: 55

minutes

PER SERVING:

243 calories.

Excellent source

of potassium,

protein and

vitamins A and

C. Good source

of calcium, iron

and niacin.

MARINADE:

1 tbsp	sesame oil	15 mL
½ cup	teriyaki sauce (page 206)	125 mL
½ cup	rice wine	125 mL

MAIN DISH:

1 ½ lb	lean flank steak	750 g
	Cookware spray	
	Peel of 1 orange, scrubbed and cut into thin slices	
½	small cauliflower, cut into florets	½
1	broccoli, cut into florets	1
3	carrots, cut into julienne strips	3
1	red pepper, seeded and cut into julienne strips	1
1	leek, cut into thin strips	1

DRESSING:

8	cloves garlic, minced	8
5 tbsp	minced fresh ginger	65 mL
¾ cup	olive oil	175 mL
1 cup	rice wine	250 mL
¼ cup	spring water	50 mL
½ cup	chopped fresh coriander	125 mL
	Pinch of chili pepper flakes	
	Black pepper, freshly ground	
8	Romaine lettuce leaves	8

1. Prepare marinade by mixing the ingredients together. Pour them over the steak, cover and refrigerate overnight.

2. Next day, spray a heavy skillet. Discard the marinade and fry the steak with the orange peel 5 minutes on each side over medium-high heat. Set steak aside. Let cool and refrigerate.

3. Steam cauliflower, broccoli and carrot for 5 minutes. Rinse with cold water and set aside.

4. Spray the frying pan again, if needed, and sauté red pepper strips and leek until tender-crisp, about 5 minutes. Set aside to cool.

5. To make the dressing, in a small saucepan, sauté garlic and ginger in olive oil for 10 minutes. Add wine, water, coriander,

chili peppers and simmer over lowest heat for 30 minutes. Season with pepper to taste and set aside to cool.

6. Wash lettuce leaves and spin dry. Arrange on serving plates.

7. Combine vegetables with dressing and toss to coat. Arrange on top of lettuce leaves.

8. Cut steak into thin strips and arrange on top of vegetables.
Yield: 8 servings.

Blue Angel Chicken Salad

PREPARATION:
15 minutes
COOKING: 55
minutes
PER SERVING:
255 calories.
Excellent source
of niacin,
potassium,
protein and
vitamin A. Good
source of
calcium and
vitamin C.

When filming, the glamorous Marlene Dietrich would often cater for fellow actors right there on the set. "One cannot project on an empty stomach," she would say. Home-made mayonnaise goes best with this recipe, which can also be used to make energy-producing sandwiches. A version of this recipe was prepared by the star for the cast of the classic film. Berlin's Marlene Dietrich Museum will open in 1996. It will include some 100,000 items and even a few pots and pans from the luminous Marlene's kitchen.

2	chicken breasts (a whole breast split in two)	2
1	chicken leg with back attached	1
2 cups	chicken stock (page 24)	500 mL
4	garlic cloves, split in two	4
1 ½ cups	Gloria Swanson's Mayonnaise (page 185)	375 mL
½ cup	no-fat plain yogurt	125 mL
2 tbsp	red wine vinegar	25 mL
2 tsp	Dijon mustard, preferably Aristocrate	10 mL
¼ cup	canola oil	50 mL
	Black pepper, freshly ground	
1	medium red pepper, finely chopped	1
1	small green pepper, finely chopped	1
2	sticks celery, finely chopped	2
1	small onion, finely chopped	1
1	apple, cored and chopped	1
2 tbsp	chopped fresh parsley	25 mL

GARNISH:

Sliced tomato, sliced cucumber and grated carrots

1. Boil chicken parts for 10 minutes in water to cover. Drain.
2. With cold water running over chicken parts, remove skin and fat. Discard. Wipe pot with paper towel.
3. Return chicken parts to the saucepan. Add chicken stock and garlic. Simmer over low heat for 45 minutes.
4. Remove chicken and allow to cool. Strain broth and reserve for soup. Discard garlic.
5. Cube chicken with a sharp knife. Place in bowl with remaining ingredients. Mix thoroughly. Chill in refrigerator overnight to accentuate flavors. Serve on bed of salad greens with garnish.

Yield: 8 to 10 servings.

JOHN BARRYMORE'S HONEY-LIME DRESSING

He starred with Greta Garbo in the classic *Grand Hotel*. He also starred in the salad department at home, as his low-cal recipe testifies. This is glorious with Saint John's United Church Salad (page 181).

PREPARATION:

3 minutes

PER TBSP (*15 mL*): *65 calories. Fair source of potassium and vitamin C.*

| ½ cup | clover honey | 125 mL |
| 2 tbsp | lime juice | 25 mL |

1. Combine honey and juice in a bowl.
2. Beat with a fork. Serve with any green salad.

Yield: 1/2 cup (125 mL).

MRS. MINIVER CARROT DRESSING

PREPARATION: 4
minutes
COOKING: 1
minute
PER SERVING:
36 calories.
Good source of
calcium,
potassium and
vitamins A
and C.

The star of the 1942 movie classic *Mrs. Miniver* was the beautiful and talented Greer Garson. Her fellow Thespians on the set recall the tasty, low-cal dressing served on the salad at the all-cast party that followed viewing of the final rushes.

1 tbsp	cornstarch	15 mL
¾ cup	fresh carrot juice	175 mL
¼ cup	chopped green onions	50 mL
3 tbsp	cider vinegar	40 mL
2 tbsp	oil (canola or safflower)	25 mL
1	clove garlic, crushed	1
⅛ tsp	black pepper, freshly ground	0.5 mL
⅛ tsp	cumin	0.5 mL
¼ tsp	Splenda granular sweetener or sugar	1 mL

1. Combine cornstarch with 1/4 cup (50 mL) carrot juice in a saucepan. Stir until blended. Add remaining juice.
2. Cook, stirring, for no more than 1 minute or until thickened. Remove immediately from heat.
3. Stir in all other ingredients. Taste and add more pepper, if desired.
4. Chill 1 hour. Shake well.
   Yield: 1 1/4 cups (300 mL) or 8 servings.

GLORIA SWANSON'S MAYONNAISE

Until her final dissolve at the age of 84, she remained the epitome of Hollywood glamour and vitality. "You are what you eat," she declared. Her riveting memoirs, *Swanson on Swanson*, trace her trajectory from silent pictures to sound and color. A true star every hour of the day, she devoted

PREPARATION:

6 to 10 minutes

PER 1/4 CUP

(50 mL): 60

calories. Fair

source of

calcium and

vitamin A.

a great deal of her money and time to worthwhile causes. We've adapted her recipe to make it even more low-cal.

2 tsp	Dijon-type mustard	10 mL
1 ½ tbsp	oil (olive preferred)	20 mL
½ cup	low-fat plain yogurt	125 mL
2 tsp	fresh lemon juice	10 mL
1 tsp	minced green onions	5 mL
1 tbsp	tomato paste or Heinz ketchup	15 mL
1 tbsp	fresh parsley, minced, or ½ tsp (2 mL) dried	15 mL
½ tsp	fresh basil, minced, or ¼ tsp (1 mL) dried	2 mL
	Black pepper, freshly ground	
	Dash of cayenne or hot pepper sauce (Tabasco)	

1. Put mustard in a blender, then gradually add the oil, pulsing 4 or 5 times for a few seconds only.
2. Add yogurt, blend thoroughly, then add all other ingredients except cayenne. Blend thoroughly until mixture is smooth.
3. Season to taste with cayenne and refrigerate.
   Yield: 1 cup (250 mL).

HOLLYWOOD TOFU MAYONNAISE

This smooth mayonnaise has no egg yolks, and therefore no cholesterol. A hit with today's health-conscious young Hollywood crowd, it can be used in any recipe calling for the dangerous kind.

1 cup	tofu	250 mL
3 tbsp	fresh lemon juice	40 mL
½ cup	canola or safflower oil	125 mL
2 tsp	Dijon-type mustard	10 mL
	Pinch of cayenne pepper	

PREPARATION: 4
minutes
REFRIGERATOR
LIFE: 3 weeks
PER SERVING:
57 calories.
Excellent source
of calcium,
folate and
potassium. Good
source of iron,
niacin, protein
and thiamin.

1. In a blender, combine tofu and 1 tbsp (15 mL) of lemon juice.
2. Blend at high speed and very slowly add, alternately, oil and remaining lemon juice until it thickens. Add mustard and cayenne to taste. Pulse once or twice.

Yield: 1 1/2 cups (375 mL).

VARIATIONS

- Green Mayonnaise: Simmer 10 sprigs washed fresh watercress, 10 spinach leaves and 10 stalks fresh tarragon or chervil for 2 minutes in a little water. Drain and rinse in cold water. Dry in a spinner. Pound in a mortar to form a pulp. Add 1 cup (250 mL) tofu mayonnaise. Use with vegetable or fish salads.
- Roquefort Cream Dressing: Add 1/2 cup (125 mL) evaporated skim milk and 2 tbsp (25 mL) Roquefort cheese to 1 cup (250 mL) tofu mayonnaise. Stir. Serve over greens or lettuce.
- Mona Lisa Dressing: To 1/2 cup (125 mL) tofu mayonnaise add 1/2 tsp (2 mL) sweet paprika, 1/2 tsp (2 mL) horseradish, 1/2 tsp (2 mL) English-type mustard and 1 tbsp (15 mL) evaporated skim milk. Stir. Serve over hearts of lettuce or Romaine.

GILLES VILLENEUVE SALAD DRESSING SENSASS

PREPARATION: 6
minutes
PER 1/4 CUP
(50 mL): 135
calories. Fair
source of
calcium,
potassium and
vitamin A.

The charismatic racing driver from Berthierville, Québec, captured the hearts of people all over the world. At Italy's Imola circuit, one challenging corner is named the Curva Gilles Villeneuve. His wife and two children accompanied him, staying in a motor home in the paddock. He took tremendous risks at the wheel of Ferraris but not with classic French cuisine. We've adapted his favorite salad dressing. (*Sensass* is French for "sensational!")

1/4 tsp	dried tarragon	1 mL
1/4 tsp	dried basil	1 mL
1 tsp	dry mustard	5 mL

1 tbsp	lemon juice	15 mL
5 tbsp	canola or safflower oil	65 mL
5 tbsp	no-fat plain yogurt	65 mL
1 tsp	minced garlic	5 mL

1. Place all ingredients in a screw-top jar and close. Shake vigorously for 5 minutes.

2. Refrigerate for 2 hours before using.

Yield: 1 cup (250 mL).

Mao Tse~Tung Salad Dressing

PREPARATION:
12 minutes or less
PER 1/4 CUP
(50 mL): 110 calories. Good source of folate, protein and vitamin A.

When he wasn't chasing down recalcitrant Nationalists, the Chinese Communist leader could whip up a poem or an unusual dressing or sauce. Forget the ideological storms of the past. His recipe, submitted to us from Sichuan province, is great on salad greens or try it on wontons or pasta.

¼ cup	white wine vinegar	50 mL
2 tbsp	sesame oil	25 mL
1 tbsp	vegetable oil	15 mL
2 tsp	Splenda granular sweetener or sugar	10 mL
½ tsp	Chinese chili sauce	2 mL
2 tbsp	minced green onion	25 mL
¼ cup	minced fresh coriander	50 mL
1 tbsp	fresh or preserved ginger, minced	15 mL
2	cloves garlic, minced	2
1 tbsp	minced fresh parsley	15 mL
1 cup	fresh spinach, washed and minced	250 mL

1. With a blender or food processor, you don't have to mince anything. Simply process until everything is well blended.

2. On the battlefield, find an oasis, a bowl with a cover or a jar. Shake everything vigorously for a few minutes and serve.

Yield: 3/4 cup (175 mL).

Prince Danilov Sauce Russe (Royal Russian Dressing)

PREPARATION:
4 minutes
MAXIMUM
REFRIGERATOR
LIFE: 4 weeks
PER TBSP (15
mL): 36
calories.

Stephen Joseph Danilov made an aristocratic splash wherever he set up a new enterprise, be it in Houston, Montréal, New York or Toronto and be it a cosmetics factory, a packaging firm or a petroleum corporation. Gregarious and kindhearted to a fault, he predicted the downfall of Soviet Communism when that system was at its peak. This marvelous old classic, which His Serene Highness had already adapted for us to make it low-cal, puts everyone in a royal mood. Serve with seafood or salads.

1 ¼ cups	Gloria Swanson's Mayonnaise (page 185)	300 mL
1 tbsp	horseradish, preferably freshly grated	15 mL
1 tsp	onion, minced	5 mL
1 tbsp	tomato paste	15 mL
1	gherkin, finely diced	1

1. Combine all ingredients and mix well.

2. Chill before serving.
   Yield: 2 cups (500 mL).

VARIATION
• Prince Danilov's Galician Dressing: Combine 1/2 cup (125 mL) finely chopped, cooked beets with 1 1/2 cups (375 mL) Gloria Swanson's Mayonnaise and 1 tbsp (15 mL) domestic or imported caviar. Add horseradish and/or Worcestershire sauce to taste. Chill.

GRETA GARBO'S THOUSAND ISLANDS DRESSING

PREPARATION:
2 minutes
PER SERVING:
35 calories.
Excellent source
of calcium,
potassium and
vitamin A.
Good source of
protein.

She claimed never to have uttered the famous words, "I vant to be alone." Ms Garbo then proceeded to do just that. Ah, well, her version of the famous dressing is definitely low-cal and makes any fresh salad sparkle. We've made it even leaner by using no-fat yogurt, now widely available.

1 cup	no-fat yogurt	250 mL
½ cup	Heinz ketchup	125 mL
2 tbsp	sweet pickle relish	25 mL
¼ cup	skim milk, fresh or reconstituted	50 mL

1. Mix all ingredients in a jar and shake until blended.

2. Chill before serving.
   Yield: 1 1/2 cups (375 mL) (10 servings).

JEANNE MANCE MIRACLE SALAD DRESSING

If you like the taste of such commercial brands as Miracle Whip and President's Choice, you'll make this low-cal one often. It's named after a great Montréal pioneer who founded the city's first hospital and was far busier in and out of the kitchen than any of the men who get far too much credit in the history books. Different versions of this recipe have been around for generations.

1 cup	spring water	250 mL
3 ½ tbsp	cornstarch	48 mL

PREPARATION:
6 minutes
REFRIGERATOR
LIFE: 3 weeks +
PER TBSP (15
mL): 42
calories. Fair
source of
calcium,
potassium,
protein and
vitamin A.

2 tbsp	Splenda granular sweetener or sugar	25 mL
1	egg	1
2 tsp	dry mustard	10 mL
1 tsp	salt or substitute (such as Mrs. Dash)	5 mL
¼ tsp	Hungarian sweet paprika	1 mL
¼ cup	cider or malt vinegar	50 mL
¾ cup	canola or safflower oil	175 mL

1. In top of double boiler, combine water and cornstarch. Bring to a boil and simmer until clear and thick, about 4 minutes.
2. Place all other ingredients in a bowl but DO NOT STIR.
3. Add cornstarch mixture and beat vigorously with an egg beater (or use an electric mixer).
4. Cool, bottle, seal and store in refrigerator.
   Yield: 2 cups (500 mL).

SARAH BERNHARDT WATERCRESS DRESSING

PREPARATION:
8 minutes
PER SERVING:
80 calories.
Good source of
calcium,
potassium and
vitamin A.

Active and vivacious throughout life, the great French actress continued to captivate hearts everywhere, even at the age of 78. This simple and delicious salad dressing helps explain how she maintained her gorgeous figure. "My life is one of passion," she moaned to Maurice Chevalier, "and watercress is my downfall."

2	bunches watercress	2
	Juice of 1 lemon	
1 tbsp	tarragon vinegar	15 mL
½ cup	canola oil	125 mL
	Black pepper, freshly ground	
½ tsp	Splenda granular sweetener or sugar	2 mL

1. Soak watercress in a sink of cold water for 20 minutes. Drain in a colander. Shake well or use a salad spinner.
2. Remove stems and mince leaves. Cover and refrigerate.
3. Combine all other ingredients in a jar and shake. Taste and add more pepper if desired.
4. Before sprinkling on your favorite salad, add watercress and shake well.

Yield: 1/2 cup (125 mL) (10 servings).

FÉLIX LECLERC RASPBERRY VINEGAR

PREPARATION: *20 minutes* MARINATION: 2 *days +* PER TBSP (15 *mL): 3 calories.*

Visitors to the home on Île d'Orléans of the distinguished and much-loved Québécois poet and singer Félix Leclerc often found him busy in the kitchen. "There's no need to import much of anything," he once declared. "There's everything here anyone could ever need if only you know how to use it." He presented friends with Christmas gifts of fruit vinegars. This one is easily made and far superior to expensive imports.

1 quart	fresh raspberries (preferably wild)	1 L
2 cups	mild cider vinegar	500 mL

1. Rinse and crush raspberries.
2. Combine raspberries and vinegar in an ovenproof or stainless steel bowl.
3. Cover and let stand in a cool spot for 1 day.
4. Heat in a moderate oven to a simmer. Remove immediately and let stand another day, tightly covered. Do not refrigerate.
5. Strain through a cheesecloth into a stainless steel pot. (Avoid aluminum, copper and iron!) Squeeze by hand until juice runs cloudy.
6. Boil for 5 minutes. Remove from heat. Pour hot liquid into clean bottles and seal. Use in vinaigrette, mayonnaise or borscht.

Yield: 4 cups (1 L).

VARIATIONS

- Use strawberries, blueberries, or peaches in season, or cranberries. Keeps for 1 year unrefrigerated, but the flavors are best retained when refrigerated.
- For tarragon vinegar, add 2 cups (500 mL) fresh or 1 cup (250 mL) dried tarragon leaves to 1 quart (1 L) of white vinegar. Steep for 3 weeks. Strain and discard leaves.
- For a more flavorful tarragon vinegar, add 1 minced garlic clove.

Sauces

Alfie Duncan's Bolognese Sauce

PREPARATION:

20 minutes

COOKING: 75

minutes +

FREEZING:

excellent

PER SERVING:

240 calories.

Excellent source

of potassium

and vitamins A

and C. Good

source of

calcium, iron,

niacin and

protein.

Alfie and his wife, Mary, were neighbors of Annie Poirier in New Brunswick. Alfie didn't venture into cooking very often but we can thank him for this low-cal version of a traditional sauce for pasta. It gets compliments galore when served hot over cooked linguine or spaghetti. Don't forget to put out freshly grated Romano cheese – expensive, yes, but a small wedge makes a big mound. Grate it in the food processor, not the blender or the spice mill! The Italian cheese is diamond-hard and will ruin all but the toughest steel blades.

	Cookware spray	
½ lb	lean ground beef	250 g
¼ lb	lean ground pork	125 g
¼ lb	lean ground veal	125 g
8 quarts	boiling hot water (to remove fat from beef)	9 L
2 cups	Alfie Duncan's El Cheapo Tomato Sauce (recipe below)	500 mL
¼ cup	dry red wine	50 mL
2 tbsp	canned tomato paste	25 mL
	Pinch of ground nutmeg (no more than 6 grains)	

1. Spray a heavy saucepan and brown the three meats, using a plastic or wooden fork to separate. Simmer for 10 minutes on very low heat or until thoroughly cooked.

2. Transfer to a colander and rinse under 8 quarts (9 L) of boiling water. Wipe saucepan with a paper towel. Shake colander vigorously.

3. Return meats to saucepan. Add

tomato sauce, wine and tomato paste. On lowest possible heat, allow sauce to "shudder" for 1 hour, barely simmering.

4. If sauce is too thick, add a little skim milk.

5. Add nutmeg and continue simmering another 20 minutes. Serve hot. To mellow flavors, cool and refrigerate overnight. *Yield: 4 to 6 servings.*

VARIATIONS

- During last 15 minutes, add 1/4 lb (125 g) of sliced mushrooms.
- For an enriched pasta sauce, add a medium carrot, grated; 2 stalks celery, chopped; and 1/2 green pepper, diced.

ALFIE DUNCAN'S EL CHEAPO TOMATO SAUCE

PREPARATION: *3 minutes*
COOKING: *45 minutes*
FREEZING: *excellent*
PER SERVING: *40 calories. Excellent source of potassium and vitamins A and C.*

Alfie's sauce can serve as a basis for Andy Warhol's Cream of Tomato Soup (page 41) or be drizzled over sausages, hamburgers, grilled meats, fish or chicken. The recipe can easily be doubled for freezing.

1	medium onion, chopped	1
	Cookware spray	
1	can tomatoes (28 oz/796 mL)	1
	(or peeled and chopped ripe tomatoes)	
2	cloves garlic, minced	2
1	large carrot, grated	1
	Black pepper, freshly ground	
1 tsp	dried basil or oregano (or a combination of both)	5 mL
1 tsp	dried thyme	5 mL
¼ tsp	celery seed	1 mL
2	cloves	2
½ cup	dry red or white wine	125 mL
1	bay leaf	1

1. Sauté onion in sprayed saucepan for 5 minutes.
2. Add other ingredients and break up tomatoes. Stir frequently. Simmer uncovered for 45 minutes. If too thick, add hot water.
3. Remove bay leaf and cloves and, if one is available, use a blender or food processor and pulse for a few minutes until the sauce is smooth. Otherwise, do what you can with a wooden fork.
4. To make a casserole, combine 1 lb (500 g) cooked meats with 1 cup (250 mL) sauce and 1/2 cup (125 mL) Cheddar cheese. Bake 30 minutes at 350°F (175°C). Otherwise, ladle as is onto cooked spaghetti or linguine and pass some grated cheese. *Yield: 6 servings.*

Carmen Miranda Hot Salsa

Preparation: 15 minutes
Cooking: 35 minutes
Freezing: excellent
Per tbsp (15 mL): 8 calories. Excellent source of potassium and vitamin A. Good source of calcium.

Salsa now outsells tomato ketchup in the United States. In their search for healthy foods, yuppies and others have sworn off fat, salt and sugar and have discovered that salsa replaces ketchup, which is often high in the last two. This salsa is so far ahead of anything sold in the stores, you'll want to refrigerate and even freeze some.

3	garlic cloves, minced	3
1	large onion, chopped	1
1	sweet banana pepper (the pale green ones)	1
	Cookware spray	
1 can	(28 oz/796 mL) plum tomatoes	1 L
1 ⅔ cups	chicken stock (page 24)	400 mL
2 tbsp	chili powder	25 mL
1 tsp	dried oregano, rubbed	5 mL
½ tsp	ground cumin	2 mL
¼ tsp	black pepper, freshly ground	1 mL
¼ tsp	cayenne or ½ fresh jalapeño pepper, minced	1 mL

1. You can use a food processor fitted with the metal blade to mince the garlic and chop the onion and banana pepper. A few pulses will do. Otherwise, use a knife and board.

2. Spray the bottom of a heavy saucepan. Sauté garlic, onion and banana pepper for 8 minutes on low heat. *Do not brown!*

3. Add all other ingredients and break up tomatoes with a fork.

4. Bring to a boil, reduce to low, simmer uncovered for 27 minutes exactly and *not a second more*. Cool.

5. Pour into sterilized jars and refrigerate or freeze.
Yield: 5 cups (1.25 L).

VARIATIONS

- For a medium hot sauce, eliminate cayenne or jalapeño pepper.
- Use beef stock (page 25) instead of chicken.
- Chop 1 green or sweet red pepper with the onion and banana pepper.
- Add a sprig or two of fresh parsley, chopped.

MANITOU HEALTH SPA
SAUCE BÉARNAISE

Loaded with butter and egg yolks, the original Sauce Béarnaise was created in southwest France. Other dairy-producing countries such as Holland followed suit. Our velvety low-cal version from Ontario is simply gorgeous. You may also eliminate the salt.

PREPARATION:
4 minutes
MAXIMUM
REFRIGERATOR
LIFE: *4 weeks*
PER TBSP (15
mL): 36
calories.

2 tsp	cornstarch	10 mL
1 tsp	polyunsaturated margarine or canola oil	5 mL
½ cup	chicken stock (page 24)	125 mL
2	egg whites at room temperature	2
⅛ tsp	white pepper, freshly ground	0.5 mL
⅛ tsp	salt	0.5 mL

BOUQUET:

¼ cup	tarragon or dry sherry wine vinegar	50 mL
¼ cup	dry white wine or dry vermouth	50 mL
1 tbsp	minced shallots or green onions	15 mL
2 tbsp	minced fresh tarragon or ½ tsp (2 mL) dried	25 mL
½ tsp	minced fresh parsley	2 mL

1. Prepare the Bouquet. Place vinegar, wine, onions, tarragon and parsley in a saucepan. Bring to a boil and simmer uncovered for 15 minutes. You should have 2 tbsp (25 mL) of concentrated Bouquet.
2. Blend cornstarch and margarine in the top of a double boiler. Add chicken stock. Stir and cook for 5 minutes to thicken.

3. Whisk egg whites for 1 minute until foamy. Blend with 2 tbps (25 mL) of thickened sauce and add gradually to remaining sauce. Cook for 2 minutes over low heat, stirring. Remove from heat and blend in Bouquet. Add pepper and salt to taste.
   Yield: 1 3/4 cups (425 mL).

SAUCE HOLLANDAISE

1. Eliminate Bouquet ingredients.

2. Blend in 1 tsp (5 mL) fresh lemon juice at end of Step 3 above.

LÉON DANTES'S SAUCE BÉCHAMEL (BASIC WHITE SAUCE)

PREPARATION:

6 MINUTES

COOKING: 13

minutes

FREEZING:

excellent

PER 1/4 CUP

(50 mL): 50

calories. Fair

source of

vitamin A.

Since it is so versatile, this is the first sauce one should learn to make. Léon used to keep it on hand when dealing with the hunger pangs of The Lakeshore Players, a Toronto theatrical group struggling to make its mark in pre–Canada Council days. He and a volunteer chef served it on dozens of delightful concoctions. With imagination, so can you!

1 ½ tbsp	canola or safflower oil	20 mL
1 ½ tbsp	cornstarch	20 mL
¼ cup	powdered instant non-fat milk	50 mL
1 cup	spring water	250 mL
1 tsp	dry sherry	5 mL
½ tsp	salt (optional)	2 mL
¼ tsp	white pepper, freshly ground	1 mL

1. Combine oil and cornstarch in a saucepan. Simmer slowly for 3 minutes.
2. Add milk and water and simmer another 10 minutes, stirring.
3. Season with sherry, salt (if using) and pepper.

Yield: 1 cup (250 mL).

VARIATIONS

- Thick Béchamel: Increase the cornstarch to 2 tbsp (25 mL).
- Sauce Mornay: Add 1/2 to 1 cup (125 to 250 mL) grated Cheddar cheese to the hot sauce and stir over low heat until melted. Season with Dijon-type mustard and Worcestershire sauce to taste.
- Sauce Velouté: Instead of water, use chicken, beef or fish stock (pages 24–26).
- Herb Sauce: Add 1 tsp (5 mL) freshly chopped herbs (parsley, dill, etc.) or 1/2 tsp (2 mL) dried herbs (thyme or oregano).
- Mustard Sauce: Combine 1 tsp (5 mL) dry mustard with the cornstarch.

MADAME CHIANG KAI~SHEK DIPPING SAUCE

PREPARATION:

3 minutes

PER 1/2 CUP

(125 mL): 32

calories. Good

source of

vitamin C.

General Chiang Kai-shek's wife insisted on freshly ironed silk sheets twice a day and total control of the kitchen. Her hubby dipped his won tons in this one; you might try spring rolls or tortellini. A delicious all-purpose dip, our version is adapted from the old Chinese stand-by.

2 tbsp	fish sauce (Oriental)	25 mL
2 tbsp	spring water	25 mL
2 tbsp	lime juice	25 mL
1 tbsp	Splenda granular sweetener or sugar	15 mL
1 tsp	Chinese chili sauce	5 mL
1	clove garlic, minced	1

1. Put all ingredients in a jar or tightly covered bowl and shake well, until ingredients are blended.

Yield: 1/2 cup (125 mL).

ANNAPOLIS VALLEY PESTO

Linguine or spaghetti with classic pesto makes a delicious side dish to accompany a pork chop, a filet mignon or a broiled trout. A green salad rounds out the meal.

4 cups	fresh basil leaves, washed, drained and loosely packed	1 L
½ cup	fresh parsley	125 mL
3	garlic cloves	3
¾ cup	oil	175 mL

PREPARATION:
6 minutes
FREEZING: not
recommended
PER SERVING:
260 calories.
Good source of
calcium and
vitamin A.

| ¼ cup | butter-flavor buds | 50 mL |
| ½ cup | Parmesan cheese, freshly grated | 125 mL |

1. Combine all items except cheese in a food processor. Blend well.
2. Just before using, stir in Parme-san cheese. Toss with drained, hot pasta. Cover and refrigerate leftover sauce.

Yield: 6 servings.

BOISSEVAIN PESTO

Just south of the town of Boissevain is a 2,000-acre park, the International Peace Garden, commemorating a 1932 pledge of peace between the people of Canada and the United States. It straddles the Manitoba–North Dakota border, whence came this outstanding recipe.

PREPARATION:
2 to 5 minutes
COOKING: 7
minutes
FREEZING: not
recommended
PER SERVING:
246 calories.
Good source of
calcium and
protein.

4 cups	fresh basil leaves, washed and drained	1 L
½ cup	oil	125 mL
2 tbsp	pine nuts	25 mL
3	garlic cloves, sliced	3
3 tbsp	butter-flavor buds or margarine	40 mL
	Dash of cayenne or black pepper	
½ cup	Parmesan cheese, freshly grated	125 mL
2 tbsp	Romano cheese, freshly grated	25 mL
½ lb	pasta	250 g

1. Mix basil, oil, pine nuts, garlic, butter-flavor buds and cayenne at high speed in a blender.
2. Transfer to a bowl. Stir in cheeses.
3. Boil pasta following directions on package.
4. Add to the pesto 2 tbsp (25 mL) boiling water from the pasta. Stir.
5. Drain pasta. Toss with pesto and serve immediately.

Yield: 6 servings.

GORDON SINCLAIR LOW-CAL BARBECUE SAUCE

PREPARATION:
6 minutes
COOKING: *3 minutes*
FREEZING: *not required*
PER TBSP *(15 mL): 14 calories. Fair source of vitamin C.*

The old curmudgeon used to get up in the morning and ask himself: "Now let's see who I can get riled up today." This basting sauce should be applied during the final 15 minutes of indoor or outdoor baking or broiling. Do not use too early.

¾ cup	Heinz ketchup	175 mL
2 tsp	celery seeds	10 mL
1	garlic clove, crushed	1
1 tbsp	Worcestershire sauce	15 mL
2 tbsp	Canadian vinegar	25 mL
2 tbsp	Splenda granular sweetener or sugar	25 mL
4	drops hot pepper sauce (such as Tabasco)	4
¼ tsp	paprika	1 mL

1. Combine all ingredients and simmer for 3 minutes. Cool before using.

2. Before storing, remove garlic.
   Yield: 1 cup (250 mL).

MICMAC CRANBERRY-CRABAPPLE SAUCE

When the new European settlers began roasting turkeys for Thanksgiving Day dinners, the natives suggested a sauce made with wild cranberries and maple syrup. For thousands of years, they had served it with wild game. The new immigrants added allspice, when it was available. Natives celebrate Thanksgiving every day, as they have done for eons. They do it by

PREPARATION:
6 minutes
COOKING: 25
minutes
FREEZING:
excellent.
PER TBSP (15
mL): 24
calories.
Excellent source
of potassium.
Good source of
calcium and
vitamin C.

thanking the Great Spirit for His bounty and by always giving "something back to Mother Earth."

12 oz	fresh or frozen cranberries	340 g
3	tart crabapples, cored and sliced	3
1 cup	maple syrup	250 mL
1 cup	spring water	250 mL
¼ tsp	ground allspice	1 mL

1. Pick any stems from cranberries and rinse them.
2. Combine crabapples, cranberries, maple syrup and water. Boil.
3. Reduce heat immediately. Simmer gently for 25 minutes, stirring occasionally.
4. When sauce is thick, stir in allspice and cool to room temperature.
5. Refrigerate a day or 2 to improve flavors.
6. Serve at room temperature.
   Yield: 3 1/2 cups (875 mL).

EMILE ZOLA HORSERADISH SAUCE

PREPARATION:
2 minutes
FREEZING: not
recommended
PER TBSP (15
mL): 16 calories.
Excellent source
of calcium,
potassium and
vitamin A.
A good source of
protein and
vitamin C.

Horseradish, a member of the mustard family, has twice the vitamin C of fresh orange juice. Its home was in eastern Europe, but the popularity of *Armoracia rusticana* is now international. The young leaves make an excellent salad, but the star attraction is the root. Grate fresh horseradish root into tomato sauce for a great seafood cocktail sauce. It's also excellent with lamb, hot or cold roast beef, corned beef and boiled beef.

½ cup	low-fat sour cream	125 mL
1 tbsp	Dijon-type mustard	15 mL
1 tbsp	tarragon vinegar	15 mL
1 tbsp or more	prepared horseradish	15 mL or more
	Black pepper, freshly ground	

1. Combine all ingredients in a bowl and season to taste.
2. Store in a tight-lidded jar in the refrigerator.

Yield: 3/4 cup (175 mL).

BERING STRAIT PLUM SAUCE

PREPARATION:
8 minutes
COOKING: *20
minutes*
FREEZING:
excellent
PER TBSP *(15
mL): 6 calories.
Excellent source
of potassium
and vitamin A.
Good source of
calcium and
vitamin C.*

Bering Strait was the pathway used by the Asian nomads thousands of years ago. Their descendants spread throughout the Americas, where they found wild plums in abundance. Our low-cal sauce, great with Oriental stir-fry dishes, uses pumpkin.

¼ cup	cooked pumpkin	50 mL
¼ cup	white vinegar	50 mL
¼ cup	spring water	50 mL
1 cup	Splenda granular sweetener or sugar	250 mL
	Grated rind and juice of 1 lemon	
2 tbsp	cornstarch	25 mL
¼ cup	spring water	50 mL
1 tbsp	Heinz ketchup	15 mL
⅛ tsp	cayenne	0.5 mL

1. In a saucepan, blend pumpkin, vinegar, water, sweetener, lemon rind and juice.
2. Bring to a boil, then stir in cornstarch mixed with water.

Simmer, stirring, until thickened and smooth – about 20 minutes. Season with ketchup and cayenne.

Yield: 2 cups (500 mL).

JERICHO TARATOR SAUCE

PREPARATION:
5 minutes
FREEZING: not
recommended
PER TBSP (15
mL): 4
calories.
Excellent
source of
potassium.
Good source of
calcium and
folate.

An essential for genuine falafel pita sandwiches. It keeps for a month in the refrigerator. Tahini is sold in health food stores, specialty shops and large supermarkets.

¾ cup	tahini (sesame seed butter)	175 mL
¾ cup	spring water	175 mL
¼ cup	lemon juice	50 mL
¼ cup	oil	50 mL
3	cloves garlic	3

1. Combine all ingredients in blender or food processor. Thin with water if necessary or thicken with more tahini.

2. Store in a lidded jar in the refrigerator. Keeps for 1 month.
   Yield: 1 3/4 cups (425 mL).

EMMIE WILKINS'S TARTAR SAUCE

PREPARATION:
8 minutes
FREEZING: not
required.
PER TBSP (15
mL): 4 calories.
Good source of
calcium,
potassium and
vitamin A.

Emmie was one of Annie Poirier's sisters; she followed Annie to North America, settling in Massachusetts "so as never to be too far from the sea." Here she married Sam Wilkins and raised two sons. During World War II, the doors to her gracious home were open to any Allied soldier who cared to drop in. Hundreds did and many of them were treated to her favorite dish – seafood. Her piquant sauce is great with any kind of crisp fish.

1 cup	Gloria Swanson's Mayonnaise (page 185)	250 mL
1 tbsp each	minced gherkin, green relish, capers, parsley and onion	15 mL each
⅛ tsp each	Hungarian sweet paprika, and freshly ground black pepper	0.5 mL each

	Small garlic clove, minced	
1 tbsp	chopped green chives (optional)	15 mL
1 tsp	minced fresh tarragon leaves	5 mL
	or	
¼ tsp	dried and crushed tarragon	1 mL
	Pinch of cumin	
	Dash of cayenne or hot pepper sauce (Tabasco)	

1. Combine all ingredients in a bowl and stir vigorously until thoroughly blended. Chill in refrigerator for at least 24 hours before using.

2. If sauce becomes too thick after a few days in the refrigerator, thin with skim milk, fresh lemon juice or tarragon vinegar. *Yield: 1 1/4 cups (300 mL).*

YOKOHAMA TERIYAKI SAUCE

PREPARATION: 6 minutes
FREEZING: not required.
PER TSP (5 mL): 4 calories. Fair source of potassium and folate.

Yes, you can buy commercial varieties but the high salt content is enough to make even an addict gag. Friends in the Japanese seaport supplied this outstanding recipe, which takes only a few minutes to prepare.

1 tbsp	finely chopped fresh ginger	15 mL
	or	
2 tsp	powdered ginger	10 mL
2	cloves garlic	2
1	medium onion	1
2 tbsp	Splenda granular sweetener or sugar	25 mL
1 cup	low sodium soy sauce	250 mL
½ cup	dry sherry	125 mL

1. Chop ginger, garlic and onion finely by hand or use a blender or food processor (a mush is entirely acceptable).

2. Combine all ingredients in a bottle, cover tightly, and refrigerate. Shake well before using. *Yield: 1 3/4 cups (425 mL).*

BREADS

UNBLEACHED FLOUR IS VITAL TO YOUR HEALTH

Since ancient times, bread has been regarded as the staff of life. The reputation is well-deserved but the modern food industry has some catching-up to do. The sad fact is that highly refined flours are not only bad for your health, they can actually reduce life expectancy.

If you're still using bleached white flour in your kitchen, switch to unbleached white flour, wholewheat flours, rice flour, potato flour, soy flour and refrigerated wheat germ. They are sold by reliable health-food stores throughout the world.

In most cases, prices are lower than bleached white flour at the supermarket. Make sure the health store has a good turnover, however, since these items can become rancid after a time.

National brands claim that their flour is "enriched." Ask yourself: "Enriched with *what*?" A host of natural vitamins and minerals has been replaced with two or three synthetic ones.

To make matters worse, most national brands are loaded with chemical softeners, whiteners, agers, fresheners, preservers and fungus-growth preventers. The fast hot-milling process destroys more than 22 nutrients. And the wheat germ – the grain's most nutritious part and an important source of the anti-cancer vitamin E – is *removed!*

The flour you use should be stone-ground to retain all the nutrients. Made from pesticide-free, organically grown wheat, this health-sustaining natural "miracle" is sold by health-food stores in two main versions: hard and soft. Use the hard flour for yeast bread and the soft one for quick breads (muffins, pancakes and biscuits). As you'll note from our tested recipes, unbleached white flour is ideal for thickening sauces. For even more nutritious meals, add wheat germ and extra skim milk (fresh or reconstituted) wherever feasible.

Never buy more flour than you can use within a week. The same is true of wheat germ, which contains oil and becomes rancid unless refrigerated. Wrap all flours tightly in plastic and refrigerate or freeze in usable quantities. Bring to room temperature before using.

OATS

Look for steel-cut oats, which are are far more nutritious than "instant" rolled oats sold under various brand names. In the rolling process, rolled oats are submitted to extremely high temperatures that destroy natural vitamins. Steel-cut oats are available in all reputable health-food stores. Use a double-boiler for a worry-free, nutritious breakfast ready to serve in twenty minutes! Use your imagination and add sugar-free apple sauce, apricot jam or your favorite conserve. If a sweetener is absolutely required, use Splenda as you would sugar.

OATMEAL "FAD" PASSÉ? NO WAY!

Don't believe the food scribes who claim that the oatmeal "fad" is passé. The fad may be less trendy but the facts are still there, more pertinent than ever. A new study from Johns Hopkins Medical Institutions in Baltimore found that people who regularly ate one small bowl of oatmeal had lower blood pressure than those who did not. The tests were conducted on 850 Yi people, an ethnic minority in southwest China, men aged 15 to 77. The Yi were chosen because they have heart disease risk factors similar to those of men in more developed regions.

To prevent and treat both hypertension and high cholesterol levels, the researchers found, it's essential to eat a bowl of oatmeal or buckwheat cereal every morning.

Our recipes are meant to encourage you to make baking at home a worthwhile and enjoyable hobby. No bread tastes better than that made from stone-ground, wholewheat flour. Wherever possible, avoid baking soda or powder in favor of yeast, a live plant. Nothing beats the aroma that fills the kitchen when you bake with this rich source of B vitamins.

Charles Dickens's Canadian Souvenir Bread

The novelist raved about this oatmeal bread when he returned to London. The recipe, which was found among his papers, originated in the Maritimes and has been adapted to cut down on fat without altering the taste or texture. It makes wonderful toast.

PREPARATION: 30 minutes + rising

BAKING: 50 minutes

FREEZING: excellent

PER SLICE: 56 calories.

Excellent source of folate and potassium. Good source of calcium, iron, niacin and protein.

1 cup	rolled oats	250 mL
½ tsp	salt (optional)	2 mL
3 tbsp	polyunsaturated margarine	40 mL
2 cups	boiling spring water	500 mL
1 tsp	Splenda granular sweetener or sugar	5 mL
½ cup	lukewarm water	125 mL
1	envelope active dry yeast	1
½ cup	molasses	125 mL
1 cup	hard wholewheat flour	250 mL
5 cups	soft wholewheat flour	1.25 mL

1. Combine rolled oats, salt (if using) and margarine. Add boiling water. Stir. Set aside.

2. Dissolve sweetener in lukewarm water. Sprinkle with yeast and let stand for 10 minutes. Stir.

3. Add molasses to oat mixture. Stir in yeast. Beat in hard flour, then 2 cups (500 mL) of the soft. Mix well. Add enough of the remaining flour to form a dough that is soft but not sticky.

4. Transfer dough to a floured surface and knead until smooth and elastic. Add more flour if needed. Spray a bowl. Shape dough into a ball and roll it around the bowl to grease all sides. Cover and let rise in a warm place for 1 1/2 hours.

5. Punch down and divide into 3 equal parts. Shape into loaves and place in sprayed 8 1/2-by-4 1/2 inch (1.5 L) loaf pans. Grease tops very lightly and let rise until doubled, about 40 minutes. Bake at 375°F (190°C) for 50 minutes or until loaves

sound hollow when rapped on bottom. Transfer to rack. Cool thoroughly before freezing.

Yield: 3 loaves.

VARIATION

• Soak 5 tbsp (65 mL) raisins or currants in hot water for 30 minutes. Drain. Work into one of the loaves as part of Step 5.

FRÈRE ANDRÉ'S EASTER BREAD

PREPARATION:
25 minutes
BAKING: 55
minutes
FREEZING:
excellent
PER SLICE: 84
calories.
Excellent source
of calcium and
potassium.
Good source of
folate, iron,
niacin, protein
and vitamin A.

Frère André was the famous healer-mystic responsible for today's Saint Joseph's Oratory in Montréal, which continues to draw the faithful by the thousands from all over the world. When he lived and prayed alone on the mountain, he did his own cooking. This is a festive loaf to help celebrate the joy of the Easter morning.

3 ½ cups	unbleached white flour	875 mL
1 cup	wholewheat pastry flour	250 mL
2 tbsp	(or 2 packages) instant yeast	25 mL
¼ cup	packed light brown sugar	50 mL
½ tsp	salt	2 mL
2 tsp	ground cinnamon	10 mL
1 ⅓	cups spring water	325 mL
2 tbsp	canola oil	25 mL
3	egg whites at room temperature	3
¾ cup	chopped pitted dates	175 mL
1	egg white for glaze	1
	Frosting (see recipe below)	
	Sliced almonds	

1. In a large bowl, mix flours and set aside 1 cup (250 mL). To remaining flour add yeast, sugar, salt and cinnamon, mixing well.

2. Heat water and oil until hot to touch. Stir hot liquids into dry ingredients; stir in egg whites. Stir vigorously and mix in enough reserved flour to make a soft dough. (Depending on the humidity in the flour and other dry ingredients, you may need slightly more than 3 1/2 cups/875 mL.)

3. Turn dough onto a floured surface and knead for 4 to 5 minutes. Gradually knead in dates and continue to knead until dough is smooth and elastic, about 5 minutes. Cover and let dough rest for 10 minutes.

4. Shape dough into a ball. Place in greased 9-inch (23 cm) round cake pan. Make a cross on top with a very sharp knife. Cover and let rise until doubled in size, about 30 minutes.

5. Brush with egg white and bake at 375°F (190°C) for 55 minutes or until done. During the last 30 minutes, cover with an inverted pan to prevent over-browning.

6. Remove and cool on wire rack. Spread frosting on top, following the mark of the cross. Arrange sliced almonds on frosting.

Yields 1 loaf.

ICING SUGAR FROSTING

In a bowl, combine and stir together 1/2 cup (125 mL) sifted icing sugar, 1 tsp (5 mL) oil and 1/2 to 1 tsp (1 to 5 mL) skim milk.

GREAT WARRIOR BANNOCK

A native tribal mainstay throughout the so-called New World, this was one of the "foods of sustenance" served by the brave women to the warriors. With the right flour and loving attention to the skillet, you, too, can ward off the evil spirits. Serve for breakfast, lunch or dinner.

2 cups	unbleached flour	500 mL
4 tsp	baking powder	20 mL
½ tsp	salt (optional)	2 mL

PREPARATION:

25 minutes

COOKING: 30

minutes

FREEZING:

excellent

PER SERVING:

260 calories.

Excellent source

of calcium and

potassium.

Good source of

protein.

½ tsp	minced fresh parsley (optional)	2 mL
½ cup	canola or safflower oil	125 mL
½ cup	spring water	125 mL
	Cookware spray	

1. In a mixing bowl, combine flour, baking powder, salt and parsley, if using.
2. Dribble in the oil. Mix. The mixture should look like oatmeal. Add water and mix to form dough.
3. Knead by hand for 15 to 20 minutes on a floured surface. Dough will be smooth. Shape into a circle to fit skillet.
4. Spray a cast-iron skillet on sides and bottom. Place over low heat.
5. Cook the dough for 15 minutes on each side but check to make sure it doesn't burn. Continue cooking until center is done. (Insert toothpick or pin; if it emerges clean, bannock is ready.)
6. Cool bannock on a rack. Serve warm.

Yield: 4 to 6 servings.

MÉTIS BANNOCK

PREPARATION:

20 minutes

BAKING: 40

minutes

FREEZING:

excellent

PER SERVING:

194 calories.

Excellent source

of potassium.

Good source of

iron, niacin and

protein.

There are as many versions of bannock as there are descendants of the more than 60 tribes – each with its own culture and language – that inhabited this part of North America prior to the arrival of the Europeans. This one is from a native of Yellowknife.

3 cups	unbleached white flour	750 mL
2 tsp	baking power	10 mL
½ cup	vegetable shortening	125 mL
2 tbsp	sugar, Splenda granular sweetener or maple syrup	25 mL
½ tsp	salt	2 mL
⅔ cup	hot spring water	150 mL

1. Heat oven to 350°F (175°C). In a large bowl, combine flour and baking powder.
2. Melt shortening in a heavy skillet.
3. Combine sugar, salt and hot water in a bowl. Add melted shortening to sugar mixture. Add sugar mixture to flour mixture and stir briefly.
4. Form dough into a ball and knead on a board or counter.
5. Shape into a circle and place in skillet.
6. Bake for 30 minutes in heated oven. Turn over. Continue baking another 10 minutes or so.
7. Serve warm with butter, margarine and/or your favorite jam or jelly.
   Yield: 8 servings.

JAMES JOYCE'S SODA BREAD

PREPARATION: *16 minutes*
BAKING: *about 1 hour*
FREEZING: *excellent*
PER SLICE: *110 calories.*
Excellent source of potassium. Good source of calcium, folate, iron, niacin, protein and vitamin A.

Even while living in Switzerland, the author of *Ulysses* insisted on this being made fresh at least twice a week. Serve it warm or toasted with your favorite low-cal jam (Joyce preferred gooseberry). When the poet Ezra Pound (who hated gooseberries) dropped in for tea, he would try to bring his own wild strawberry jam.

2 cups	unbleached white flour	500 mL
2 cups	stone-ground wholewheat flour	500 mL
1 ¼ tsp	salt	6 mL
2 ½ tsp	baking soda	12 mL
2 tbsp	canola oil	25 mL
1 ½ cups	buttermilk or sour skim milk	375 mL
3	egg whites, beaten	3
3 tbsp	corn syrup or honey	40 mL
¾ cup	raisins	175 mL
1 tbsp	caraway seeds	15 mL
	Cookware spray	

1. In a large bowl, combine flours, salt and baking soda. Mix well and stir in oil, blending until mixture is coarse.
2. In a small bowl, combine milk, egg whites and syrup. Add raisins and caraway seeds.
3. Stir liquid mixture into flour mixture. Beat well and turn dough on to floured surface. Knead, adding 1/3 to 1/2 cup (75 to 125 mL) additional white flour until dough is soft. (It should not be sticky.) Flatten into a circular shape and place on a sprayed baking sheet.
4. With a sharp knife, cut an X across the top 1/4 inch (0.5 cm) deep.
5. Bake at 350°F (180°C) for 1 hour or until loaf sounds hollow when tapped with a fork. *Yield: 1 loaf.*

WINDSOR SCONES

PREPARATION:
20 minutes +
refrigeration
BAKING: 12
minutes
FREEZING:
excellent
PER SERVING:
92 calories.
Excellent source
of calcium,
potassium and
protein. Good
source of folate,
niacin and
vitamins A
and C.

These are traditionally served with Devon cream and lemon curd, but remember that the Duchess once declared, "One can never be too rich or too thin." The Duke must have had other ideas, because he loved them. We've named our low-cal version for the Duke and Duchess of Windsor – she would like them for their non-fattening ingredients, he for their taste and texture.

1 cup	rolled oats	250 mL
1 cup	wholewheat pastry flour	250 mL
¼ cup	Splenda granular sweetener or sugar	50 mL
3 tsp	baking powder	15 mL
¼ tsp	salt	1 mL
	Rind of 1 orange, grated	1
¼ cup	polyunsaturated margarine, chilled	50 mL
½ cup	golden raisins	125 mL
½ cup	evaporated skim milk	125 mL
	Cookware spray	

1. In a bowl, measure and combine oats, flour, sweetener, baking powder, salt and finely grated rind. Stir well to mix.
2. Cut in margarine until pieces are the size of small peas.
3. Stir in raisins. Add milk and mix until dough is formed.
4. Pat to a 1-inch (2.5 cm) thickness. Cut into small rounds. Refrigerate for 2 hours.
5. Put the scones on a lightly sprayed baking sheet and bake at 425°F (220°C) until golden brown, about 12 minutes. Serve warm.

Yield: 12 scones.

Henry Scadding Fruit Scones

Nothing could be more traditionally British than hot scones with thick cream and good berry jam (a delight called Devonshire Cream Tea). The original uses clotted cream; our low-cal version tastes wonderful with low-cal jam and plain no-fat yogurt. Serve them at brunch or tea-time.

Henry Scadding, who was born in England but lived most of his life in Canada, was Toronto's first historian.

PREPARATION:
6 minutes
BAKING: 25 to
30 minutes
minutes
FREEZING:
excellent
PER SERVING:
150 calories.
Excellent source
of potassium
and vitamin A.
Good source of
calcium, folate,
niacin and
protein.

1 ¾ cups	unbleached wholewheat flour	425 mL
2 tbsp	Splenda granular sweetener or sugar	25 mL
2 tbsp	baking powder	25 mL
2 tbsp	natural wheat germ	25 mL
¼ tsp	ground allspice	1 mL
¼ cup	polyunsaturated margarine	50 mL
¼ cup	golden sultana raisins or other dried fruit, softened in hot water and drained	50 mL
¼ tsp	grated lemon rind	1 mL
¾ cup	skim milk, fresh or reconstituted	175 mL
	Cookware spray	

SURFACE COATING:

1	egg white	1
1 tbsp	Splenda granular sweetener or sugar	15 mL

1. In a large bowl, combine flour, sweetener, baking powder, wheat germ and allspice.
2. Rub in margarine until mixture is crumbly (a food processor may be used). Add fruit, rind and milk. Mix only until just moistened.
3. Turn dough onto floured surface and knead with the heel of your hand 6 times. Pat out to a round 3/4 inch (2 cm) thick and cut into 8 wedges with a floured knife. Place on sprayed baking sheet.
4. Brush surfaces with egg white and sprinkle with sweetener.
5. Bake in 400°F (200°C) oven for 25 to 30 minutes or until golden brown. Serve warm.
   Yield: 8 scones.

yukon Sourdough Biscuits

PREPARATION:
4 minutes + 1 hour rising
BAKING: *20 minutes*
FREEZING: *excellent*
PER SERVING: *180 calories. Excellent source of folate and potassium. Good source of iron, niacin and protein.*

If you pity our "poor" pioneers because they had no supermarket bakeries, try this simple recipe and you'll never buy these biscuits in a store again.

1 ½ cups	white flour	375 mL
2 tsp	baking powder	10 mL
¼ tsp	baking soda	1 mL
¼ tsp	salt	1 mL
¼ cup	polyunsaturated margarine	50 mL
1 cup	sourdough starter (page 218)	250 mL
	Cookware spray	

1. Sift dry ingredients into a bowl, then stir in margarine and starter. Mix well.
2. Knead dough on a floured board until smooth. Roll out to 1/2-inch (1 cm) thickness and cut with floured 3-inch (7.5 cm) cutter.
3. Place in sprayed baking pan or on cookie sheet.
4. Cover, keep warm and leave for 1 hour to rise.
5. Bake at 425°F (220°C) for 20 minutes until golden.
   Yield: 8 biscuits.

Fort Rouge Sourdough Hamburger Buns

PREPARATION:
10 minutes
BAKING: 8 to 10
minutes
FREEZING:
excellent
PER SERVING:
180 calories.
Excellent source
of calcium and
potassium.
Good source of
iron, niacin and
protein.

These outperform hamburger buns sold in commercial bakeries because they're fresher and more nutritious. They can also be served as biscuits.

1 cup	soft wholewheat flour	250 mL
2 tbsp	natural wheat germ	25 mL
2 ½ tsp	baking powder	12 mL
1 cup	sourdough starter (page 218)	250 mL
¼ cup	canola or safflower oil	50 mL

1. In a bowl, combine dry ingredients. Mix well.
2. Add sourdough starter and oil. Stir to combine.
3. Knead dough for 3 minutes on a floured board.
4. Divide dough into 6 even lots and shape into rounds.
5. Bake at 425°F (220°C) on ungreased cookie sheet until lightly browned, 8 to 10 minutes.

Yield: 6 hamburger buns.

VARIATIONS

- For dinner biscuits, after Step 3, pat dough until 1/2-inch (1 cm) thick. Cut with biscuit or cookie cutter. Continue with Step 5. Yield: 14 biscuits.
- For cheese biscuits, add 1/2 cup (125 mL) grated old Cheddar or Parmesan cheese.
- For onion biscuits, add 1/2 cup (125 mL) finely chopped onion. For cheese and onion biscuits, add 1/4 cup (50 mL) of each. You may also add caraway seeds but boil them for 5 minutes first.

Sourdough Lifetime Starter

PREPARATION:

3 minutes

FERMENTATION:

2 days

1 tbsp	dry yeast	15 mL
2 cups	unbleached white flour	500 mL
2 tbsp	granulated sugar	25 mL
2 cups	spring water	500 mL

1. Combine all ingredients in a glass bowl. Beat with a large spoon.
2. Cover and let stand for 2 days in a spot no colder than 65°F (18°C).
3. To keep the starter going forever (after removing a cup to make biscuits), stir in 2 cups (500 mL) flour and 2 cups (500 mL) water. Beat again and set aside, covered.

Yield: 3 1/2 cups (875 mL).

Walter Huston's Original Graham Crackers

Forget the artificial, salty kind you buy in the store. After you try these, you and your family and friends will never want the commercial ones. Walter was born at 11 Major Street in Toronto and appeared in more than 50 films. After an actress made some graham crackers and brought them to the set, he asked her for the recipe, which we've adapted.

¼ cup	soy milk (or ordinary skim milk)	50 mL
1 tsp	fresh lemon juice	5 mL
¼ cup	canola or sunflower oil	50 mL
¼ cup	maple syrup (or Splenda granular sweetener)	50 mL
2 cups	soft wholewheat flour	500 mL
½ tsp	baking soda	2 mL

PREPARATION:

35 minutes

BAKING: 10 to

15 minutes

MAXIMUM

STORAGE: 3

weeks

PER CRACKER:

46 calories.

Excellent source

of calcium and

protein. Good

source of iron,

niacin and

protein.

½ tsp	baking powder	2 mL
¼ tsp	sea salt	1 mL
	Cookware spray	

1. Combine milk and lemon juice. Let stand for 5 minutes to sour.
2. Whisk oil and maple syrup in a small bowl.
3. In a slightly larger bowl, sift dry ingredients. Make a well in the center and pour in the liquid mixtures. Stir very gently until mixture becomes sticky and forms a ball.
4. Set oven to 350°F (175°C).
5. Spray several cookie sheets very, very lightly.
6. Sprinkle the clean counter with a small amount of flour and roll the dough to the thickness desired (we like 1/8 inches/4 mm). Cut in squares or use a cookie cutter to create favorite shapes.
7. Place on sprayed sheets and prick with a fork.
8. Bake for 10 to 15 minutes or until lightly browned.
9. Transfer crackers to racks. Cool thoroughly. Store in clean containers with tight covers.
   Yield: approximately 20 crackers.

VARIATION

- Omit lemon juice and milk. Instead, use buttermilk or low-fat yogurt.

A·J· CASSON'S BANANA BRAN BREAD

He was a year older than the century and the last of the Group of Seven artists who brought the Canadian landscape to a jaded world. "If you're painting the north country, you've got to have a bold approach to it," he once declared. On frequent camping trips, this was one of Casson's comfort foods.

1 cup	bran breakfast cereal	250 mL
1 cup	unbleached white flour	250 mL
½ cup	stone-ground wholewheat flour	125 mL

PREPARATION:
15 minutes
BAKING: 45 to
50 minutes
FREEZING:
excellent
PER SLICE: 55
calories.
Excellent source
of potassium.
Good source of
iron, niacin,
protein and
vitamin A.

3 tsp	baking powder	15 mL
½ tsp	baking soda	2 mL
¼ tsp	salt	1 mL
1	egg	1
½ cup	warm skim milk	125 mL
3 tbsp	canola oil	40 mL
1 cup	mashed ripe bananas (about 3 large)	250 mL
½ cup	chopped nuts (optional)	125 mL
½ cup	honey or molasses	125 mL
	Cookware spray	

1. Heat oven to 350°F (180°C).
2. While oven is heating, combine dry ingredients in a large bowl.
3. Beat together egg, milk, oil and bananas. Add nuts, if using, and honey.
4. Add liquid mixture to dry ingredients and blend but don't overdo it; batter should be slightly lumpy.
5. Pour into 1 or 2 sprayed loaf pans or – if you're in the woods – baked-bean cans. Do not fill more than two-thirds full. Use custard cups for any extra batter.
6. Bake 45 to 50 minutes (25 minutes for cups) or until a toothpick inserted in the center comes out clean.
   Yield: 1 or 2 loaves.

NOTE
• When ready to use, thaw frozen loaves in the refrigerator overnight.

OLD HAVANA LEMON LOAF

This is so addictive, you may want to double the recipe and freeze the extra loaf. We made some healthful changes to the traditional Cuban treat but taste and texture are sublime as ever. It's fantastic toasted for breakfast or late afternoon tea.

1	egg	1
4	egg whites	4
¼ cup	honey or Splenda granular sweetener	50 mL

PREPARATION:
10 minutes
BAKING: 60
minutes
FREEZING:
excellent
PER SLICE: 54
calories.
Excellent source
of potassium
and protein.
Good source of
calcium, folate,
iron, niacin and
vitamin E.

2 tbsp	lemon juice	25 mL
2 tbsp	grated lemon rind	25 mL
1 cup	skim milk	250 mL
¼ cup	canola oil	50 mL
½ cup	chopped nuts	125 mL
1 ½ cups	wholewheat pastry flour	375 mL
2 tbsp	wheat germ	25 mL
¼ tsp	salt	1 mL
1 tsp	baking powder	5 mL
	Cookware spray	

GLAZE:

| 2 tbsp | Splenda granulated sweetener or sugar | 25 mL |
| 2 tbsp | lemon juice | 25 mL |

1. In a large bowl, beat eggs and egg whites. Add honey, lemon juice and rind, milk and oil.
2. In a smaller bowl, combine dry ingredients. Blend well. Add to egg mixture, stirring.
3. Spoon into sprayed 8-by-4-inch (1.5 L) loaf pan.
4. Bake at 350°F (175°C) until done. Cool for 10 minutes before glazing. To glaze, stir together sweetener and lemon juice and apply with a pastry brush. Remove from pan when cool.

Yield: 1 loaf.

ARMAGEDDON LOAF

This is not only a delicious loaf to serve shortly after the tolling of the final bell in the last steeple on Earth; it's one to be enjoyed now, while there is still time and the population explosion has not yet completed the extinction of all other life forms (and hence our own). Give thanks before eating.

1 cup	skim milk, fresh or reconstituted	250 mL
¼ cup	vegetable shortening	50 mL
⅓ cup + 2 tsp	Splenda granular sweetener or sugar	75 mL + 10 mL

PREPARATION:

26 minutes + 4

hours rising

BAKING: *30 to*

35 minutes

FREEZING:

excellent

PER SLICE: *63*

calories.

Excellent source

of calcium,

potassium and

vitamin A.

Good source of

niacin, protein

and vitamins C

and E.

¼ cup	corn syrup	50 mL
1 cup	lukewarm spring water	250 mL
2	envelopes dry yeast	2
3	egg whites	3
1	egg	1
2 cups	unbleached white flour	500 mL
½ tsp	cinnamon	2 mL
¼ tsp	nutmeg	1 mL
¼ tsp	salt	1 mL
1 cup	golden raisins	250 mL
½ cup	chopped candied cherries	125 mL
½ cup	chopped mixed peel	125 mL
½ cup	raw wheat germ	125 mL
5 ½ cups	soft wholewheat pastry flour	1.125 L
	Cookware spray	

1. Heat milk but do not boil. Transfer to a bowl. Add shortening. When it melts, stir. Add 1/3 cup (75 mL) Splenda and corn syrup. Stir and cool.

2. Place lukewarm water in a small bowl. Stir in 2 tsp (10 mL) Splenda. Sprinkle yeast on top; set aside for 10 minutes. Stir and add to milk mixture.

3. Beat egg whites and eggs until frothy and add to liquid mixture. Mix in 2 cups (500 mL) flour with cinnamon, nutmeg and salt and beat into eggs. Stir in raisins, cherries, peel and wheat germ. Stir in enough of the remaining flour to form a dough; turn onto floured surface. Knead for 10 minutes until satiny.

4. Shape dough into a ball and place in a sprayed bowl, rotating to grease all sides. Cover with a slightly dampened cloth. Let rise in a warm spot until doubled in size (2 hours).

5. Punch down and divide into 3 loaves. Placed in sprayed 9-by-5-inch (2 L) pans; cover with a damp cloth. Let rise for 2 hours.

6. Bake in 375°F (190°C) oven for 30 minutes or until golden.
   Yield: 3 healthy, low-fat loaves.

Mount Eisenhower Cinnamon Rolls

PREPARATION:
6 minutes
BAKING: 15
minutes
FREEZING:
excellent
PER SERVING:
145 calories.
Excellent source
of potassium.
Good source of
niacin, protein
and vitamin C.

Take some with you the next time you go cycling, hiking or mountain climbing. Not only will the aroma of cinnamon rekindle childhood memories but the rolls will give you an energy lift. In the heart of the Rockies, the Alberta mountain was named after President Dwight D. Eisenhower of the United States.

¼ cup	Splenda granular sweetener or sugar	50 mL
1 ½ tsp	cinnamon	7 mL
1	pkg refrigerated pizza dough (10 oz /283 g)	1
¼ cup	chopped pecans or local nuts	50 mL
	Cookware spray	

TOPPING:

¼ cup	unsweetened apple juice	50 mL
1 tbsp	clover honey	15 mL
½ cup	Splenda granular sweetener or sugar	125 mL
1 tsp	cinnamon	5 mL
¼ cup	polyunsaturated margarine, melted	50 mL

1. Prepare topping first by stirring together juice, honey, sweetener and cinnamon. Add melted margarine. Mix well and set aside.

2. For rolls, stir together the sweetener and cinnamon.

3. Unroll pizza dough and stretch to form an 11-inch (27.5 cm) square. Sprinkle it with the cinnamon mixture. With a sharp knife, cut into 8 strips.

4. Roll each strip into a loose spiral. Dip one side of each into nuts and place, nutty side down, in a sprayed 9-inch (23 cm) round cake pan. Leave space between each roll for rising.

5. Pour topping over spirals. Each should be well moistened. Bake at 425°F (220°C) for 15 minutes or until tops are browned.

Remove from oven and let stand for 3 minutes. Invert and serve warm.

Yield: 8 rolls.

Saint Joseph's Resurrection Morning Buns

PREPARATION:
30 minutes + 40 minutes rising
BAKING: 25 *minutes*
FREEZING: *excellent*
PER SERVING: *140 calories. Excellent source of calcium, potassium and vitamin A. Good source of folate, iron, niacin and protein.*

Most countries have a patron saint and Saint Joseph is Canada's. The original recipe for these hot cross buns was developed by the Sisters of Saint Joseph, who founded Toronto's renowned Saint Michael's Hospital in 1862. The nuns came from Philadelphia, but the mother house is in France.

6 ¼ cups	stone-ground wholewheat pastry flour	1.6 L
¼ tsp	salt	1 mL
1 ¼ tsp	cinnamon	6 mL
½ tsp	nutmeg	2 mL
½ tsp	ground cloves	2 mL
	Grated rind of 1 orange (scrubbed and washed)	
2	packages quick-rise instant yeast (0.56 oz/16 g)	2
1 ½ cups	skim milk	375 mL
1 cup	spring water	250 mL
¼ cup	oil	50 mL
¼ cup	clover honey	50 mL
4	egg whites, slightly beaten	4
1 cup	raisins	250 mL
1 cup	mixed candied (glacé) fruit peel	250 mL
1	egg white, slightly beaten	1
	Cookware spray	

1. In a large bowl, combine flour, salt, cinnamon, nutmeg, cloves, orange rind and yeast.
2. Heat milk, water, oil and honey until hot to touch. Stir into dry mixture. Add 4 egg whites, raisins, peel and enough additional flour to make a soft dough. Knead on floured surface for 5 minutes or until smooth.
3. Cover. Let rest for 10 minutes.
4. Divide and shape dough into 24 balls. Cut shallow cross in each. Place 1 1/4 inches (3.5 cm) apart on sprayed baking sheets. Cover with a cloth and let rise for 40 minutes or until doubled.
5. Bake at 350°F (175°C) for 25 minutes or until done.
6. Remove from pans to wire rack. Brush tops with egg white and reserve what remains. When slightly cool, frost, if desired. *Yield: 24 buns.*

SAINT JOSEPH'S FROSTING

Combine 1 1/2 cups (375 mL) icing sugar, reserved egg white, 1/4 tsp (1 mL) vanilla and skim milk, if needed. Stir well and pipe frosting over crosses.

TANTRAMAR THANKSGIVING LOAF

This delicious loaf will help you celebrate any festive occasion – even a grandchild's birthday. You can double the recipe and freeze one for future enjoyment.

2 cups	stone-ground wholewheat pastry flour	500 mL
2 tsp	baking powder	10 mL
¼ tsp	salt	1 mL
3 tsp	orange peel (scrubbed, washed and grated)	15 mL
½ cup	clover honey	125 mL
2 tbsp	canola oil	25 mL
	Juice of the above orange plus enough spring water to make ¾ cup (175 mL)	
2	egg whites, beaten	2

PREPARATION:
15 minutes
BAKING: 70
minutes
FREEZING:
excellent
PER SLICE: 90
calories.
Excellent source
of potassium
and protein.
Good source of
calcium, iron,
niacin and
vitamins A
and C.

1 ½ cups	sharp grated Cheddar cheese	375 mL
1 cup	cranberries (fresh or frozen/thawed)	250 mL
¾ cup	local nuts	175 mL
	Cookware spray	

1. Heat oven to 350°F (175°C).
2. In a large bowl, combine flour, baking powder, salt and orange peel. Add honey and oil. Stir well. Add orange juice mixture, egg whites and cheese. Mix thoroughly but do not beat.
3. Add cranberries and nuts. Blend and turn into sprayed 9 1/2-by-5 1/2-inch (23.5 x 13.3 x 7 cm) loaf pan.
4. Bake for 70 minutes or until toothpick comes out clean. Cool in pan for 15 minutes on cool surface. Remove from pan onto rack to finish cooling.
5. Once thoroughly cool, wrap tightly in plastic. Let stand for 10 hours before slicing.
   Yield: 1 loaf.

THOUSAND ISLANDS WILD RICE BREAD

The Thousand Islands in the St. Lawrence River used to be home to many natives who lived on an abundance of fish and the bounties of the land. This recipe survives and we've adapted it for modern times.

	Cookware spray	
½ cup	hazelnuts	125 mL
4	egg whites	4
1 cup	skim milk, fresh or reconstituted	250 mL
2 tbsp	plain low-fat yogurt or sour cream	25 mL
⅔ cup	Splenda granular sweetener or sugar	150 mL
¼ cup	polyunsaturated margarine, melted	50 mL
1 tsp	vanilla	5 mL
1 cup	wholewheat flour	250 mL

PREPARATION:
15 minutes
BAKING: *1 hour*
FREEZING:
excellent
PER SLICE: *96*
calories.
Excellent source
of potassium,
protein and
vitamin A.
Good source of
calcium, niacin
and vitamins C
and E.

1 ¼ cups	unbleached white flour	300 mL
2 tbsp	fresh wheat germ	25 mL
2 tsp	baking powder	10 mL
½ tsp	baking soda	2 mL
¼ tsp each	ground cloves and nutmeg	1 mL each
1 cup	cooked native wild rice	250 mL
½ cup	raisins or dates, chopped	125 mL
1 tsp	grated lemon rind	5 mL

1. Spray a 9-by-5-inch (2 L) loaf pan. Line bottom with sprayed waxed paper.
2. Toast hazelnuts in 350°F (175°C) oven for 12 minutes. Rub vigorously in a clean kitchen towel to remove most of the skins. Chop.
3. In a large bowl, whisk together egg whites, milk, yogurt, sweetener, melted margarine and vanilla.
4. In another bowl, stir dry ingredients and add chopped nuts, rice, raisins and lemon rind. Sprinkle over the milk mixture.
5. Stir carefully without beating until blended.
6. Pour into pan and bake at 325°F (160°C) for 1 hour or until a toothpick inserted in the center comes out clean. The loaf should be bronzed. Remove from oven and cool in the pan for 15 minutes.
7. Remove from pan and place on a rack. When thoroughly cool, wrap and store in a cool, dry place for a day before slicing. Do not refrigerate.

Yield: 1 loaf.

NOTE
If freezing, follow Step 7, wrap, label and freeze.

GABRIELLE ROY'S OATMEAL MUFFINS

PREPARATION:

10 minutes

BAKING: 25

minutes

FREEZING:

excellent

PER SERVING:

106 calories.

Excellent source

of calcium,

potassium and

vitamin A.

Good source of

folate, niacin

and protein.

Oat bran helps reduce low-density lipoproteins or LDLs – the bad form of cholesterol. The great novelist, born on the prairies, used to make a huge batch of these muffins and freeze them. With breakfast out of the way, she could tackle a new work first thing in the morning.

1 cup	rolled oats	250 mL
1 cup	oat bran cereal	250 mL
½ cup	wholewheat pastry flour	125 mL
1 tbsp	baking powder	15 mL
¼ cup	Splenda granular sweetener or sugar	50 mL
½ cup	chopped nuts	125 mL
3	egg whites	3
1 cup	buttermilk or skim milk	250 mL
2 tbsp	canola oil	25 mL
½ cup	skim milk	125 mL
	Cookware spray	

1. Heat oven to 425°F (220°C).
2. In a large bowl, mix together the dry ingredients, including the nuts.
3. In a separate bowl, beat egg whites. Add buttermilk, oil and skim milk. Mix well.
4. Pour liquid ingredients over dry ones and beat with a spoon for 30 seconds. Ignore the lumps.

Do not beat until smooth!

5. Lightly spray a 12-muffin tin. Fill each muffin cup three-quarters full. Bake for 25 minutes or until a toothpick inserted in the center comes out clean. Cool and wrap in plastic if freezing.
Yield: 12 muffins.

VARIATIONS

- Add cranberries, apples, pitted prunes or whole blueberries in Step 3.
- Instead of Splenda, add the same amount of orange juice concentrate.
- Add 1 tbsp (15 mL) grated lemon or orange rind in Step 3.

Manitoulin Island Breakfast Muffins

PREPARATION:
6 minutes
BAKING: 45
minutes
FREEZING:
excellent
PER SERVING:
130 calories.
Excellent source
of potassium
and vitamin A.
Good source of
calcium, iron,
niacin, protein
and vitamin C.

One of these will get you going even on a blue Monday morning. Try it with Jerusalem Instant Marmalade (page 245).

2 cups	sliced carrots	500 mL
1 cup	orange juice	250 mL
1	egg	1
	or ¼ cup (50 mL) Farm-Fresh egg substitute (page 12)	
2	egg whites	2
¼ cup	brown rice flour	50 mL
1 tsp	vanilla extract	5 mL
¼ tsp	ground coriander	1 mL
1 tsp	canola oil	5 mL
3 ½ cups	rolled oats	875 mL
½ cup	chopped dates	125 mL
	Cookware spray	

1. Chop carrots finely in food processor.
2. Add juice, egg, egg whites, flour, vanilla, coriander and oil. Pulse to mix well. Transfer to a bowl.
3. Stir in oats and dates.
4. Spray 18 muffins cups and place 1/4 cup (50 mL) batter in each. Bake at 350°F (175°C) for 45 minutes until nicely browned.
Yield: 18 muffins.

MONTAIGNE

RAISIN-BRANANA MUFFINS

PREPARATION:

18 minutes

BAKING: 20

minutes

FREEZING:

excellent

PER SERVING:

103 calories.

Excellent source

of calcium,

potassium and

vitamin A.

Good source of

niacin and

vitamin C.

An early devotee of health food, the French essayist (1533–1592) is the one who declared: "The greatest thing in the world is to know how to be one's self." A good place to start is at the breakfast table with one of these unusual muffins. The oat bran actually reduces cholesterol in the body. Serve hot.

2 ½ cups	oat bran	625 mL
¼ cup	soft wholewheat flour	50 mL
1 tsp	Splenda granular sweetener or sugar	5 mL
1 tbsp	baking powder	15 mL
¾ tsp	baking soda	4 mL
1 tsp	cinnamon	5 mL
1 ⅔ cups	skim milk, fresh or reconstituted	400 mL
1	large ripe banana, mashed	1
½ cup	chopped unpeeled apples	125 mL
¼ cup	raisins	50 mL
1 tbsp	canola or safflower oil	15 mL
	Cookware spray	

1. Heat oven to 400°F (200°C).
2. Mix together dry ingredients. Stir thoroughly.
3. Mix wet ingredients in a separate bowl. Stir thoroughly.
4. Combine the two and mix *very lightly*. Do not beat!
5. Spray 12 muffin cups lightly and dust with oat bran.
6. Fill cups two-thirds full with batter. Bake for 20 minutes until lightly browned.
7. Remove and set on a wooden board. Cool for 10 minutes. Serve immediately or turn onto wire racks, cool 1 hour, wrap and freeze.
Yield: 12 muffins.

Saguenay Wild Blueberry Muffins

PREPARATION:
4 minutes
BAKING: 25 to
30 minutes
FREEZING:
excellent
PER SERVING:
104 calories.
Excellent source
of calcium,
potassium and
vitamin A.

The awesome Lac Saint Jean region north of Québec City is so renowned for its wild blueberries that the inhabitants refer to each other jokingly as *nous autres, les Bleuets*. This recipe also uses another Québec delicacy, authentic maple syrup, and is as low-cal as we can make it. Our version delivers far fewer calories than commercial muffins.

3	egg whites	3
⅓ cup	canola or safflower oil	75 mL
⅓ cup	Splenda granular sweetener or sugar	75 mL
¼ cup	Québec maple syrup (preferably No. 1 Grade)	50 mL
1 ½ cups	skim milk (fresh or reconstituted)	375 mL
½ cup	oat bran flakes	125 mL
	(the non-cereal kind sold in health stores)	
1 ½ cups	Québec wild blueberries	375 mL
	(fresh or frozen, unsweetened)	
¼ tsp	cinnamon	1 mL
2 cups	soft wholewheat flour	500 mL
1 tbsp	baking powder	15 mL
	Cookware spray	

1. In a large bowl, beat egg whites. Add oil, sweetener, syrup and milk. Mix well. Add bran flakes and blueberries. Mix gently.
2. In another bowl, stir together cinnamon, flour and baking powder.
3. Add flour mixture to liquid mixture. Stir until just blended and no more!
4. Fill 18 sprayed muffin cups about two-thirds full.
5. Bake at 375°F (190°C) for 25 minutes or until lightly browned. Remove from tins and cool on wire rack. Wrap each individually in plastic if freezing.

Yield: 18 muffins.

MANITOULIN WILD RICE PANCAKES

PREPARATION:

10 minutes

COOKING: 8

minutes per

pancake

FREEZING: *good*

FREEZER LIFE: *1*

month

PER SERVING:

110 calories.

Excellent source

of potassium.

Good source of

calcium, iron,

niacin and

vitamins C

and E.

This is a low-cal version of an old Ojibwe recipe for a highly nutritious and satisfying breakfast – one guaranteed to start your day right!

2 cups	unbleached white flour or soft wholewheat flour	500 mL
2 tsp	Splenda granular sweetener or sugar	10 mL
2 tsp	baking powder	10 mL
½ tsp	baking soda	2 mL
2 tsp	raw wheat germ	10 mL
3	egg whites	3
2 ⅔	cups buttermilk or skim milk	650 mL
2 tbsp	canola oil	25 mL
¾ cup	cooked native wild rice	175 mL
½ cup	wild blueberries, fresh or frozen	125 mL
	Cookware spray	

1. In a large bowl, stir flour, sweetener, baking powder, soda and wheat germ.
2. In another bowl, beat egg whites, then whisk in milk and oil. Add to dry ingredients.
3. Sprinkle rice and blueberries over mixture and stir lightly, just enough to blend wet and dry together. *Do not beat!*
4. Spray a griddle or frying pan and place on medium heat.
5. After 3 minutes, make pancakes by ladling the batter, 1/4 cup (50 mL) at a time, on to the skillet. Fry until golden brown underneath. Flip and continue cooking. (Note: To freeze, allow pancakes to cool thoroughly. Place between sheets of waxed paper. Seal and freeze. Small pancakes can be toasted.)
6. Serve with calorie-reduced, maple-flavored syrup.
Yield: 14 6-inch (15 cm) pancakes.

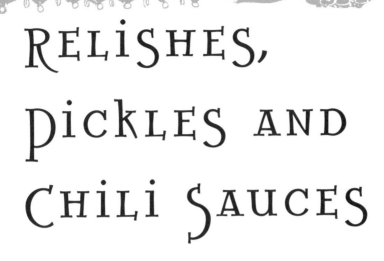

RELiSHES, PiCKLES AND CHiLi SAUCES

COUSiN LOUiSE'S HAMBURGER RELiSH

PREPARATION:
35 minutes +
overnight
standing
COOKING: 30
minutes + 5-
minute water
bath
PER TBSP (15
mL): 12 calories.
Excellent source
of potassium
and vitamin A.
Good source of
iron, niacin and
vitamin C.

Louise Calvert was Tante Marie's adopted daughter. Marie was one of Étienne Poirier's five sisters. Louise was born in Eel River, ironically in the same house where her beleaguered aunt, Annie Poirier – the *raison d'être* of the Annie & Etienne Poirier Foundation – spent some of the last 17 months of her life. Served with home-made hamburgers, this relish puts every international fast-food chain to shame. It is simply outstanding.

10 cups	firm zucchini, grated or chopped	2.5 L
4 cups	grated or chopped onion	1 L
4 tbsp	coarse salt (the pickling kind)	50 mL
4 ½ cups	white sugar or Splenda sweetener	1.12 L
2 ¼ cups	white vinegar	550 mL
1 tbsp	nutmeg	15 mL
1 tbsp	powdered mustard	15 mL
1 tbsp	turmeric	15 mL
1 tbsp	cornstarch	15 mL
1 ½ tsp	celery salt	7 mL
½ tsp	white or black pepper	2 mL

| 1 | green pepper, chopped | 1 |
| 1 | red pepper, chopped | 1 |

1. Put the zucchini, onions and pickling salt into a large porcelain or glass punch bowl. Stir with a wooden spoon and leave in a cool spot overnight.
2. Next morning, drain and rinse in three or four batches of cold water. (If water consumption is unmetered, allow cold water to pour over the mixture until it becomes clear.)
3. Drain one last time and place in a large stainless steel pot (definitely not aluminum!) with everything else and bring to a boil. Simmer uncovered for 30 minutes or until the sauce reaches the consistency you prefer on a freshly grilled, lean-beef hamburger.
4. Pour into sterilized pint jars (6, 7 or 8 should do). Seal. Place the jars in boiling water for 5 minutes. Remove with tongs and let cool. Store in a cool, dry cupboard.

MON ONCLE JULES'S RELISH

PREPARATION:
15 minutes +
overnight
standing
COOKING: 8
minutes

Jules Girouard was married to Étienne Poirier's sister, Anna, and lived in Québec City at historic 26, rue des jardins, believed by many to be the oldest stone house in the urban area and designated by UNESCO as a World Heritage Site. When Jules died, Anna became a successful life insurance sales person but she was best known for her entertaining. Every world-renowned opera singer and boulevardier visiting Québec City made a bee-line for Anna's enclave, where hospitality and comradeship reigned supreme. The glamorous Anna served this relish – concocted by her husband after travels in the United States in the 1940s – with her own version of Québec *tourtière*. Along with *filet mignon* and wild blueberry pie, the relish became one of her trademarks. Totally unique, it is well worth making and keeping on hand for "important guests."

10 cups	zucchini, chopped	2.5 L
2 cups	onions, chopped	500 mL
1	red pepper, chopped	1
¼ cup	pickling salt	50 mL
5 tbsp	cornstarch	65 mL
2 ½ cups	white vinegar	625 mL
4 cups	granulated sugar or Splenda sweetener	1 L
1 tbsp	dry mustard	15 mL
1 tbsp	turmeric	15 mL
1 tbsp	celery seed	15 mL
	Dash of cumin (optional)	
¼	tbsp cayenne (a must)	4 mL

1. Place zucchini, onions and pepper in a glass or porcelain bowl and sprinkle with the pickling salt. Next day, run cold water over the lot, drain and rinse. (You must get rid of the salt, which causes heart problems.)

2. In a bowl, mix cornstarch and vinegar until smooth; add to mixture along with sugar and seasonings. Heat and simmer gently for 8 minutes (or a few minutes longer, if you prefer thicker consistency). At this point, it's important to keep stirring or you'll end up with a bowl of glue. Stir!

3. Pour into hot sterilized jars and seal. Label and store in a cool, dry place.
Yield: 8 pints (4 L).

MARGIE BENNETT'S COCKNEY RELISH

Margie Bennett, Annie Poirier's niece, was forced to abandon sweets due to diabetes, an inability to absorb sugar and starch. After many trials, she came up with a relish that beats anything sold in stores. Not only does it link us with the culinary glories of the "good old days," but it's a tastebud triumph with hamburgers and any cold meat loaf, sliced or cut into chunks.

PREPARATION:
10 minutes +
overnight
standing
COOKING: 5 to
10 minutes + 10
minutes water
bath
PER TBSP (15
mL): 6 calories.
Excellent source
of potassium
and vitamin A.

Enough firm zucchini to make 10 cups (2.5 L) chopped

4 cups	chopped onion	1 L
1	red pepper, diced	1
¼ cup	coarse salt	50 mL
3 ½ cups	Splenda granular sweetener	875 mL
2 ¼ cups	white vinegar	550 mL
⅓ cup	light raisins	75 mL
1 tbsp	dry mustard	15 mL
1 tbsp	cornstarch	15 mL
1 tsp	celery seed	5 mL
½ tsp	turmeric	2 mL

1. Scrub zucchini but do not peel. Chop them in a food processor or chop finely by hand. (Don't overdo; it should not be reduced to mush!) Measure *exact* amount.

2. Place zucchini, onion and red pepper in a glass bowl and sprinkle with salt. Cover and let stand overnight at room temperature.

3. Next morning, rinse in running cold water and drain thoroughly in a colander.

4. Transfer to a stainless steel saucepan (not aluminum!). Add all other ingredients and bring to a boil.

5. Reduce heat immediately to very low and simmer until vegetables are clear, 5 to 10 minutes. Again, don't overdo!

6. Stir with a wooden spoon and pour into sterilized jars. Seal and place in a water bath. Bring to a boil and simmer for 10 minutes.

7. Remove with jar tongs and cool on racks away from drafts. Label and store in a cool dark place. *Yield: 7 pints (3 L).*

TANTE MARiE'S
COUNTRY GARDEN RELiSH

PREPARATION:
10 to 15 minutes
COOKING: 5
minutes
PER TBSP (15
mL): 18
calories.
Excellent source
of calcium,
potassium and
vitamin C.
Good source of
folate and iron.

Anyone who ate this relish by Marie Synnott (Annie Poirier's sister-in-law) swore that it could turn the most mundane leftovers into pure gastronomic delights. Here then is the original recipe, a closely guarded family secret for generations.

2 cups	cooked beets, chopped	500 mL
	(if inconvenient, use a can of whole beets)	
2 cups	raw cabbage (finely shredded and packed)	500 mL
1 ½ cups	cider or white wine vinegar	375 mL
1 ¼ cups	granulated sugar or Splenda sweetener	300 mL
1	small clove garlic, shredded	1
3 tbsp	bottled horseradish (or make your own)	40 mL
1 tsp	salt (optional)	5 mL
½ tsp	cayenne or Tabasco sauce	2 mL

1. Place all ingredients in a cast iron or stainless steel saucepan. Meanwhile, sterilize two 1-pint (500 mL) jars.
2. Bring mixture slowly to a boil.

When it boils, pack immediately into the jars. Seal and store in a cool place. To be safe, store in the refrigerator.

Yield: 2 pints (1 L).

WELLiNGTON KiWi CHUTNEY

PREPARATION:

12 minutes

COOKING: 1 1/2

hours

FREEZING:

excellent

PER TBSP (15

mL): 19

calories.

Excellent source

of calcium,

potassium and

vitamin C.

Good source of

iron and

vitamin A.

As everyone knows, the first kiwi fruit came from New Zealand and are still the sweetest. They are by no means a new fruit (kiwi is a recent Maori name). Climate and soil are vital factors, of course, and some people with jaded tastebuds don't give a hoot. They are chock-full of vitamin C and a number of essential minerals.

9	ripe kiwi fruit	9
2 cups	brown sugar	500 mL
½ cup	Splenda granular sweetener or white sugar	125 mL
1 cup	cider vinegar	250 mL
1 cup	raisins (seedless Californian will do)	250 mL
4 tbsp	finely chopped ginger root	50 mL
2 tbsp	finely chopped garlic	25 mL
1 tsp	cayenne	5 mL
½ tsp	sea salt	2 mL
½ tsp	cloves	2 mL

1. Peel and slice kiwi fruit.
2. Combine kiwi fruit with sugar and sweetener. Let stand for 20 minutes.
3. Combine all other ingredients in a saucepan. Fold in fruit mixture.
4. Bring to a boil. Lower heat and simmer uncovered for 1 1/2 hours.
5. Spoon into sterilized jars and seal. When cool, label and date. Store in a cool place or freeze. (Note: If freezing, leave space at top of jar for expansion!)
Yield: 3 pints (1.5 L).

Grey Nuns' Autumn Pickles

PREPARATION:
22 *minutes +*
overnight
standing
COOKING: *90*
minutes
FREEZING: *not*
appropriate
PER TBSP (*15*
mL): *5 calories.*
Excellent source
of potassium
and vitamin A.
Good source of
calcium and
niacin.

Les Soeurs Grises were the first to pitch in and help the destitute and the sick in the early days of Montréal. This ancient recipe from one of the convents can now be made with a modern sweetener for the diet-conscious. Your guests will rave if you serve it with hot or cold beef, sandwiches and even shepherd's pie.

15	firm apples in season	15
31	green tomatoes	31
7	onions (large)	7
½ cup	coarse sea salt	125 mL
4	cloves garlic, chopped	4
4 cups	brown sugar or Splenda granular sweetener	1 L
¼ cup	pickling spices	50 mL
	White vinegar	

1. Scrub, wash, rinse and dry apples and tomatoes. Set apples aside.
2. Slice onions and tomatoes. Place them in a non-metal container. Add salt and let stand overnight, covered.
3. Next morning, drain thoroughly and shake in a colander. Transfer to a large pot (not aluminum or copper). Add unpeeled, sliced apples, garlic, sugar and spices tied in a cheesecloth bag.
4. Add vinegar so the ingredients are about three-quarters covered.
5. Simmer for 90 minutes.
6. Ladle into hot, sterilized jars. Seal and apply labels. Store on the floor of a cool, dark closet. *Yield: 14 pints (7 L).*

LABRADOR FROZEN PICKLES

PREPARATION:
20 minutes + 4
hours standing

COOKING: 2
minutes

PER TBSP (15
mL): 1.6
calories.
Excellent source
of potassium
and vitamin A.
Good source of
calcium, iron
and vitamin C.

If you find these too mild, wrap the pickling spices in cheesecloth and add to vinegar when boiling. Discard before freezing.

12 cups	sliced cucumbers	3 L
3	stalks celery, cut into 1-inch (2.5 cm) pieces	3
3	green peppers, seeded and chopped	3
3 tbsp	salt	40 mL
2 cups	white vinegar	500 mL
3 tbsp	pickling spices (optional)	40 mL
3 cups	Splenda granular sweetener or sugar	750 mL

1. Combine cucumbers, celery and peppers. Sprinkle with salt and let stand for 4 hours.
2. Heat vinegar and spices (if using). Add sweetener. Heat only until it dissolves.
3. Drain and rinse vegetables with cold water. Pack into small freezer containers. Add vinegar. Date, label and freeze. Thaw in refrigerator.

Yield: 8 pints (4 L).

ACAJUN CHILI SAUCE

Developed by the deported Acadiens in the wilds of Louisiana, this is one of the best chili sauces to accompany roast game, chicken, ham, cheese and Sunday morning sausages.

12 lb	tomatoes	6 kg
6	ripe peaches	6
6	ripe pears	6
2	bunches celery (4 cups/1 L)	2
2 ½ cups	small onions, ground	625 mL

PREPARATION:

15 minutes

COOKING: 2

hours + 5

minutes water

bath

PER 1/4 CUP

(50 mL): 74

calories.

Excellent source

of potassium

and vitamins A

and C. Good

source of

calcium, iron

and niacin.

3	green peppers, ground	3
3	red bell peppers	3
4 ½ cups	brown sugar (2 lb/1 kg)	1.125 L
4 cups	cider vinegar	1 L
1	stick cinnamon, 1/2 inch (1 cm)	1
1 cup	pickling spices	250 mL
5	bay leaves	5
3 tsp	curry powder	40 mL
1 tbsp	dry mustard	15 mL

1. Wash fruits and vegetables. Scald and skin tomatoes if you insist (a waste of minerals, vitamins and time, in our opinion).
2. Use a food processor or chop fruits and vegetables finely.
3. Stir sugar into vinegar until dissolved; pour over fruits and vegetables.
4. Tie cinnamon, spices and bay leaves in cheesecloth. Add to mixture along with curry powder and mustard. Simmer gently for 2 hours. Stir now and then. Leave uncovered so the sauce thickens.
5. Remove bag. Fill hot pint jars, leaving 1/2-inch (1 cm) headspace; adjust lids.
6. Process in boiling water bath for 5 minutes (start timing when water returns to boil). Cool. Label and store.
   Yield: 9 pints (4.5 L).

BETTE DAVIS'S MILD CHILI SAUCE

The indomitable star loved her corner of Maine more than the men in her life. "If I ever get hooked again," she vowed, "I'll wear black and scream all the way to the altar." She enjoyed this chili sauce, an old New England tradition.

14 lb	ripe tomatoes	7 kg
4 cups	chopped celery (1 lb/500 g)	1 L
2 ½ cups	small onions, ground	625 mL
2 ½ cups	ground green peppers	625 mL

PREPARATION:
20 minutes
COOKING: 3
hours, 20
minutes
FREEZING:
excellent

PER 1/4 CUP
(50 mL): 30
calories.
Excellent source
of potassium
and vitamin A.
Good source of
folate and
vitamin C.

6 inches	cinnamon stick	15 cm
4 ½ cups	brown sugar	1.125 L
4 cups	cider vinegar	1 L
3 tbsp	salt	40 mL
1 tbsp	dry mustard	15 mL
1 ½ tsp	ground cloves	7 mL

1. Scald tomatoes. Peel them and chop in chunks, putting them into a large kettle (not aluminum). (Coring is not necessary unless you hate the seeds.)
2. Cook for 15 minutes. Drain off 6 cups (1.5 L) of the juice and refrigerate it for cooking or drinking.
3. Add celery, onion and green pepper. Simmer for 1 1/2 hours.
4. Tie cinnamon in cloth. Add it to the kettle with the remaining ingredients.
5. Continue simmering for 1 1/2 hours.
6. Remove cinnamon.
7. Fill hot jars, leaving 1/2-inch (1 cm) headspace. Adjust lids.
8. Place jars in a warm water bath. Bring to a boil, start counting and process for exactly 5 minutes.

Yield: 9 pints (5 L).

TYRONE POWER'S SPANISH TOMATO CHILI SAUCE

The handsome actor loved Spain and its cuisine. We've adapted one of his favorite recipes to make it as low-cal as possible. This is perfect for the end of the season when green and ripe tomatoes make you wonder what to do with the abundance.

12 quarts	ripe tomatoes	13 L
9	onions	9
¾ cup	coarse sea salt	175 mL
4 tbsp	pickling spices	50 mL
3 cups	cider vinegar	750 mL

PREPARATION:

26 minutes

COOKING: 2

hours

FREEZING: *not*

required

PER TBSP (15

mL): 3 calories.

Excellent source

of potassium and

vitamin A. Good

source of calcium

and vitamin C.

2 lb	brown sugar or Splenda granular sweetener	1 kg
3	cloves garlic, chopped	3
½ tsp	cayenne	2 mL

1. Scrub, wash and drain tomatoes.
2. Slice onions and tomatoes.
3. Sprinkle them with the salt and let stand overnight.
4. Next morning, drain thoroughly.
5. Tie pickling spices in a cheesecloth bag. Add to a large saucepan along with all other ingredients.
6. Simmer for 2 hours.
7. Remove from heat. Stir in sweetener.
8. Ladle into hot, sterilized jars. Label and store in a cool, dry place.

Yield: 16 pints (8 L).

MEMORY LANE DIJON-STYLE MUSTARD

PREPARATION:

6 minutes

¼ cup	powdered black, brown or white mustard seeds	50 mL
3 tbsp	verjuice* or tarragon vinegar (page 193)	40 mL
1 oz	cayenne (optional)	28 g
1 tbsp	fresh mace, thyme or parsley (optional)	15 mL
1	slice fresh lemon	1

1. In a cup, combine the powdered mustard seeds (any combination) with the verjuice to form a smooth paste.
2. For more zip, add optional ingredients. If mustard is too hot, tone it down with 1 tsp (5 mL) of canola oil.
3. Transfer to a container with a close-fitting cover. Place a lemon slice on top, seal and store. (Refrigeration is not required.) Replace the slice of lemon once a week.

*Verjuice (or *verjus* in French) was used to make the original *Sauce Verte* sold on the streets of the Old World centuries ago. It's the acidic juice from unripened grapes, available today in home wine-making stores.

PRESERVES, CONSERVES AND MARMALADES

COTTAGE COUNTRY PRUNE JAM

PREPARATION:
5 minutes
COOKING: 40
minutes
FREEZING:
excellent
PER TBSP (15
mL): 15 calories.
Excellent source
of calcium and
potassium.
Good source of
iron, niacin and
vitamin C.

Easy to make in minutes, this low-cal jam is terrific with muffins, toast and waffles. The original recipe goes back to at least 748 A.D. Any friend or relative will bless you when offered a jar as "a gift from my own kitchen."

2 cups	prunes	500 mL
4 cups	spring water	1 L
½	small orange	1/2
2 cups	Splenda granular sweetener or white sugar	500 mL

1. Rinse and drain prunes. Cover with 3 cups (750 mL) water and simmer 15 minutes. Drain. Reserve liquid.
2. Remove pits and chop prunes.
3. Scrub and dry orange. Quarter and remove seeds. In a blender or food processor, grind the unpeeled orange with 1 cup (250 mL) water.
4. Boil the orange and water mixture for 10 minutes. Stir in prunes and reserved liquid and simmer for 15 minutes until thickened. Add sweetener and stir well. Pour into clean jars and seal. When cool, label and refrigerate or freeze.

Yield: 2 1/2 cups (625 mL).

Judy LaMarsh's Conserve

PREPARATION:
20 minutes +
overnight
standing
COOKING: 1 1/2
hours
FREEZING:
excellent

Strictly speaking, a conserve is a jam that contains more than one kind of fruit. Surprisingly, this unusual recipe calls for vegetable marrow. The great-hearted politician made it often.

6 lb	vegetable marrow, cubed	3 kg
5 ½ lb	Splenda granular sweetener or sugar	2.5 kg
8 oz	preserved ginger, chopped	240 mL
	Juice and chopped rind of 3 scrubbed lemons	
¼ tsp	cayenne	1 mL

1. Cover vegetable marrow cubes with sweetener and let stand overnight.
2. Add all ingredients to a saucepan and simmer gently, uncovered, for 1 1/2 hours or until clear. Stir often.

3. Spoon into hot, sterilized jars. Seal with paraffin wax. Date, label and store in a cool, dark place.

   Yield: 5 pints (2.5 L).

Jerusalem Instant Marmalade

PREPARATION:
6 minutes
COOKING: 15
minutes
FREEZING:
excellent
PER TBSP (15
mL): 18
calories.

Some Seville-orange purists insist that no marmalade is valid without time-consuming preparation and cooking. We beg to differ. This delectable spread from the Holy Land, favored for centuries, takes only 21 minutes and will make your day...every day.

2	navel oranges	2
½ cup	dates, chopped	125 mL
½ cup	apple-juice concentrate, thawed	125 mL
1 tsp	Splenda granular sweetener or white sugar	5 mL

1. Scrub oranges under warm water. Dry. Do not peel. Chop and place in food processor with dates. Blend until finely chopped.
2. Put fruit in saucepan with concentrated apple juice and sugar and cook, stirring, over medium-low heat for 15 minutes or until thick.
3. Store in lidded jar. Will keep for a week in refrigerator.
   Yield: 1 cup (250 mL).

MEMRAMCOOK MARMALADE

In the early days of the French colonies in North America, lemons and oranges were unknown. Wild apples, gooseberries and other fruit were used to make *le p'tit déjeuner* palatable. This modern adaptation of an old Acadien breakfast recipe gives a sunny lift to wholewheat muffins and toast any time of day.

Make it in the spring when fresh rhubarb is plentiful.

4 cups	shredded carrot	1 L
4 cups	diced rhubarb	1 L
6	lemons, sliced and shredded	6
2	oranges, sliced and shredded	2
6 cups	white sugar or Splenda granular sweetener	1.5 L
1 ½ cups	spring water	375 mL

1. Scrub carrots, rhubarb, lemons and oranges. (The best brush for this and other kitchen uses is a stiff one with a handle, sold in hardware stores to clean white-wall car tires. Other so-called vegetable brushes are practically useless.) Shred in a food processor or by hand.
2. Combine all ingredients in a saucepan and bring to a boil. Stir with a wooden spoon. Simmer, uncovered, for 5 minutes. Continue stirring to make sure the mixture doesn't stick.
3. Pour into hot, sterilized jars. Seal. Cool. Label. Store in a cool, dark place.
   Yield: 6 pints (3 L).

Tante Clémentine's
Unset Jam Corrective

It happens now and then to the best of us. Whether the fruit was at fault or we didn't follow a recipe, the jam or jelly won't set. This "corrective" can make your day – as long as you measure every ingredient carefully.

¼ cup	spring water	50 mL
4 tsp	powdered pectin	20 mL
4 cups	unset jam or jelly	1 L
¼ cup	granulated sugar	50 mL

1. Mix water and pectin.
2. Bring to a boil, stirring. Add jam or jelly and sugar.
3. Bring to a full boil and continue boiling for 60 seconds.
4. Remove from heat. Skim, if necessary, and pour into sterilized jars. Seal.

DESSERTS

TIPS FOR REPLACING SUGAR WITH HONEY

You can substitute honey for sugar or sweetener in most recipes, unless you're diabetic or on a sugar-free diet.

- Substitute honey for up to half the sugar called for.
- Since honey adds moisture, cut back on the liquid called for (1/4 cup/150 mL for each cup of honey).
- In baking, add 1/2 tsp (2 mL) baking soda for each cup (250 mL) of honey. Reduce oven temperature by 25°F (10° to 20°C) to avoid burning baked goods.
- Before measuring honey, spray cup lightly with vegetable cooking spray. This prevents the honey from sticking.
- Store honey at room temperature. If it crystallizes, remove lid, place in warm water and heat gently until crystals dissolve.

See also Honey versus Sugar on page 19.

AFRICVILLE COBBLER

We have no tangible proof but it's our contention that this delectable dessert originated among the first Afro-American settlers in Nova Scotia. People of African descent first came to New France around 1610. Many settled near the city of Halifax in a place that was named Africville. Our historical contention regarding the dessert is based on the fact that Halifax was an early center of the worldwide spice trade. All the women there (and now some of the men) are A-1 chefs and culinary artists who have originated and developed a distinct, utterly delicious, non-fattening cuisine that gives zip to Maritime food.

PREPARATION:

6 minutes

BAKING: 50

minutes

FREEZING:

excellent

PER SERVING:

182 calories.

Excellent source

of potassium

and vitamin C.

Good source of

vitamin A.

6 cups	thinly sliced, scrubbed, unpeeled apples	1.5 L
¼ cup	clover honey or brown sugar	50 mL
3 tbsp	fresh lemon juice	40 mL
¼ tsp	cinnamon	1 mL
	Cookware spray	
¼ cup	Splenda granular sweetener or sugar	50 mL
1	egg	1
½ cup	buttermilk	125 mL
¼ cup	molasses	50 mL
2 tbsp	oil	25 mL
1 cup	unbleached white flour	250 mL
½ tsp	baking soda	2 mL
½ tsp	baking powder	2 mL
½ tsp	ground ginger	2 mL
¼ tsp	ground nutmeg	1 mL
	Whipped "cream" (page 285)	

1. In a bowl, coat the apples with the honey, lemon juice and cinnamon by swirling them around gently.
2. Spread the apple mixture in a sprayed 9-inch (23 cm) dish and bake at 350°F (175°C) for 20 minutes.
3. Using a fork, in a bowl mix sweetener, egg, buttermilk, molasses and oil.
4. In another bowl, stir together flour, baking soda, baking powder and spices. Add this to the egg mixture and beat until the whole thing is smooth.
5. After 20 minutes (and no longer!), remove apples from oven, but do not turn oven off.
6. Spoon the batter over the apples. Return the dish to the oven.
7. Bake no more than 30 minutes. Remove from oven.
8. Slice with a sharp knife and serve before the cobbler cools. Add generous dollops of whipped, vanilla-laced "cream." *Yield: 10 servings.*

Apple Jonathan

PREPARATION:

15 minutes

BAKING: *40*

minutes

FREEZING:

excellent

PER SERVING:

132 calories.

Excellent

source of

carbohydrates,

potassium and

vitamins A

and C.

A version of this fabulous dessert exists in Nova Scotia, where it is called Apple Annapolis. It is simple to make and simply delicious to eat. The thick batter topping forms a bottom crust as well.

6 to 8	tart apples, washed, unpeeled and sliced (6 cups/1.5 L)	6 to 8
⅓ cup	Splenda granular sweetener or sugar	75 mL
¾ tsp	ground cinnamon	4 mL

TOPPING:

½ cup	Splenda granular sweetener or sugar	125 mL
1 ½ cups	unbleached flour	375 mL
2 tsp	baking powder	10 mL
¼ cup	canola oil	50 mL
	Skim milk	

GARNISH:

Splenda sweetener or granulated sugar,
cinnamon, nutmeg and chopped cherries

1. Spread apples into a greased 9-inch (23 cm) pie plate. Sprinkle with 1/3 cup (75 mL) sweetener and cinnamon.
2. To make the topping, in a bowl, blend 1/2 cup (125 mL) sweetener, flour and baking powder. Add oil and enough milk to make a cup (250 mL) of batter.
3. Pour batter over apples and bake at 350°F (175°C) for 40 minutes.
4. Invert on serving plate and sprinkle with sweetener, cinnamon, nutmeg and chopped cherries.
5. Serve with custard sauce. *Yield: 8 to 10 servings.*

HUGH GARNER

CABBAGETOWN APPLE CRISP

PREPARATION:

10 minutes

BAKING: *30 to*

35 minutes

FREEZING:

excellent

PER SERVING:

220 calories.

Excellent source

of calcium,

potassium and

vitamin C.

His realistic "dirty thirties" novel helps us understand an earlier Hogtown. This outstanding low-cal recipe, named in his honor, helps us understand sound nutrition. And young writers should read his autobiographical *One Damned Thing After Another* before quitting that fairly good job. Writing, like the art of cooking, is not for dilettantes.

	Cookware spray	
4	tart apples, unpeeled and sliced	4
¼ cup	fresh orange juice	50 mL
½ cup	quick-cooking rolled oats	125 mL
3 tbsp	natural wheat germ	40 mL
⅓ cup	Splenda granular sweetener or sugar	75 mL
¼ cup	soft wholewheat flour	50 mL
1 tsp	cinnamon	5 mL
¼ tsp	ground cloves	1 mL
¼ tsp	grated orange rind	1 mL
2 tbsp	polyunsaturated margarine, softened	25 mL
1 tbsp	canola or safflower oil	15 mL
¼ cup	chopped nut meats	50 mL

1. Lightly spray a 1 1/2 quart (1.5 L) casserole.
2. Place apples in the casserole and drizzle with orange juice.
3. In a bowl, combine oats, wheat germ, sweetener, flour, cinnamon, cloves and orange rind. Add margarine and oil. Blend to a crumbly consistency, using fingers and/or a fork.
4. Add the nuts and sprinkle over the apple mixture.
5. Bake at 375°F (190°C) for 30 to 35 minutes or until apples are tender. Serve with whipped topping or plain low-fat yogurt. *Yield: 4 servings.*

MICROWAVE METHOD

1. Prepare as above in microwave-safe dish.

2. Microwave, uncovered, on high for 8 to 10 minutes, turning dish once after 4 minutes.

TANTRAMAR CRANBERRY CRISP

PREPARATION:
8 minutes
BAKING: 30
minutes
FREEZING:
excellent
PER SERVING:
359 calories.
Excellent source
of calcium,
potassium and
vitamin A.

For something colorful and tasty that can be put together in a few minutes, try our low-cal version of the traditional festive crisp. It's delicious with a dollop of vanilla-laced no-fat yogurt, sweetened with Splenda.

4 cups	cranberries, fresh or frozen	1 L
3 tbsp	Splenda granular sweetener or sugar	40 mL
1 tbsp	polyunsaturated margarine, melted	15 mL
1 tbsp	canola oil	15 mL
½ cup	coarsely chopped pecans or other nuts	125 mL

TOPPING:

1 cup	wholewheat pastry flour	250 mL
¾ cup	brown sugar	175 mL
½ cup	rolled oats	125 mL
½ cup	canola oil	125 mL

1. Heat oven to 375°F (190°C).
2. Wash cranberries in a colander and, if frozen, thaw in cold water. Drain. Spread in a greased 8-inch (2 L) baking dish.
3. In a bowl, combine sweetener, melted margarine, oil and chopped nuts. Spread the mixture over the cranberries.
4. For topping, in a bowl combine flour, sugar, oats and oil. Spread over the dish. Bake for 30 minutes or until topping browns.
Yield: 4 to 6 servings.

Ojibwe Fruit Gratin

PREPARATION:
4 minutes
BAKING: 45
minutes
FREEZING:
excellent
PER SERVING:
146 calories.
Excellent source
of calcium,
potassium and
vitamin C.

Complement your fabulous dinner with this outstanding dessert, created on Manitoulin Island (*Odawa-Minniss* in the Ojibwe language), ancestral home of the Odawa nation. Then inform the delighted guests that each serving has only only 145 or so calories and no cholesterol! Leftovers can be served for breakfast and you won't conk out at ten in the morning.

⅔ cup	dried apricots, diced	150 mL
1 cup	spring water	250 mL
3	tart apples	3
2 tbsp	raisins	25 mL
2 tsp	lemon juice	10 mL
½ tsp	cinnamon	2 mL
½ tsp	allspice	2 mL
1 tsp	Splenda granular sweetener or sugar (optional)	5 mL
¾ cup	low-fat granola	175 mL
¾ cup	no-fat vanilla yogurt	175 mL

1. In a saucepan, soak apricots in water for 1 hour. Cover and simmer for 15 minutes.
2. Scrub apples under warm water, rinse under cold water and slice.
3. To apricots, add apples, raisins, juice, cinnamon, allspice and sweetener, if using. Cook for 20 minutes. Stir.
4. Pour into a 1-quart (1 L) baking dish. Spread granola on top. Bake at 350°F (175°C) for 10 minutes. Top with yogurt when serving.

Yield: 6 servings.

Poirier New World Crumble

PREPARATION:
10 minutes
BAKING: 45
minutes
FREEZING:
excellent
PER SERVING:
264 calories.
Excellent source
of calcium,
potassium and
vitamin C.

"Poirier," of course, means "pear tree" in English. The Poiriers have been in Canada and the United States for generations and brought many pear recipes with them from France. The cranberries give it that North American piquant touch.

TOPPING:

²⁄₃ cups	unbleached white flour	150 mL
½ tsp	grated nutmeg	2 mL
½ tsp	cinnamon	2 mL
2 cups	rolled oats	500 mL
1 cup	Splenda granular sweetener or sugar	250 mL
½ cup	oil	125 mL

FILLING:

6	ripe pears, unpeeled, sliced	6
2 tbsp	lemon juice	25 mL
½ cup	cranberries, fresh or frozen	125 mL
2 tbsp	Splenda granular sweetener or sugar	25 mL

1. Heat oven to 375°F (190°C). Prepare the topping in a bowl by combining flour and spices.
2. Add oats, sweetener and oil. Mix thoroughly by hand. Depending on flour used, you may need a touch more oil. Set topping aside until ready to bake.
3. In a lightly greased pie plate or other dish, combine pears, lemon juice, cranberries and sweetener. Add topping, spreading it evenly over top of filling.
4. Bake for 45 minutes or until brown. Serve warm with no-fat yogurt. The dish can be baked, cooled and reheated.

Yield: 10 servings.

GROS MORNE RHUBARB COBBLER

PREPARATION:
30 minutes
COOKING: 30
minutes
FREEZING:
excellent
PER SERVING:
199 calories.
Excellent source
of calcium,
potassium and
vitamin A.

You can share a morning break with a moose in Newfoundland's magnificent Gros Morne National Park, watch icebergs tower above the water, photograph a rainbow or make a wish the first time you spot a sea dragon floating in a cove. A single serving of this cobbler will recharge the most exhausted hiker; two will send him or her jogging at full speed!

8 cups	rhubarb, cut in ½-inch (1 cm) pieces	2 L
1 cup	Splenda granulated sweetener or sugar	250 mL
½ cup	unbleached white flour	125 mL
	Grated rind of 1 orange	

TOPPING:

1 ½ cups	unbleached white flour	375 mL
1 tsp	baking powder	5 mL
½ tsp	baking soda	2 mL
¼ tsp	salt (optional)	1 mL
½ cup	Splenda granulated sweetener or sugar	125 mL
4 tbsp	canola or safflower oil	50 mL
3	egg whites	3
1 cup	buttermilk or sour skim milk	250 mL
1 tsp	vanilla	5 mL
2	drops almond extract	2
¼ cup	blanched almonds, sliced	50 mL
	No-fat yogurt or whipped skim milk (see page 285)	

1. In a bowl, combine rhubarb with sweetener, flour and orange rind. Set aside for 30 minutes. Rhubarb will release its juices.

2. Spoon rhubarb mixture into a sprayed 9-by-13-inch (3.5 L) baking dish.

3. In a bowl, thoroughly combine flour, baking powder, baking soda, salt and sweetener. In another bowl, add oil to egg whites, buttermilk, vanilla and almond extract. Mix the dry and liquid ingredients together thor-

oughly and spoon over fruit. Sprinkle with almonds.

4. Bake at 400°F (200°C) for 30 minutes or until topping is browned. Serve warm with low-fat yogurt or whipped milk.

LUMINA'S MONTH OF MAY CRISP

PREPARATION:
8 minutes
BAKING: 40
minutes
FREEZING:
excellent
PER SERVING:
177 calories.
Excellent source
of calcium,
potassium and
vitamins A
and C.

Lumina Drapeau, of course, grew the finest rhubarb and sold her produce door-to-door. The boys (and girls, too) lined up for encores when Lumina dished out this treat, hot from the oven. (And, yes, this luminous *chef extraordinaire* was *really* named Lumina.)

3 cups	fresh or frozen rhubarb (½-inch/1 cm pieces)	750 mL
1 cup	fresh or frozen raspberries	250 mL
⅔ cup	Splenda granular sweetener or sugar	150 mL
⅓ cup	unbleached white or wholewheat pastry flour	75 mL

TOPPING:

1 cup	stone-ground wholewheat flour	250 mL
¼ cup	Splenda granular sweetener or sugar	50 mL
½ cup	rolled oats	125 mL
⅛ tsp	cinnamon	0.5 mL
¼ cup	low-fat margarine or canola oil	50 mL
	Skim milk	

1. In a bowl combine rhubarb, raspberries, sweetener and flour.
2. Spray a 9-inch square (2.5 L) baking pan. Spoon in mixture.
3. Combine ingredients for topping and mix well with fingers. If mixture appears to be too dry (due to variations in flour and humidity), add a little skim milk and continue working the mixture until it is thoroughly moist. Layer over the top of the fruit mixture.
4. Bake at 375°F (190°C) for 40 minutes or until golden.
5. Serve with no-fat yogurt.
   Yield: 6 servings.

Balmoral Compote
(Apricots and Cherries)

PREPARATION:
5 minutes
COOKING: 5
minutes
FREEZING:
excellent
PER SERVING:
55 calories.
Excellent source
of potassium
and vitamins A
and C.

Serve this healthy Memory Lane delight with pancakes and waffles for a hearty breakfast. Simply terrific, too, with any cooked cereal and plain, non-fat yogurt. Both Grandma and Grandpa will bless you!

8	canned or fresh apricots, quartered	8
¾ cup	dried sour cherries	175 mL
½ cup	spring water	125 mL
1 tbsp	lemon juice	15 mL
1 tsp	clover honey	5 mL
1 tsp	Splenda granular sweetener or sugar	5 mL
½ tsp	grated lemon rind	2 mL

1. Combine all ingredients in a saucepan.
2. Cook over medium heat for 5 minutes. Serve warm.

Yield: 4 servings.

Linus Pauling International
Fruit Compote

This delicious compote is one way of boosting your intake of the miracle vitamin C so dear to the heart of Dr. Linus Pauling, two-time Nobel laureate. In the old days, compotes were usually stewed. Our version keeps everything fresh and eye-appealing.

PREPARATION:
10 minutes
FREEZING: not
appropriate
PER SERVING:
80 calories.
Excellent source
of potassium
and vitamins A
and C.

1	fresh pineapple, peeled, cored and cut into chunks	1
2	seedless oranges, peeled, sectioned and cut into small wedges	2
3	kiwi fruits, peeled and cut into wedges	3
¼ cup	fresh orange juice	50 mL
1 tbsp	fresh lemon juice	15 mL
1 tbsp	Splenda granular sweetener or sugar	15 mL
1	banana	1

1. In a glass salad bowl, toss together pineapple, oranges and kiwi fruit.

2. Combine fruit juices with sweetener. Stir well and pour over fruit.

3. Slice banana and toss with other ingredients to coat.
   Yield: 6 servings.

MAE CLARKE MACÉDOINE OF FRUIT

She played the quintessential gun moll in the classic movie *The Public Enemy* where James Cagney used her face as a grapefruit juicer. The 1931 picture also starred platinum bombshell Jean Harlow. Take no chances; serve your lover this balanced *macédoine* and relax. You won't even need expensive musicians.

PREPARATION:
10 minutes
MARINATING:
2 hours
FREEZING: not
appropriate
PER SERVING:
55 calories.
Excellent source
of calcium,
potassium and
vitamin C.

½ cup	dry vermouth	125 mL
¼ cup	Splenda granular sweetener or sugar	50 mL
¼ tsp	cinnamon	1 mL
1	small pineapple, cut in wedges	1
2	navel oranges, peeled and cut in sections	2
1	pink grapefruit, peeled and cut in sections	1
18	large seedless grapes, halved	18

1. In a saucepan, combine vermouth, sweetener and cinnamon. Bring to a boil, then remove pronto (immediately!) from heat. Cool and let stand in refrigerator for 1 hour.

2. Pour liquid over fresh fruit and marinate for at least 1 hour in refrigerator.

Yield: 6 servings.

TiTANiC BRANDiED PEACH PUDDiNG

PREPARATION:
6 minutes
COOKING: 4
minutes
FREEZING:
excellent
PER SERVING:
100 calories.
Excellent source
of calcium,
potassium and
vitamin A.

Yes, this was on the menu for dinner that night when the behemoth of the sea struck the iceberg and sank to the bottom of the Atlantic. You can recreate it without that sinking feeling. Thanks to our low-cal version, your pampered guests will glide away on wings of gossamer.

3 tbsp	quick-cooking tapioca	40 mL
2 cups	skim milk, fresh or reconstituted	500 mL
½ tsp	cinnamon	2 mL
2	egg whites, beaten	2
1 tsp	Splenda granular sweetener or sugar	5 mL
3	drops maple extract	3
½ tsp	brandy extract	2 mL
½ tsp	vanilla extract	2 mL
3 cups	unsweetened, frozen peaches, thawed overnight in refrigerator and drained	750 mL

1. In top of double boiler, sprinkle tapioca over skim milk. Set aside for 5 minutes.

2. Stir in cinnamon, egg whites and sweetener. Bring to a boil and stir constantly.

3. Simmer, covered, over medium heat for 10 minutes or until mixture thickens. Stir often.

4. When thickened, remove from heat. Stir in extracts. Taste for sweetness and adjust by adding more sweetener, a little at a time. Stir. Cool to lukewarm and fold in peaches. Cover and chill 2 hours.

Yield: 6 servings.

Shining Star Strawberry Short-cake

PREPARATION:
6 minutes
BAKING: 15
minutes
FREEZING: not
required
PER SERVING:
212 calories.
Excellent source
of calcium,
potassium and
vitamin C.

We've adapted this delicate and absolutely delicious traditional Ojibwe recipe. It was provided by Brian Waindubence, whose grandmother called him Shining Star. If wild strawberries are not available, use fresh cultivated ones from the garden or the market.

2 cups	pastry flour	500 mL
3 ½ tbsp	baking powder	45 mL
3 oz	light cream cheese	90 mL
1 tbsp	polyunsaturated margarine	15 mL
2	egg whites, beaten	2
⅓ cup	skim milk, fresh or reconstituted	75 mL
1 tbsp	soft polyunsaturated margarine	15 mL
1 quart	wild strawberries or freshly picked cultivated ones	1 L
1 tsp	Splenda granular sweetener or sugar	5 mL
	Whipped topping (page 285)	

1. In a bowl, sift flour and baking powder. Cut in cream cheese and margarine finely, using pastry blender or 2 knives.

2. In another bowl, beat egg whites and add milk. Gradually add this mixture to the flour-cheese one, combining lightly with a fork. Dough should be soft but not sticky. If required, add more milk.

3. Knead dough about 20 seconds. Cut with floured cutter, 3 1/2 inches (9 cm) in diameter.

4. Spread half the rounds with margarine and top with remaining rounds. Place on ungreased pan and bake at 425°F (220°C) for 15 minutes. Remove to a cooling rack.

5. When cold, split each round apart and place on large serving plate.

6. If necessary, wash, hull and split strawberries. (Wild ones will have no hulls and should not require washing.) Add sweetener and let stand for 10 minutes.

7. Spoon strawberry mixture between and on top of rounds. Apply topping just before serving.

Yield: 6 shortcakes.

VARIATIONS

- In season, use slightly crushed raspberries, sliced peaches or wild blueberries.

ELMYR TOMPKINS SUNDAY SWEET POTATOES

PREPARATION:
12 minutes
COOKING: *30 minutes (plus cooking time for potatoes)*
FREEZING: *excellent*
PER SERVING: *225 calories. Excellent source of potassium and vitamin A. Good source of calcium, niacin and protein.*

The Annie & Etienne Poirier Foundation was set up to help elderly people such as Elmyr Reese Tompkins, a 94-year-old widow in Georgia who complained she had been confined by a relative and forced to sign a new will. Her $20-million estate, originally willed to charities working for blind and handicapped children, was the subject of a notorious court case. We've named this dessert in honor of Mrs. Tompkins, for sweet potato was one of her favorite foods. Our chefs triple-tested and pronounced it "absolutely fantastic." The original recipe was submitted by Nancy Craig Reaves, Mrs. Tompkins's cousin.

3 cups	cooked sweet potatoes, mashed	750 mL
1 cup	sugar or Splenda granulated sweetener	250 mL
¼ cup	skim milk	50 mL
⅓ cup	polyunsaturated margarine	75 mL
4	egg whites	4
1 tsp	pure vanilla extract	5 mL
	Cookware spray	

TOPPING:

1 cup	shredded coconut	250 mL
1 cup	chopped pecans	250 mL

1 cup	brown sugar	250 mL
	or	
¾ cup	Splenda granulated sweetener	175 mL
½ cup	soft, unbleached wholewheat flour	125 mL

1. Scrub and wash potatoes but do not peel. Steam until cooked.
2. Mash the potatoes and measure them into a bowl, adding sugar, milk, margarine, egg whites and vanilla.
3. Transfer to a lightly-sprayed 8-by-12-inch (3.5 L) baking dish.
4. Mix topping ingredients. Spread over mixture.
5. Bake at 350°F (175°C) for 30 minutes or until lightly browned.

Yield: 10 servings.

SACKVILLE BAPTIST PUDDING

PREPARATION: *8 minutes*
BAKING: *75 minutes*
FREEZING: *not recommended*
PER SERVING: *91 calories. Excellent source of calcium, potassium and vitamin A.*

First marketed in 1897, Grape-Nuts cereal was one of our first "convenience foods." The ladies at the Baptist church in Sackville, N.B., developed this easy-to-make puff pudding which is still an international favorite, decades after it was first published.

	Cookware spray	
¼ cup	polyunsaturated margarine	50 mL
½ cup	Splenda granular sweetener or sugar	125 mL
2	eggs, separated	2
1 tsp	grated lemon rind	5 mL
3 tbsp	lemon juice	40 mL
2 tbsp	unbleached white flour	25 mL
¼ cup	Post Grape-Nuts cereal	50 mL
1 cup	skim milk	250 mL

1. Spray a 6-cup (1.5 L) baking dish.
2. In a blender, cream margarine and sweetener. Add egg yolks; beat until fluffy. Blend in lemon rind and juice, flour, cereal and milk. (Ignore the curdled look of the mixture.)
3. In a bowl, beat egg whites until peaks form. Fold into cereal mixture. Pour gently into baking dish. Place dish in larger pan half-filled with hot water.
4. Bake uncovered at 350°F (175°C) for 75 minutes until top springs back when touched.
   Yield: 4 servings.

SAGUENAY BLUEBERRY FOOL (MOUSSE AUX BLEUETS DE SAGUENAY)

PREPARATION:
8 minutes +
chilling
COOKING: 5
minutes
FREEZING: not
appropriate
PER SERVING:
55 calories.
Excellent source
of potassium
and vitamins A
and C.

The British have called this type of dessert a *fool* since at least the 1700s. The French call it *une mousse*. Regardless of the name, this old-fashioned low-calorie dessert is a delightful way to serve the vitamin-rich blueberry.

2 cups	fresh or frozen wild blueberries	500 mL
¼ cup	Splenda granular sweetener or sugar	50 mL
¼ cup	skim milk (or reconstituted from powder)	50 mL
½ tsp	pure vanilla extract	2 mL
1	envelope low-cal topping (to make 1 cup/250 mL)	1

1. In a saucepan, combine blueberries and sweetener. Stir.
2. Cover and simmer for 5 minutes until berries are tender.
3. Set aside to cool.
4. When cool, purée in blender or food processor.
5. Combine blueberry mixture with milk and vanilla in a chilled bowl. Whip until fluffy.
6. Set out 4 dessert glasses and spoon in alternate layers of the blueberry purée and topping. Do not stir. Chill for 1 hour.
   Yield: 4 servings.

Lumina Drapeau's "Mois de Marie" Sorbet

PREPARATION:
10 minutes
COOKING: 30 minutes
FREEZING: 4 1/2 hours
PER SERVING: 113 calories. Excellent source of calcium, potassium and vitamins A and C.

May is the Month of Mary, when a welcome newcomer at farmers' markets is the pink-tinged rhubarb. Lumina's exotic sorbet won't add any flab to the waistline, either, as long as you don't use sugar.

6 cups	diced rhubarb, or 1 ½ lb (750 g)	1.5 L
1 ½ cups	Riesling wine	375 mL
¾ cup	Splenda granular sweetener or sugar	175 mL
2 tbsp	fresh lemon juice	25 mL

1. Wash rhubarb, dice it and put the slices in an ovenproof non-aluminum dish. Cover and bake at 375°F (190°C) for 30 minutes or until soft. Cool and purée in blender or food processor.

2. Add wine, sweetener and lemon juice. Taste and add more sweetener if you wish.

3. Freeze for 1 hour until the edges begin to harden. Beat in mixing bowl until frothy. Cover and refreeze for 30 minutes.

4. Remove from freezer and beat again.

5. Cover and freeze for 3 hours before serving.
   Yield: 6 servings.

NOTE

An ice-cream maker can be used. Follow manufacturer's instructions.

Bea Lillie Peach Sorbet

PREPARATION:
15 minutes
COOKING:
none
FREEZING: 6
hours
PER SERVING:
32 calories.
Excellent source
of potassium
and vitamins A
and C.

Born at 68 Dovercourt Road, Toronto, she reigned for decades as an international comedienne and revue star. Songs such as "There Are Fairies at the Bottom of Our Garden" and "It's Better with Your Shoes Off" are classics. And so is this delightful sorbet.

2 ½ cups	fresh or frozen unsweetened peaches, peeled, pitted and sliced	625 mL
3 tbsp	fresh lemon juice	40 mL
1 cup	Splenda granular sweetener or sugar	250 mL
1 cup	boiling spring water	250 mL
1 cup	dry white wine	250 mL
1 ½ tsp	grated orange peel	7 mL

GARNISH:

Long, thin strips of orange peel, fresh raspberries or kiwi fruit slices

1. If using frozen peaches, let stand for 20 minutes at room temperature.
2. Combine peaches and lemon juice in a blender or food processor. Pulse or blend until smooth.
3. In a bowl, combine sweetener and boiling water. Stir until dissolved. Stir in peach mixture, wine and grated orange peel.
4. Turn into 9-by-9-by 2-inch (2.5 L) pan. Cover and freeze for 4 hours.
5. Break frozen mixture into chunks. Transfer to a mixing bowl or food processor. Beat on medium-high until smooth. Return to pan. Cover and freeze for 2 hours until firm.
6. Let stand for 20 minutes before scooping into dessert dishes. Garnish with orange strips, raspberries or kiwi fruit.
   Yield: 8 servings.

PRINCE ALBERT YOGURT "ICE CREAM"

PREPARATION:
6 minutes plus
freezing time
FREEZING:
excellent
PER SERVING:
163 calories.
Excellent source
of calcium and
vitamin A.

The honey adds a silkiness to this unusual low-cal treat. The original used to be made with cream in the Saskatchewan city. To preserve fresh ginger, chop and cover with dry sherry.

3 ½ cups	no-fat plain yogurt	875 mL
½ cup	clover honey	125 mL
½ cup	chopped ginger preserved in sherry	125 mL

1. Combine yogurt, honey and chopped ginger.
2. Pour into ice-cream maker and follow manufacturer's instructions for ice cream.
3. Serve as is or with mashed fruit or no-sugar syrup (sold in stores).
   Yield: 6 servings.

PIE PASTRY

PREPARATION:
6 minutes +
chilling
FREEZING:
excellent
PER SERVING:
304 calories.
Fair source of
calcium and
vitamin A.

This is an easy-to-make traditional recipe and, although heavy on calories and cholesterol, it is a winner. Our dietitians recommend Low-Cal Pie Crust I and Low-Cal Pie Crust II (see below).

2 cups	all-purpose flour	500 mL
	(or 1 ½ cups/375 mL and ½ cup/125 mL cake or pastry flour)	
¾ cup	butter (6 oz/170 g), diced, chilled	175 mL
2 tbsp	sugar	25 mL
¼ cup	vegetable shortening (2 oz/60 g), chilled	50 mL
½ cup	iced spring water	125 mL

1. Measure flour, butter and sugar into a food processor. Pulse 5 or 6 times. Add shortening and pulse again 4 times.
2. Add water and pulse 4 times.
3. Form dough into ball, wrap in plastic and chill for 2 hours.
4. Roll on floured board.
   Yield: 2 crusts (8 servings).

Low-Cal Pie Crust I

PREPARATION:

15 minutes +

refrigeration

time

FREEZING:

excellent

PER SERVING:

97 calories.

Excellent source

of calcium and

vitamin A.

This is the best and most versatile to come out of Québec's *nouvelle cuisine* school. It is just as flaky and rich-tasting as any made with butter or shortening. The inexpensive flours are sold in health stores.

2 cups	rice flour (8 oz/240 g)	500 mL
2 cups	fine rye flour (8 oz/240 g)	500 mL
2 cups	dry non-fat cottage cheese (16 oz/454 g)	500 mL
2 cups	polyunsaturated margarine (16 oz/454 g)	500 mL
	Cookware spray	

1. All ingredients should be at room temperature.
2. Aerate flours for 2 minutes in a blender or sift 5 times.
3. Transfer flours to a bowl and incorporate the other ingredients gradually, adding a little at a time, mixing with a fork until it forms a solid dough. Divide and form into 4 balls, wrap in waxed paper and refrigerate overnight.
4. Next day, cover rolling area with a pastry cloth or waxed paper. Press dough on the cloth to form a circle about 1/4 inch (1 cm) thick.
5. Cover with another sheet of waxed paper. Roll from the center to the outer edges. Lift the roller back to the center each time instead of rolling. You should have about an extra 2 inches (5 cm) all around the pie plate. (Measure by inverting it.)
6. Spray the pie plate, remove top sheet of waxed paper and invert crust into the plate. Carefully peel off the remaining paper.
7. Fill with *tourtière* or other mixture and repeat the procedure with remaining 3 balls.
   Yield: four 9-inch crusts.

NOTES

- For a one-crust pie, trim outer edges to within 1 inch (2.5 cm) of the rim. Fold outer edges under rim. Crimp with a fork and anchor the edging at 6 or 7 points to prevent shrinkage. Prick bottom of shell with a fork. Sprinkle bottom with about 24 uncooked beans to prevent puffing. Bake in preheated oven at 450°F (230°C). Cool before filling.
- You can re-roll extra dough, cut into strips and use these to create a lattice top. Tears can be repaired by moistening with a little water. Press together.

LOW-CAL PIE CRUST II

This is a terrific pie shell but if you happen to be in a foul mood, forget it. Postpone your pie project until happy days are here again. The recipe can be difficult but practice makes perfect.

PREPARATION:
15 minutes +
chilling
FREEZING:
excellent
PER SERVING:
40 calories.
Good source of
calcium.

2 tbsp	polyunsaturated margarine	25 mL
¼ cup	wholewheat pastry flour	50 mL
¼ cup	unbleached white flour	50 mL
5 to 8 tsp	iced spring water	25 to 40 mL

1. In a bowl, cut margarine into flours with a pastry blender until crumbly.
2. Add chilled water a teaspoon at a time and continue blending until dough clings together.
3. Form into a round, flatten with a hand, wrap in plastic or waxed paper and chill for 2 hours.
4. Place dough between 2 sheets of waxed paper and roll as in Low-Cal Pie Crust I above. Remove top paper.
5. If using as bottom crust, invert crust (paper side UP) over pie plate. USE BOTH HANDS – ONE ON BOTTOM AND ONE ON TOP! Remove paper and press gently against sides of plate. Check your pie recipe to see if crust must be baked before filling. If so, bake 10 minutes at 425°F (220°C).
6. If the pastry is to go on top of a filling, keep paper side UP and deposit gently. Remove paper, crimp edges and cut vents.

Yield: 1 bottom or top crust.

- Double the recipe if that prize-winning pie you're creating for dinner tonight requires both a bottom and a top crust.

ERNEST HEMINGWAY KEY LIME PIE

PREPARATION:
10 minutes
COOKING: 15
minutes
FREEZING: not
recommended
PER SERVING:
230 calories.
Excellent source
of calcium,
potassium and
vitamin C.

As a young journalist for the *Toronto Star*, Hemingway lived at 1599 Bathurst Street in Toronto. When he moved to Florida and then Cuba, he developed a fondness for white rum, seafood and the famous Key West Lime Pie. If you're afraid of the cholesterol, use an egg substitute (sold in frozen foods department).

1 cup	Splenda granulated sweetener or sugar	250 mL
¼ cup	unbleached white flour	50 mL
3 tbsps	cornstarch	40 mL
2 cups	spring water	500 mL
3	egg yolks	3
1 tbsp	polyunsaturated margarine	15 mL
¼ cup	fresh lime juice	50 mL

Grated rind of 1 lime
Baked 9-inch (23 cm) Low-Cal Pie Shell (page 268)
Meringue pie topping (page 270)

1. In the top of a double boiler, combine sweetener, flour and cornstarch and gradually stir in the water. Cook over medium heat, stirring, until thickened.

2. In a bowl, beat the egg yolks, then gradually stir cooked mixture into beaten egg yolks. Return to double boiler and cook, stirring, another 3 minutes.

3. Stir in margarine, lime juice and rind. Cool to lukewarm. Pour into baked shell and cool thoroughly.

4. Top with meringue and brown under oven broiler.
Yield: 8 servings.

CHE'S LEMON MERINGUE PIE:

Use lemon rind and juice instead of lime rind and juice. Proceed as above.

Meringue Pie Topping

PREPARATION:
4 minutes
BROWNING: *10 to 15 minutes.*
PER SERVING:
106 calories.
Good source of calcium.

6 tbsp	Splenda granulated sweetener or sugar	75 mL
1 tbsp	cornstarch	15 mL
½ cup	cold spring water	125 mL
4	egg whites	4
¾ tsp	vanilla extract	4 mL

1. Heat oven to 350°F (180°C).
2. In a saucepan, combine 2 tbsp (25 mL) sweetener with cornstarch and water. Stir until cornstarch dissolves. Cook over medium heat for 3 minutes or until thickened and clear. Set aside to cool.
3. Beat egg whites with vanilla until light. Beat in remaining sweetener, a little at a time. Add cornstarch mixture and beat until stiff peaks form and meringue is shiny.
4. Pile on cooled filling. Spread right to the edges to prevent shrinking.
5. Bake until top browns, 10 to 15 minutes.

Lucy Maud Montgomery
Riverside Flan

PREPARATION:

12 minutes

BAKING AND

COOKING: *15 +*

8 minutes

CHILLING: *3*

hours +

PER SERVING:

200 calories.

Excellent source

of vitamin C.

Good source of

calcium,

potassium and

vitamin A.

The creator of *Anne of Green Gables* spent her final years on Riverside Drive in Toronto's west end. She loved P.E.I. strawberries, and this gorgeous flan is adapted from a Down East recipe.

CRUST:

1 cup	unbleached white flour	250 mL
¼ cup	Splenda granular sweetener or sugar	50 mL
⅓ cup	polyunsaturated margarine	75 mL

FILLING:

2 tbsp	cornstarch	25 mL
¼ cup	Splenda granular sweetener or sugar	50 mL
1 ½ cups	skim milk, fresh or reconstituted	375 mL
1	egg, beaten	1
1 tsp	vanilla extract	5 mL
1	drop yellow food coloring (optional)	1

TOPPING:

1 pint	fresh strawberries, sliced	500 mL
2	kiwi fruit, peeled and diced	2
⅓ cup	low-calorie apricot jam	75 mL

1. To make the crust, combine flour and sweetener. Cut in margarine until mixture is crumbly (a food processor can be used). If too dry, sprinkle with a little iced spring water.
2. Press firmly into a 9-inch (23 cm) flan pan with removable base.
3. Bake at 375°F (190°C) for 15 minutes. Cool.
4. Combine cornstarch and sweetener to make the filling. Add milk gradually, whisking until

smooth. Cook and stir over medium heat until mixture boils. Whisk into beaten egg and return filling to saucepan and place over heat.

5. Stirring constantly, simmer for 2 minutes over low heat. Remove. Stir in vanilla and food coloring (if using).

6. Pour into bowl and cover with plastic wrap. Chill.

7. Remove wrap, pour filling into crust.

8. Arrange fruit on surface.

9. Heat jam in small saucepan until melted. Brush over fruit. Chill for 2 hours before serving.

Yield: 1 9-inch (23 cm) flan.

Cabot Trail Energy Cookies

PREPARATION:

22 minutes

COOKING: *20*

minutes

FREEZING:

excellent

PER COOKIE:

47 calories.

Excellent source

of calcium,

niacin,

potassium and

protein. Good

source of

vitamins A

and C.

These old favorites are simply marvelous on hiking trips or to boost energy levels at school recess periods. They're chewy, naturally sweet and extremely nutritious. No child should go to school without them.

1 ¼ cups	pitted dates (8 oz/250 g)	300 mL
½ cup	spring water	125 mL
1 cup	grated unpeeled apple	250 mL
¾ cup	canola or safflower oil	175 mL
1 tsp	vanilla extract	5 mL
½ cup	chopped walnuts or local nuts	125 mL
2 cups	rolled oats	500 mL
1 cup	oat bran	250 mL

1. Put dates in a saucepan and cover with water. Simmer for 6 minutes. Mash well.

2. Add grated apple and oil. Beat until smooth.

3. Add vanilla, nuts oats and oat bran and let stand for 15 minutes.

4. Meanwhile, heat oven to 325°F

(160°C).

5. Mix thoroughly and drop one level teaspoonful (5 mL) at a time close to each other on ungreased baking sheets.

6. Bake until brown around the edges, about 20 minutes. Cool on paper towels.

Yield: 70 cookies.

CAVENDISH GINGERSNAPS

PREPARATION:
20 minutes
BAKING: *12*
minutes
FREEZING:
excellent
PER COOKIE:
65 calories.
Excellent source
of of calcium,
folate and
niacin.

Soft and tasty, these are not for the diet-conscious but a treat now and then won't kill you. Folks have been making them for generations. To cut down on cholesterol, use our Farm-Fresh Egg Substitute (page 12). Unbleached flours are sold in health stores.

1 ½ cups	vegetable shortening	375 mL
2 cups	Splenda granular sweetener or sugar	500 mL
2	eggs	2
	or	
½ cup	Farm Fresh Egg Substitute (page 12)	125 mL
½ cup	molasses	125 mL
4 cups	unbleached white flour	1 L
2 tsp	baking soda	10 mL
2 tsp	cinnamon	10 mL
2 tsp	ground cloves	10 mL
2 tsp	ground ginger	10 mL
	White sugar for dipping	
	Cookware spray	

1. Heat oven to 375°F (190°C).
2. In a bowl, cream shortening and sweetener. Add eggs and molasses. Beat until fluffy.
3. In another bowl, combine flour, baking soda, cinnamon, cloves and ginger. Stir into shortening mixture.
4. Roll dough into 1-inch (2.5 cm) balls. Dip in sugar. Set on lightly sprayed baking sheets. Bake for 12 minutes.

Yield: 80 gingersnaps.

Zippy Rickety Uncles

PREPARATION:
2 minutes
COOKING: 3
minutes
FREEZING:
excellent
PER SERVING:
58 calories.
Good source of
carbohydrates
and potassium.

Delightfully chewy, they're similar to crispy peanut butter bars sold in stores. No one seems to know why they're called Rickety Uncles. Great for Hallowe'en treats, and we've eliminated the granulated sugar without losing texture or flavor. If you do not make your own, the peanut butter should be purchased fresh in a health store. It should have no additives whatsoever.

½ cup	Splenda granular sweetener or sugar	125 mL
1 cup	corn syrup	250 mL
1 cup	unsalted crunchy peanut butter	250 mL
1 tsp	vanilla extract	5 mL
4 cups	corn flakes, preferably Kellogg's	1 L

1. In a saucepan, bring sweetener and syrup to a boil while stirring. Remove immediately from heat.
2. Stir in peanut butter. Add vanilla and stir. Add corn flakes and mix well.
3. Put spoonfuls onto waxed paper. Cool, wrap and refrigerate.

Yield: 48 Rickety Uncles.

BARBARA FRUM

"AS IT HAPPENS" RAISIN SQUARES

PREPARATION:

16 minutes

BAKING: *40*

minutes

FREEZING:

excellent

PER SERVING:

202 calories.

Excellent source

of calcium,

carbohydrates

and potassium.

Not only are these delicious, they're low-cal thanks to the Splenda sweetener. We've named them in honor of the late radio and TV journalist who fell in love with them on one of her out-of-town sojourns.

1 lb	raisins	500 g
¾ cup	Splenda granular sweetener or sugar	175 mL
1 cup	spring water	250 mL
1 cup	vegetable shortening	250 mL
1 cup	Splenda granular sweetener or sugar	250 mL
3	egg whites	3
½ tsp	vanilla	2 mL
2 ½ cups	soft wholewheat flour	625 mL
1 tsp	baking soda	5 mL
2 tsp	cream of tartar	10 mL
	Cookware spray	

1. Heat oven to 400°F (200°C).
2. Chop raisins on a wooden board using a large knife, or pulse once or twice in a food processor using the sharp blade. Transfer to a saucepan and mix with sweetener and water. Simmer over low heat until thick. Set aside.
3. In a bowl, combine shortening, sweetener, egg whites and vanilla. Beat thoroughly.
4. In a separate bowl, sift dry ingredients. Combine with egg white mixture to form a dough. Divide in half. Roll half the dough to fit a 10-inch by 15-inch (2 L) pan, sprayed lightly.
5. Spread raisin filling over dough.
6. Roll second half of dough to the same size; cover filling with it.
7. Bake for 40 minutes or until dough is golden. Cool.
8. If freezing, cut squares and wrap each tightly in plastic. Label and freeze. To use, thaw overnight in refrigerator.
   Yield: 18 squares.

DOROTHY DIX CHEESECAKE FOR THE LOVELORN

PREPARATION:
8 minutes

COOKING: *6 to*
8 minutes

FREEZING:
excellent

PER SERVING:
74 calories.
Excellent source
of calcium,
potassium and
vitamin C.

She was born years ahead of Ann Landers and became the adviser to millions via her newspaper columns. A native Southerner, she was a very wise and kindhearted lady; her columns and books should be reprinted for today's so-called Generation X. One taste of this delicious cheesecake will convince even the most dyed-in-the-tarmac skeptical yuppy that life is worth living.

CRUST:

6 tbsp	melted, polyunsaturated margarine	75 mL
1 ½ cups	Cavendish Gingersnaps, crumbled (page 273)	375 mL
6 tbsp	brown sugar	75 mL

FILLING:

1 cup	unsweetened apple juice	250 mL
⅔ cup	Splenda granular sweetener or sugar	150 mL
1 tbsp	unflavored gelatin	15 mL
6	egg whites	6
½ tsp	vanilla extract	2 mL
1 tbsp	fresh lemon juice	15 mL
1	package light (low-calorie) cream cheese (8 oz/250 g)	1
¾ cup	evaporated skim milk, chilled	175 mL
1 cup	cooked pumpkin	250 mL
⅓ tsp	each: cloves, cinnamon and ginger	1.5 mL

GARNISH:

Semisweet chocolate or carob shavings

1. Prepare the crust by combining ingredients. Press three-quarters of the mixture into a 9-inch (23 cm) springform pan and chill. Set aside the rest for the topping.
2. In the top of a double boiler, combine juice, sweetener and gelatin. Heat and stir until gelatin dissolves.
3. Beat egg whites for 3 minutes and add gradually to gelatin mixture. Cook until slightly thickened. Stir constantly. Remove from heat and add vanilla.
4. In a blender or food processor, blend lemon juice and cheese. Add gelatin mixture and pulse a few times until smooth. Chill until it thickens.
5. Using a chilled bowl and beaters, whip skim milk until stiff.
6. Fold the two mixtures together, then stir twice only. Pour into springform pan; top with remaining crumb mixture and chill for 1 hour.
7. Remove from pan. Decorate with shavings.
   Yield: 10 servings.

MADAME DE GAULLE LOW-CAL CHEESECAKE WITH RASPBERRY SAUCE

It was up to his devoted spouse to worry about the French leader's diet. Le Grand Charles had a weakness for desserts and this adaptation proves you don't need to use sugar to gain the upper hand. A serving is only 125 calories.

PREPARATION:
10 minutes
BAKING: 45 minutes
FREEZING: excellent
PER SERVING: 125 calories. Excellent source of calcium, niacin, protein and vitamin A. Good source of vitamin C.

	Cookware spray	
¼ cup	raw almonds (see note below)	50 mL
2 cups	2% cottage cheese	500 mL
½ cup	no-fat plain yogurt	125 mL
3	eggs	3
½ cup	Splenda granular sweetener or sugar	125 mL
2 tbsp	unbleached white flour	25 mL
1 tsp	grated lemon rind	5 mL
½ tsp	almond extract	2 mL

1   package frozen, unsweetened raspberries, thawed (10 oz/300 g)   1
½ cup   Splenda granular sweetener or sugar   125 mL

1. Heat oven to 350°F (180°C).
2. Spray an 8-inch (20 cm) spring-form pan.
3. Spread unskinned raw almonds in the springform pan and bake for 5 minutes. Remove from oven and slice. There is no need to skin. Return almonds to pan, spreading them evenly to form a bottom "crust."
4. In blender or food processor, blend cottage cheese until smooth. Add remaining ingredients and blend until smooth. Pour over almonds.
5. Bake 45 minutes or until set.
6. Remove from oven and run knife around edge to loosen. Cool on rack in pan. Chill 2 hours or more.
7. Purée raspberries in blender or food processor. Remove seeds if you wish by pressing through a sieve. Stir in sweetener. Chill. Spoon sauce over cut wedges.
Yield: 8 servings.

NOTES
- Since raw almonds go rancid, buy yours in a busy store, seal tightly and refrigerate or freeze.
- If freezing the cheesecake, make the sauce after thawing.

FRONT LINE LOVE CAKE

Without eggs, butter or milk to go stale, this cake was shipped by the thousands to the soldiers in World War I and World War II. Even in the damp trenches, it kept well and contributed to morale and, alas, homesickness, too. Developed in 1916, the recipe was quickly picked up by newspapers everywhere.

PREPARATION:

10 minutes

BAKING: 30

minutes

FREEZING:

excellent

PER SERVING:

204 calories.

Excellent source

of calcium,

carbohydrates

and potassium.

	Cookware spray	
1 cup	spring water	250 mL
1 cup	packed brown sugar	250 mL
1 ½ cup	raisins	375 mL
¼ cup	oil	50 mL
1 tsp	cinnamon	5 mL
½ tsp	nutmeg	2 mL
¼ tsp	each allspice and ground cloves	1 mL
1 ¾ cups	wholewheat pastry flour	425 mL
1 tsp	baking soda	5 mL
	Icing sugar	

1. Spray and dust lightly with flour an 8-inch (2 L) square pan.
2. In a saucepan, combine water, sugar, raisins, oil, cinnamon, nutmeg, allspice and cloves. Bring to a boil, stirring. Set aside and cool to lukewarm.
3. In a bowl, combine flour and baking soda; add to raisin mixture and stir briefly.
4. Pour into pan and bake at 350°F (175°C) for 30 minutes. Cool in pan. Sprinkle with icing sugar.
Yield: 12 squares.

QUEEN ELIZABETH CAKE

One of the easiest to make, this dessert never fails. It became popular during World War II and many believed the recipe came from the Queen Mother herself. Despite wartime rationing, the ingredients were fairly easy to come by. Our version cuts down on calories and is guaranteed to boost morale.

PREPARATION:

20 minutes

BAKING: 30

minutes

FREEZING:

excellent

PER SERVING:

157 calories.

Excellent source

of calcium and

potassium.

	Cookware spray	
1 cup	chopped dates	250 mL
1 cup	boiling water	250 mL
1 tsp	baking soda	5 mL
¼ cup	polyunsaturated margarine, at room temperature	50 mL

1 cup	sugar or Splenda sweetener	250 mL
1 tsp	vanilla extract	5 mL
1 ½ cups	cake and pastry flour	375 mL
1 tsp	baking powder	5 mL
¼ tsp	salt	1 mL
½ tsp	chopped walnuts	2 mL

TOPPING:

¼ cup	polyunsaturated margarine	50 mL
½ cup	brown sugar	125 mL
3 tbsp	evaporated skim milk	40 mL
½ cup	sweetened shredded coconut	125 mL

1. Spray an 8-inch (2 L) square baking pan.
2. In a bowl, combine dates, boiling water and baking soda. Mix.
3. In a larger bowl, cream margarine and sugar until fluffy. Stir in vanilla.
4. In a third bowl, sift flour, baking powder and salt. Add date mixture and flour mixture alternately in 2 batches to margarine mixture. Stir in walnuts. Pour into pan. Bake at 350°F (175°C) for 30 minutes.
5. For topping, melt margarine and brown sugar with milk in a saucepan over medium heat. Bring to a boil, stirring, then remove immediately. Stir in coconut. Spread over warm cake.
6. Heat oven broiler. When red hot, place cake under it and broil until topping bubbles. Watch that it doesn't burn. Cool.

Yield: 14 squares.

SANTA'S NORTH POLE CHRISTMAS CAKE

PREPARATION:

7 minutes

BAKING: 60

minutes

FREEZING:

excellent

PER SERVING:

148 calories.

Excellent source

of calcium,

potassium and

protein. Good

source of

vitamin A.

Christmas rekindles fond memories and stokes dreams to be treasured for life. This year, start a new tradition with this fantastic recipe!

2 ½ cups	wholewheat pastry flour	625 mL
½ cup	seedless raisins	125 mL
½ cup	candied cherries, chopped	125 mL
½ cup	pecans, chopped	125 mL
1 ¾ cups	granulated sugar or Splenda sweetener	425 mL
2 tsp	baking powder	10 mL
¼ tsp	salt	1 mL
½ cup	oil	125 mL
1 cup	skim milk	250 mL
2 tsp	rum or brandy extract	10 mL
6	egg whites	6
1	egg	1
	Cookware spray	

1. In a bowl, mix 2 tbsp (25 mL) of the flour with fruits and nuts.
2. In food processor, combine the rest of the flour with sugar, baking powder and salt. Add oil, milk and extract. Blend to mix. Add egg whites and egg. Pulse or beat for a minute, then stir in fruit mixture. Blend.
3. Spoon batter into sprayed, floured pan.
4. Bake for 60 minutes at 350°F (175°C) or until toothpick inserted in center comes out clean. Cool 15 minutes in pan. Turn out on wire rack and finish cooling before frosting with glaze or sprinkling with icing sugar.

Yield: 20 slices and two for Santa.

GRACIE FIELDS YULETIDE FRUITCAKE

PREPARATION:
25 minutes +
aging
COOKING: *1 1/2*
to 2 hours
FREEZING: *not*
recommended.
PER SERVING:
127 calories.
Good source of
calcium and
vitamins A
and C.

If you have any of Gracie's recordings, bring them out in November when the time comes to prepare this wonderful cake. (Many stores feature new CDs of her nostalgic old songs in the Yuletide season.) Don't be daunted by the list of ingredients; remember, Christmas comes but once a year.

2 ½ cups	pitted dates, chopped	625 mL
2 cups	candied citron peel, chopped	500 mL
2 cups	seeded raisins	500 mL
1 ½ cups	currants	375 mL
1 ½ cups	raw almonds	375 mL
1 ½ cups	maraschino cherries, drained	375 mL
	(reserve liquid) and chopped	
½ cup	brandy	125 mL
1 can	crushed pineapple (19 oz/540 mL), undrained	1
2 cups	Splenda granulated sweetener or sugar	500 mL
½ cup	liquid reserved from maraschino cherries	125 mL
1 cup	low-cal raspberry or strawberry jam	250 mL
	Cookware spray	
4 cups	unbleached white flour	1 L
1 ½ tsp	baking soda	7 mL
2 tsp	cinnamon	10 mL
¼ tsp	salt	1 mL
½ tsp	ground cloves	2 mL
½ tsp	ground allspice	2 mL
2 cups	polyunsaturated margarine	500 mL
2 cups	Splenda granular sweetener or sugar	500 mL
8	eggs	8
4	egg whites	4
	Brandy	

Day 1

1. In a bowl, combine dates, citron peel, raisins, currants, almonds and cherries. Stir in brandy. Cover tightly and let stand at room temperature overnight.

2. In a saucepan, combine pineapple and sweetener and bring to a boil. Simmer uncovered for 40 minutes. Remove from heat and stir in cherry liquid and jam. Cover and refrigerate overnight.

Day 2

1. Spray and line five 9-by-5-inch (2 L) loaf pans with waxed paper. Spray lining.

2. In a bowl, combine flour, baking soda, cinnamon, salt, cloves and allspice. Add 1 cup (250 mL) of the flour mixture to the date mixture and stir or toss to coat fruits.

3. In a large bowl, cream margarine and 2 cups (500 mL) sweetener. Beat in eggs and egg whites gradually. While doing so, stir in small amounts of flour and pineapple mixtures. Mix thoroughly. Stir in date mixture. Spoon batter into pans.

4. Place a large shallow pan, half-filled with water, on bottom rack of oven. Heat to 275°F (140°C).

5. Place loaves on middle rack and bake for 1 1/2 to 2 hours or until a toothpick inserted in the center of each loaf comes out clean.

6. Remove from oven and cool for 15 minutes. Remove from pans and peel off paper. Place on racks to continue cooling.

7. Wrap each cake in cheesecloth soaked in brandy. Place a second wrap of plastic on each, followed by a third wrap of foil. Store in a cool dry closet and moisten cheesecloth once a week with brandy. By Christmas week, the cakes will have "aged" to perfection; Gracie will then reward you with a smile of gratitude and a lovely old song for the holidays.
Yield: 5 cakes.

Cottage Cheese Frosting

PREPARATION:
3 minutes
FREEZING: not
recommended
PER TBSP (15
mL): 10 calories.
Excellent source
of calcium, potas-
sium, protein and
vitamin A.

Amazing what can be done with common ingredients! You needn't tell unless they ask.

½ cup	low-fat cottage cheese	125 mL
2 tbsp	Splenda granulated sweetener or sugar	25 mL
1 tsp	vanilla extract	5 mL

1. Combine all ingredients in blender or food processor. Blend until smooth.

2. For decoration, pipe around the rim as well as on top.

Devon "Cream"

PREPARATION:
15 minutes +
overnight chilling
FREEZING:
excellent
PER TBSP (15
mL): 26 calories.
Excellent source
of calcium,
potassium and
vitamin A. Good
source of protein.

This requires overnight refrigeration, but the superb results are well worth the wait. And the calories? A fraction of the real thing! Resembles the thick English cream or the *crème fraîche* loved by the French. If freezing, allow to thaw completely and beat again.

¾ cup	evaporated milk	175 mL
1 tsp	unflavored powdered gelatin	5 mL
2 tbsp	cold spring water	25 mL
1 tsp	clover honey	5 mL
	Splenda granulated sweetener or sugar (optional)	
¼ tsp	vanilla extract	1 mL

1. Heat the milk, preferably in the top of a double boiler.
2. Dissolve gelatin in cold water and add to hot milk.
3. Stir thoroughly, cover and chill overnight in refrigerator.
4. Just before serving, transfer to a mixing bowl and beat for 5 minutes or until light and fluffy. Add honey, sweetener to taste and vanilla.

Yield: 3/4 cup (150 mL).

VARIATION

• Instead of vanilla, use almond extract or a favorite liqueur.

DIET WHIPPED "CREAM"

PREPARATION:

3 to 5 minutes

PER TBSP (15

mL): 3 calories.

Excellent source

of calcium,

potassium and

vitamin A.

This one will delight you and the guests. Honey gives it the consistency of real whipped cream.

1 can	evaporated skim milk (20 oz/385 mL)	1
1 tbsp	clover honey at room temperature	15 mL
1 ½ tsp	vanilla extract	7 mL

1. Chill beaters, bowl and milk in refrigerator overnight.
2. Beat milk until foamy. Add honey and vanilla and beat

until thick. Serve immediately.

Yield: 6 cups (1.5 L).

More Food For Thought

These "best books" are available in all public libraries and fine bookstores. According to our panelists, they are the best of the 85 titles they've assessed in recent years anywhere in the world, in English or French. They provide ample evidence of the body's need for foods grown without the use of pesticides, the life-sustaining value of unpolluted spring water, the horrifying dangers of poisons present in common foods and the immense importance to everyone's health of organically grown farm crops.

Circle of Poison. David Weir and Mark Schapiro. San Francisco, CA: Institute for Food and Departmental Policy, 1981. Documents what alert citizens are doing to end the international marketing of dangerous pesticides.

Creative Food Experiences for Children. Mary Goodwin and Gerry Pollen. Washington, DC: CSPI, 1980. Activities, recipes and games foster good eating habits among children aged three to ten.

Drinking Water Hazards. John Cary Stewart. Hiram, OH: Envirographics, 1990. How to determine if contaminants are present in drinking water and how to conduct testing.

Eating Clean: Overcoming Food Hazards. Center for Study of Responsive Law, 1987. ($8 U.S. from the Center at Box 19367, Washington, DC 20036). Excellent compendium by Ralph Nader and colleagues on food safety and nutrition.

The Fast-Food Guide. Michael F. Jacobson and Sarah Fritschner. New York, NY: Workman Publishing, 1991. Analysis of foods offered by fast-food chains.

Is Your Water Safe to Drink? Raymond Gabler, Ph.D., and the editors of Consumer Reports Books. Fairfield, OH: Consumers Union, 1988. Information on drinking-water problems, bottled water, tests for purity and *Consumer Reports* ratings of common filters.

The New Organic Grower. Eliot Coleman. Post Mills, VT: Chelsea Green Publishing Company, 1989. Tools and techniques for small-scale farming or home gardening: crop rotation, green manures, market strategy, part-time help and other important topics.

ORGANIZATIONS

Annie Poirier Home Cooking Institute, Box 461, Grand Bay, NB, Canada EOG 1WO. Affiliate of the non-profit Annie & Etienne Poirier Foundation. Conducts Memory Lane cooking demonstrations in community centers, churches, schools and synagogues. Sponsors the international Memory Lane low-calorie recipe contest. Groups active in major world cities. Free information package. Enclose SASE with American, Canadian or European stamps or IRC from local post office.

Center for Science in the Public Interest (CSPI), **1875 Connecticut Ave., N.W., Suite 300, Washington,** DC 20009. Membership organization prompted measures to curb illegal drugs in milk, use of unsafe additives and promotes improved food labelling. Publishes the award-winning *Nutrition Action Newsletter*, 10 times a year ($9.95 with membership).

Rachel Carson Council, Inc., 8940 Jones Mill Road, Chevy Chase, MD 20815. (301) 652-1877. Fights use of pesticides, lead and other contaminants.

Greenpeace, 1726 Commercial Drive, Vancouver, BC V5N 4A3. Founded in 1971, Greenpeace is an international organization with offices in 30 countries worldwide. Campaigns for clean food, economic and ecological renewal. Free newsletter.

HOTLINES

1-800-4-CANCER: National Cancer Institute (NCI). Answers questions on diagnosis, treatment and diet. Free publications.

1-800-622-DASH: Mrs. Dash Sodium Information Hotline. Tackles queries on health menace of salt and some 10,000 foods. Free brochure and coupons.

1-800-288-0718: National Organization Mobilized to Stop Glutamate (NOMSG) **Hotline.** Educational and advocacy organization formed by MSG-sensitive sufferers. Newsletter to members.

1-800-561-0070: SPLENDA Information Centre, P.O. Box 1390, Guelph, Ontario N1H 7L4. Send for free coupons and brochure on the new sugar substitute.

1-800-426-4791 or, in Washington, D.C., (202) 382-5533: EPA Safe Drinking Water Hotline. Handles questions on water purity and locates local labs for testing. Free publications.

SOFTWARE

Nutrition Software, by Ohio Distinctive Software ($11 postpaid). Displayed at 1991 American Dietetic Association annual meeting/exhibition. For any IBM PC compatible. Computes ideal weight, recommends daily calorie level and exercise to reach goals, creates menu plans (even for diabetes, hypertension, pregnancy). Database of 3,500 foods including fast foods and frozen dinners. Two-disk set (5.25" or 3.5"). Ohio Distinctive Software, P.O. Box 20201, Columbus, OH 43220 / P.O. Box 4016, Stn E, Ottawa, Ont. K1S 5B1, (614) 459-0453.

INDEX

A.J. Casson's Banana Bran Bread, 219
Acajun Chili Sauce, 240
Africville Cobbler, 248
Africville Chicken, 97
alcohol, 20–22
Alfie Duncan's El Cheapo Tomato Sauce, 195
Alfie Duncan's Bolognese Sauce, 194
Alfred Hitchcock's Salmon Loaf, 116
Alice Marcotte Sainte-Croix Linguine with Chicken, 128
Alice B. Toklas's Borjupaprikas, 53
allergies, 4
aluminum, 10
Andy Warhol's Cream of Tomato Soup, 41
animal protein, 5
Annapolis Valley Pesto, 200
Annie Poirier's Clam Chowder, 27
apples, 11–12
Apple Jonathan, 250
Armageddon Loaf, 221
Authentic Amsterdam Coleslaw, 174
Ava Gardner's Paella Valenciana, 141

Balmoral Compote, 257
Barbara Frum "As It Happens" Raisin Squares, 275
Basic Chicken Stock, 24
Basic Chinese-Style Stock, 26
Basic Beef Stock, 25

Basic Fish Stock, 26
Bay of Fundy Gourmet Meat Loaf, 66
Bayou Cajun Burgers, 69
Bea Lillie Peach Sorbet, 265
beans: baked, Laurentian, 148; baked Lima, Rudolph Valentino, 149; Balmoral Style, 153; chili, Kedgwick Vegetarian, 151; chili, Truman Capote, 150; dried, 146–147; Evangeline, 137; green, 153; green, à la Gaspésienne, 154; and rice, Cajun, 138;
beef: barbecued, Robert Morley's, 57; brisket, Corner Brook, 55; burgers, Route 66, 70; burgers, First, 67; burgers, Bayou Cajun, 69; burgers, Camillien Houde's, 68; cabbage rolls, Lazy Bones, 60; chili, Charles Boyer, 62; goulash, Alice B. Toklas's, 53; meat loaf, Bay of Fundy, 66; meat loaf, Hollywood, 64; meat loaf, Jean Cocteau's, 65; salad, Fort Edmonton, 181; and sauce, Calgary Stampede, 56; sirloin, Jean Drapeau, 58; sloppy Joes, P'tit Montreal, 71; sloppy Joes, San Francisco, 72; sloppy Joes, Mountain Brook, 74; sloppy Joes, Chinatown, 73; soup, Ma Parker, 43; stock, Basic, 25; stroganoff, Café Budapest, 59; tacos, Red Deer, 61;

Benny Hill Plat du Jour, 115
Bering Strait Plum Sauce, 204
Berkshire Hills Side Dish, 157
Bette Davis's Mild Chili Sauce, 241
biotechnology, 3–4
Blue Angel Chicken Salad, 183
Boissevain Pesto, 201
bread: banana bran, A.J. Casson's, 219;
     bannock, Great Warrior, 211; ban-
     nock, Métis, 212; buns, Saint
     Joseph's, 224; Charles Dickens's,
     209; cinnamon rolls, Mount Eisen-
     hower, 223; Easter, Frére André's,
     210; graham crackers, Walter Hus-
     ton's, 218; lemon loaf, Old Havana,
     220; loaf, Tantramar Thanksgiving,
     225; loaf, Armageddon, 221; soda,
     James Joyce's, 213; sourdough bis-
     cuits, Yukon, 216; Sourdough Life-
     time Starter, 218; sourdough
     hamburger buns, Fort Rouge, 217;
     wild rice, Thousand Islands, 226
budgets, 1–2
broccoli: cancer prevention, 23, 146;
     fettucine, California, 126

Cabot Trail Energy Cookies, 272
Café Budapest Boeuf Stroganoff, 59
Cajun Beans and Rice, 138
calcium, 4–5, 22–23
Calgary Stampede Beef and Sauce, 56
California Broccoli Fettuccine, 126
Camillien Houde's Mont-Royal
     Burgers, 68
Canadian Brass Glazed Ham, 92
cancer prevention, 5–6, 23, 146
Caribana Rice and Peas, 162
Carleton-sur-mer Fish Chowder, 28
Carmen Miranda Hot Salsa, 196
Carole Lombard Hollywood Purée,
     156
Cavendish Gingersnaps, 273
Célina Fournier's Amqui Tourtière, 90

Charles Boyer Real Chili, 62
Charles Dickins's Canadian Souvenir
     Bread, 209
Chéticamp Garden-Fresh Corn, 161
chicken: Africville, 97; with brandied
     pears, 104; coq au vin, Marc Foisy's,
     100; Grand Pré, 106; Henri iv, 103;
     Judy Garland Rainbow, 98; with lin-
     guine, 128; Mae West, 105; pie,
     Point Pelée Birders', 108; salad, Blue
     Angel, 183; soup, Mata Hari, 42;
     soup, Mary Pickford's 49; stir-fry,
     Red Flag, 105; stock, Basic, 24;
     White House, 102
chili: Charles Boyer, 62; Kedgwick
     Vegetarian, 151; Saskatoon Vegetari-
     an, 168; Truman Capote 4-Alarm,
     150; verde, Lupe Velez, 88
chili sauce: Acajun, 240; Bette Davis's
     Mild, 241; Tyrone Power's Spanish
     Tomato, 242
Chinatown Sloppy Joes, 73
clams: Ava Gardner's Paella Valen-
     ciana, 141; chowder, Annie Poirier's,
     27; Linguine Charlo, 129
Cliff Barlow's Smoked Fish Dinner,
     119
conserves (see also marmalades): Judy
     Lamarsh's, 245; jam, Cottage Coun-
     try Prune, 244; jam corrective, Tante
     Clementine's, 247
corn: about, 158–159; garden-fresh,
     Cheticamp, 161; on the cob, 160;
     pie, Lancaster County, 161
Corn on the Cob, 160
Corner Brook Brisket of Beef, 55
Cottage Country Prune Jam, 244
Cottage Cheese Frosting, 284
Cousin Louise's Hamburger Relish,
     233

dairy products, 5,15–16
Delhi Curried Pork, 84;

desserts: apple crisp, Hugh Garner, 251; Apple Jonathan, 250; Blueberry Fool, Saguenay, 263; cake, Queen Elizabeth, 279; cake, Santa's North Pole Christmas, 281; cake, Front Line Love, 278; cheesecake for the Lovelorn, 276; cheesecake with Raspberry Sauce, 277; cobbler, Africville, 248; cobbler, Gros Morne Rhubarb, 255; compote, Balmoral, 257; compote, Linus Pauling, 257; cookies, Cabot Trail Energy, 272; cranberry crisp, Tantramar, 252; "cream," Diet Whipped, 285; "cream," Devon, 284; crisp, Lumina's Month of May, 256; crumble, Poirier New World, 254; flan, Lucy Maud Montgomery, 271; frosting, Cottage Cheese, 284; fruit gratin, Ojibwe, 253; fruitcake, Gracie Fields, 282; gingersnaps, Cavendish, 273; key lime pie, Ernest Hemingway, 269; macédoine, Mae Clarke Fruit, 258; pie pastry, 266; pie crust I, Low-Cal, 267; pie crust II, Low-Cal, 268; pie topping, Meringue, 270; pudding, Titanic Brandied Peach, 259; pudding, Sackville Baptist, 262; raisin squares, Barbara Frum, 275; rickety uncles, Zippy, 274; shortcake, Shining Star Strawberry, 260; sorbet, Bea Lillie Peach, 265; sorbet, Lumina Drapeau's, 264; sweet potatoes, Elmyr Tompkins Sunday, 261; topping, Strawberry Fields, 287; yogurt "Ice Cream," Prince Albert, 266

Devon "Cream," 284

Diet Whipped "Cream," 285

Dorothy Dix Cheesecake for the Lovelorn, 276

Dr. Banting's July Heat Wave Soup, 50

eating alone, 23

egg substitute, 12

eggs, 12

Elmyr Tompkins Sunday Sweet Potatoes, 261

Emile Zola Horseradish Sauce, 203

Emmie Wilkins's Tartar Sauce, 205

Ernest Hemingway Key Lime Pie, 269

Étienne's World-Famous Spaghetti Sauce, 133

Evangeline Health Luncheon, 137

Fast-and-Speedy Niagara Falls Ham, 93

fat, 13–14

Felix Leclerc Raspberry Vinegar, 192

Fettuccine Toronto, 127

Fèves au Lard Laurentiennes, 148

First Nations' Manomin Potage, 45

fish: chowder, Carleton-Sur-Mer, 28; fillets, Viking Trail, 119; plat du jour, Benny Hill, 115; salmon noodle casserole, Juneau, 118; salmon loaf, Alfred Hitchcock, 116; salmon cakes, John Lennon, 117; smoked dinner, Cliff Barlow's, 119; Sole Duglère de Percé, 113; soup, Percé, 29; stock, Basic, 26; Tourtière Marco Polo, 121; Tourtiére Chéticamp, 120;

Flin Flon Baked Potatoes, 165

flour, 207–208

Fort Edmonton Ginger Beef Salad, 181

Fort Rouge Sourdough Hamburger Buns, 217

food poisoning, 7–8

Foundation's $100 Seafood Pasta Sauce, 135

Fredericton Ham Casserole, 94

Frére André's Easter Bread, 210

Front Line Love Cake, 278

Gabrielle Roy's Oatmeal Muffins, 228

Gates Marinated Vegetable Salad, 180
Gilles Villeneuve Salad Dressing Sensass, 187
Gloria Swanson's Mayonnaise, 185
Gordon Sinclair Low-Cal Barbecue Sauce, 202
Gracie Fields Yuletide Fruitcake, 282
Great Warrior Bannock, 211
Green Beans, Balmoral Style, 153
Green Beans à la Gaspésienne, 154
Green Gables Scalloped Potatoes, 164
Greta Garbo's Thousand Islands Dressing, 190
Grey Nuns' Autumn Pickles 239
Gros Morne Rhubarb Cobbler, 255
ground beef, 14–15

Hamburg's First Burger, 67
heart disease, preventing, 5–6, 20–22
Henry Scadding Fruit Scones, 215
herbs and spices, 13
Hollywood Meat Loaf, 64
Hollywood Tofu Mayonnaise, 186
honey versus sugar, 19–20, 262
Hong Siu Chu Yuk, 81
Hugh Garner Cabbagetown Apple Crisp, 251

Ingrid Bergman's Roast Pork, 77
irradiated food, 2

Jambalaya Acadien, 85
James Joyce's Soda Bread, 213
James Cagney Turkey Rolls, 109
Janetville Pasta with Fiddleheads, 132
Jean Cocteau's Montmartre Meat Loaf, 65
Jean Drapeau Bifteck au Poivre Vert, 58
Jericho Tarator Sauce, 205
Jerusalem Instant Marmelade, 245
John G. Tames Classic Greek Salad, 175

John Barrymore's Honey-Lime Dressing, 184
John Wayne Sweet and Sour Pork, 79
John Lennon Salmon Cakes, 117
Joséphine Savoie Cajun Jambalaya, 139
Judy LaMarsh's Conserve, 245
Judy Garland Rainbow Chicken, 98
Juneau Salmon Noodle Casserole, 118

Kedgwick Vegetarian Chili, 151
kitchen equipment, 8–10
Klondike Strata, 95
Klondike Kate's Turnip and Apples, 167

Labrador Frozen Pickles, 240
Lancaster County Corn Pie, 161
Las Vegas Cucumber Soup, 33
Lazare Poirier's Oyster Chowder, 30
Lazy Bones Casserole Cabbage Rolls, 60
lead crystal plates and glasses, 10
leftovers, 6–7
Léon Dates's Sauce Béchamel, 199
Linguine Charlo, 129
Little Current Wild Rice Pilaf, 143
Louis Aragon Baked Potatoes with Yogurt, 163
Low-Cal Pie Crust I, 267
Low-Cal Pie Crust 11, 268
Lucy Maud Montgomery Riverside Flan, 271
Lumina Drapeau's "Mois de Marie" Sorbet, 264
Lumina's Month of May Crisp, 256
Lupe Velez Chili Verde, 88

Ma Parker Quick-Getaway Beef Soup, 43
Madame Chiang Kai-Shek Dipping Sauce, 200

Madame de Gaulle Low-Cal Cheese-
    cake, 277
Mae Clarke Macédoine of Fruit, 258
Mae West "Come-up-and-see-me-
    sometime" Chicken, 99
Magnificent Snowbirds Moose Jaw
    Rice Salad, 176
manitou water, 16–170
Manitou Health Spa Sauce Bernaise,
    197
Manitoulin Wild Rice Pancakes, 232
Manitoulin Island Breakfast Muffins,
    229
Mao Tse-tung Salad Dressing, 188
Marc Foisy des Forges's Coq au Vin,
    100
Margie Bennett's Cockney Relish, 235
marmalades (see also conserves):
    Jerusalem Instant, 245; Meramcook,
    246
Mary Pickford's University Avenue
    Potage, 49
Mata Hari Chicken Soup, 42
mayonaise: Gloria Swanson's, 185;
    tofu, Hollywood, 186
Memory Lane Dijon-Style Mustard,
    243
Memramcook Marmelade, 246
Meringue Pie Topping, 270
Métis Bannnock, 212
Miami Golden Girls Filling, 286
Micmac Cranberry-Crabapple Sauce,
    202
microwave ovens, 8
milk, 2–3
minerals, 4–5, 23
Mishima's Tofu "Ground Beef," 170
Mon Oncle Jules's Relish, 234
Montaigne Raisin-Branana Muffins,
    230
Montmagny Barbecued Spareribs, 78
Mount Eisenhower Cinnamon Rolls,
    223

Mountain Brook Sloppy Joes, 74
Mrs. Miniver Carrot Dressing, 185
muffins: breakfast, Manitoulin Island,
    229; oatmeal, Gabrielle Roy, 228;
    raisan-banana, Montaigne, 230; wild
    blueberry, Saguenay, 231

Navajo Marinated Tomatoes, 178
Norman Bethune's Chop Suey, 83
nutrition, 4–5

oatmeal, 208
Ocean Limited Turkey, 110
Ojibwe Fruit Gratin, 253
Old Havana Lemon Loaf, 220
Orlando Lemon Filling, 286
osteoporosis, 4

pasta: Fettuccine Toronto, 127; fet-
    tucine, California Broccoli, 126;
    with fiddleheads, 132; Linguine with
    Chicken, 128; Linguine Charlo, 129;
    spaghetti, Étienne's World-Famous,
    133; spaghetti alla Putanesca, 136;
    Woodstock Balsamic Penne, 131
P'tit Montréal Sloppy Joes, 71
Pennsylvania German Carrot-Parsnip
    Casserole, 155
Pie Pastry, 266
pickles: Grey Nuns' Autumn, 239;
    Labrador Frozen, 240
Point Pelée Birders' Pie, 108
Poirier New World Crumble, 254
pork: and apple pie, WLMK's, 87;
    chili verde, Lupe Velez, 88; chop
    suey, Norman Bethune's, 83; chops,
    Raymond Massey Festive, 75; Chops
    Sensass, 76; curried, Delhi, 84;
    ham, Canadian Brass Glazed, 92;
    ham Casserole, Fredericton, 94;
    ham, Fast-and-Speedy Niagara Falls,
    93; Jambalaya Acadien, 85; roast,
    Ingrid Bergman's, 77;

spareribs, Montmagny Barbecued, 78; stew, Chinese Red (Hong Siu Chu Yuk), 81; stew, Ragoût de Porc Saint-Maure, 80; strata, Klondike, 95; sweet and sour, John Wayne, 79; tourtière René Lévesque, 89; tourtière, Thérèse Pitre's, 91; tourtière, Père Godin's, 91; tourtière, Célina Fournier's Amqui, 90; value of lean Canadian pork, 17–18; Yu Xiang, Sichuan, 82–83

Pork Chops Sensass, 76

Potage Haut-Balmoral, 47

Potage Bas-Balmoral, 46

Potage Saint-Quentin, 35

potatoes; baked, with yogurt, 163; baked, Flin Flon, 165; pie, Richard Hatfield, 166; scalloped, Green Gables, 164; sweet, Elmyr Tompkins, 261

Poulet Henri IV, 103

Poulet de Grand Pré, 106

pressure cooker, 8,9

Prince Albert Yogurt "Ice Cream," 266

Prince Danilov Sauce Russe, 189

Prosilac, 2–3

Queen Elizabeth Cake, 279

Ragoût de Louisborg, 32

Ragoût de porc Saint-Maure, 80

Raymond Massey Festive Pork Chops, 75

Red Flag Chicken Stir-fry, 105

Red Deer Taco Mix, 61

Red Deer Tacos, 62

Red River Vegetarian Loaf, 169

relishes: chutney, Wellington Kiwi, 238; country garden, Tante Marie's, 237; hamburger, Cousin Louise's, 233; Margie Bennett's Cockney, 235; Mon Oncle Jules's, 234;

rice: Jambalaya Acadien, 85–86; Jam-

balaya, Joséphine Savoie Cajun, 139; paella, Valenciana, 141; and peas, Caribana, 162; Risotto de Florence, 144; salad, Shoal Lake, 177; salad, Magnificent Snowbirds, 176; wild, bread, Thousand Island, 226; wild, pancakes, Manitoulin, 232; wild, pilaf, Little Current, 143; wild, soup, First Nations', 45

Richard Hatfield Potato Pie, 166

Risotto de Florence, 144

Robert Morley's Barbecued Sirloin, 57

Route 66 Hamburgers, 70

Rudolph Valentino Baked Lima Beans, 149

Sackville Baptist Pudding, 262

Saguenay Blueberry Fool, 263

Saguenay Wild Blueberry Muffins, 231

Saint John's United Church Salad, 181

Saint Joseph's Resurrection Morning Buns, 224

salads: caesar, Santa Monica, 173; chicken, Blue Angel, 183; coleslaw, Authentic Amsterdam, 174; ginger beef, Fort Edmonton, 181; greek, John G. Tames Classic, 175; rice, Magnificent Snowbirds, 176; rice, Shoal Lake, 177; Saint John's United Church, 181; tomatoes, Navajo Marinated, 178; vegetable, Gates Marinated, 180

salad dressings: carrot, Mrs. Miniver, 185; galician, Prince Danilov, 189; Gilles Villeneuve, 187; honey-lime, John Barrymore's, 184; Jeanne Mance Miracle, 190; Mao Tse-Tung, 188; mayonnaise, Gloria Swanson's, 185; mayonnaise, Hollywood Tofu, 186; mayonnaise, green, 187; Mona Lisa, 187; raspberry vinegar, Félix Leclerc, 192; Roquefort Cream, 187; Sauce Russe,

Prince Danilov, 189; Thousand Islands, Greta Garbo's, 190; watercress, Sarah Bernhardt, 191
salt and sugar, 18–19
Salt Lake City Melon Soup, 52
San Francisco Sloppy Joes, 72
Santa Monica Caesar Salad, 173
Santa's North Pole Christmas Cake, 281
Sarah Bernhardt Watercress Dressing, 191
Saskatoon Vegetarian Chili, 168
sauces: barbecue, Gordon Sinclair Low-Cal, 202; béarnaise, Manitou Health Spa, 197; béchamel, thick, 199; béchamel, Léon Dantes's, 199; Bolognese, Alfie Duncan, 194; cranberry-crabapple, Micmac, 202; dipping, Madam Chiang Kai-Shek, 200; Herb, 199; Horseradish, Emile Zola, 203; Mornay, 199; Mustard, 199; pesto, Boissevain, 201; pesto, Annapolis Valley, 200; plum,, Bering Strait, 204; salsa, Carmen Miranda Hot, 196; tarator, Jericho, 205; tartar, Emmie Wilkins's, 205; teriyaki, Yokohama, 206; tomato, Alfie Duncan, 195;
Veloutée, 199
Saugeen Cream of Mushroom Soup, 37
scones: Henry Scadding Fruit, 215; Windsor, 214
Shining Star Strawberry Shortcake, 260
Shoal Lake Rice Salad, 177
Sichuan Yu Xiang Pork, 82
Sir Harry Oakes's Bahamian Soup, 51
Sloppy Joes, 71
Soeur Saint-Victor's Heavenly Carrot Soup, 34
Sole Duglère de Percé, 113
soup: banana, Sir Harry Oakes's Bahamian, 51; beef, Ma Parker Quick-Getaway, 43; cabbage, Potage Saint-Quentin, 35; carrot, Soeur Saint-Victor's, 34; chicken, Mata Hari, 42; chicken, Mary Pickford's, 49; chowder, Annie Poirier's Clam, 27; chowder, Beauséjour Tomato, 39; chowder, Ragoût de Louisbourg, 32; cream of mushroom, Saugeen, 37; cream of tomato, Andy Warhol's, 41; cucumber, Las Vegas, 33; Dr. Banting's July Heat Wave, 50; fish chowder, Carleton-Sur-Mer, 28; fish, Percé, 29; garlic and pepper, Verdi's, 36; herb, lentil and tomato, 47; lentil, Potage Bas-Balmoral, 46; melon, Salt Lake City, 52; oyster chowder, Lazare Poirier's, 30; pea, La Bolduc's, 38; wild rice, First Nations', 45
Soupe aux pois de la Bolduc, 38
Soupe aux Poissons de Percé, 29
Sourdough Lifetime Starter, 218
Spaghetti alla Putanesca, 136
Splenda granular sweetener, 19–20
stock: beef, 25; chicken, 24; Chinese-Style, 26; fish, 26, turkey, 25
Strawberry Fields Topping, 287

Tante Marie's Country Garden Relish, 237
Tante Clémentine's Unset Jam Corrective, 247
Tantramar Cranberry Crisp, 252
Tantramar Thanksgiving Loaf, 225
Thousand Islands Wild Rice Bread, 226
Titanic Brandied Peach Pudding, 259
tofu: burgers, Tokyo, 171; greek salad, John G. Tames, 175; "ground beef", Mishima's, 170; mayonnaise, Hollywood, 186
Tokyo Tofu Burgers, 171

Tomato Chowder Beauséjour, 39
tomatoes: chili verde, Lupe Velez, 88;
    chowder beauséjour, 39; greek
    salad, John G. Tames, 175; Navajo
    Marinated, 178; sauce, Alfie Dun-
    can El Cheapo, 195; soup, cream of,
    41; soup, herb and lentil, 47
Tourtière René Lévesque, 89
Tourtière Cheticamp, 120
Tourtière Marco Polo, 121
Truman Capote 4-Alarm Tex-Mex
    Chili, 150
Tugboat Annie Chicken with
    Brandied Pears, 104
turkey: Ocean Limited, 110; rolls,
    James Cagney, 109; stock, 25
Turkey Stock, 25
Tyrone Power's Spanish Tomato Chili
    Sauce, 242

unbleached flour, 207–208

Vancouver Ouzeri, 123
Verdi's Garlic and Pepper Soup, 36
Viking Trail Fillets, 114
vitamins, 22–23

Walter Huston's Original Graham
    Crackers, 218
Wellington Kiwi Chutney, 238
whipped cream, 15–16
White House Hot or Cold Chicken,
    102
Windsor Scones, 214
WLMK's Pork and Apple Pie, 87
Woodstock Balsamic Penne, 131

Yokohama Teriyaki Sauce, 206
Yukon Sourdough Biscuits, 216

Zippy Rickety Uncles, 274